PlPlease re
GEOFFREY VALE CHAF
32 Victoria Road M
Tel. 01621 859059   F
Email. geoff.vale@

LIVING T
CHRISTIAN !

LIVING THE CHRISTIAN STORY

The Distinctiveness of Christian Ethics

JOHN E. COLWELL

T&T CLARK
EDINBURGH & NEW YORK

T&T CLARK LTD

A Continuum imprint

59 George Street
Edinburgh EH2 2LQ
Scotland

www.tandtclark.co.uk

370 Lexington Avenue
New York 10017–6503
USA

www.continuumbooks.com

First published 2001

ISBN 0 567 08790 5

British Library Cataloguing-in-Publication Data
A catalogue record for this book is available from the British Library

Typeset by Fakenham Photosetting Ltd, Fakenham, Norfolk
Printed and bound in Great Britain by MPG Books, Bodmin

Contents

Preface

Given the title of this book it will be interesting to see where, within a library, it is placed. It's just possible that a librarian in a hurry may note the reference of its title to the Christian story and file it under the heading of Christology. Of course one would expect it to be placed within the 'ethics' section of a library but there may be some justification for it being filed under 'salvation', or 'Christian discipleship', or 'sanctification', or perhaps 'Pneumatology', and I even hope that our hypothetically careless librarian may not have made a total categorical error in placing it within the 'Christology' section.

Naturally libraries need some form of classification system – it would not be helpful simply to file all books alphabetically according to author or editor – but, contrary to the impression given by such systems, together with the similar impression given by not a few books on theology and not a few college courses, theology is a single discipline which ought not to be sub-divided categorically.[1] What, as a Christian, I believe about God is identified by what I believe about Christ and this, in turn, ought to inform what I believe about everything else. And if this is true of Christian belief it is similarly true of Christian practice. Christian ethics, like ecclesiology, should derive its shape and its content from the gospel. Correspondingly, the work of theology has not been properly done unless and until it has taken concrete form in an understanding of the Church and of the manner of Christian living. Sadly this integration of faith and practice is often obscured by the manner in which Christian doctrine is presented: there may be a focus on the concrete actuality of the gospel story

---

[1] Stanley Hauerwas comments that, as a 'self-conscious activity', Christian ethics is a 'rather recent development': '... being a Christian always involved moral claims, but rarely before the nineteenth century was it thought necessary to analyze the conceptual and logical relation between Christian belief and action': Stanley Hauerwas, *A Community of Character: Toward a Constructive Christian Social Ethic* (Notre Dame: University of Notre Dame Press, 1981), p. 89.

(though even this cannot always be taken for granted) but too frequently there is little or no focus on the concrete actuality of the Christian community. Just as sadly, the reverse of this dynamic is even more common: accounts of Christian ethics are given which only in the most general manner appear to take their shape from the concrete actuality of the gospel story and its significance. It is with an attempt at an explanation for the reasons behind this lack of integration that this book begins.

Certainly this is not a universal failing: both Thomas Aquinas and Karl Barth – whose sometimes conflicting genius underlies so much of this book – offer accounts of the Christian life that are thoroughly integrated with their accounts of the gospel. But they both pursued this goal over a series of volumes rather than the more modest (though perhaps more ambitious) project of attempting this integration within a single book.

Consequently what is offered here cannot pretend to be more than a cursory outline of the shape of Christian living that seeks to be a response to the gospel. While I attempt to engage with key authors who have contributed to this theme I can only do so in the briefest form and can only apologize to those who have written similarly but whose contribution, merely through economy of space, remains unmentioned.

As always, no work is written in isolation and anything here that is of any worth derives from the stimulus of conversations with family, church, students and colleagues together with the stimulus of authors I have never met. I never met Karl Barth, I certainly didn't meet Thomas Aquinas or John Calvin, I haven't even met Stanley Hauerwas (though I have been present when he has lectured and we have exchanged letters) but this book is a humble attempt to engage in conversation, though inevitably a one-way conversation, with each of them. Colin Gunton, who supervised my doctoral studies (many years ago) remains a good friend whose writings and conversation have probably been the principal influence behind my own thinking. I cannot adequately express the value I place on his support and on the responses he has made to this present text. I am particularly grateful for the friendship and encouragement of Ian Randall and Stephen Holmes, two of my colleagues on the staff of Spurgeon's College, whose criticisms and comments as the text has taken shape have preserved me from the worst errors and excesses (though responsibility for whatever dross remains is mine and not theirs). Similarly, and especially, I am grateful to Rosemary, Sarah and Tim who have read the text, argued with me, and who, together with Philip, have provided the happiest possible family context in which writing and thinking can take place.

John E. Colwell
Easter 2001

Abbreviations

CD　　　　Karl Barth, *Church Dogmatics*, vols. I–IV, Eng.
　　　　　trans. eds. G. W. Bromiley and T. F. Torrance
　　　　　(Edinburgh: T&T Clark, 1956–1975)

Institutes　John Calvin, *Institutes of the Christian Religion*,
　　　　　ed. J. T. McNeill, trans. F. L. Battles
　　　　　(Philadelphia: Westminster Press, 1960)

JTS　　　*Journal of Theological Studies*

SJT　　　*Scottish Journal of Theology*

ST　　　St. Thomas Aquinas, *Summa Theologica*, trans.
　　　　　by Fathers of the English Dominican Province
　　　　　(Westminster, Maryland: Christian Classics,
　　　　　1981)

Part One

PARTICULARITY AND DISTINCTIVENESS

1
Morality and Rationalism

Is there such a topic as 'Christian Ethics'? That is to say: is there an approach to ethics that is specifically and distinctively Christian? Or, to be more precise: is there a distinctive approach to ethics that derives from Christian commitment and Christian identity?

To some who read this book the answer to the question may seem obvious. Our actions and attitudes derive from our beliefs; what we do is an expression of what we believe and what we think. Since our beliefs take a specific shape this will inevitably (or should inevitably) determine, or at least influence, our attitudes and our actions. Christian ethics cannot validly identify itself as 'Christian' unless its reflection derives directly and consciously from the fact that Jesus Christ died and rose again.[1] Indeed, perhaps the matter should be expressed more strongly: to define what it means to be a Christian merely in terms of beliefs, commitments and attitudes is inadequate. My identity as a Christian is just that, a matter of identity, a matter of being, and not merely a matter of belief or opinion. To be a Christian is to be a disciple of Christ, to follow him, to be like him, to be indwelt by his Spirit. Consequently, it is not merely that being a Christian implies ethical commitments: to be a Christian is an ethical commitment.[2]

---

[1] 'The foundations of Christian ethics must be evangelical foundations; or, to put it more simply, Christian ethics must arise from the gospel of Jesus Christ. Otherwise it could not be *Christian* ethics': Oliver O'Donovan, *Resurrection and the Moral Order: An Outline for Evangelical Ethics* (Leicester: IVP, 1986), p. 11.

[2] 'The task of Christian ethics is to help us see how our convictions *are* in themselves a morality. We do not first believe certain things about God, Jesus, and the church, and subsequently derive ethical implications from these beliefs. Rather our convictions embody our morality: our beliefs are our actions. We Christians ought not to search for the "behavioral implications" of our beliefs. Our moral life is not comprised of beliefs plus decisions; our moral life is the process in which our convictions form our character to be truthful': Stanley Hauerwas, *The Peaceable Kingdom: A Primer in Christian Ethics* (London: SCM Press, 1984), p. 16.

However, even if there are those who are puzzled by the question (a puzzlement which may evidence either perception, naïveté, or intellectual isolation) there will undoubtedly be some for whom the question is genuine.

On the one hand there may be those who will have found the assertions of the previous paragraph concerning the identity of theology and ethics deeply disturbing. Might not this imply a reduction of Christianity to a moral code and a consequent betrayal of the gospel? Properly understood, Christianity focuses upon what God has done rather than upon what we do. The cross of Christ exposes our righteousness as 'rubbish' (Phil. 3.8). Ought we not therefore to be suspicious of any concentration on ethics as a thinly disguised attempt at self-justification? Is not the very idea of a Christian ethic consequently self-contra-dictory? A response to this form of the question will be attempted in the third chapter of this section but, before that form of questioning can properly be considered, there is another, and perhaps more persistent, form in which the question is posed.

To identify a specifically Christian ethic would seem to imply that there are concepts of moral rightness and goodness that are distinctive for a particular community, the Church, rather than accessible and applicable to society as a whole. Even if that ethic is deemed (by Christians) to be applicable to society as a whole, it would seem not to be accessible to society as a whole. But if this is the case, on what basis can Christians seek to impose their values on society as a whole? If these values are integral to Christian belief and identity, then these values are not shared by society as a whole or accessible to society as a whole. Moreover, if there is validly a Christian ethic there is also validly a Hindu ethic, a Buddhist ethic, a Marxist ethic. How is society to choose between these rival truth claims? What is required, if notions of moral rightness and goodness are to be applicable to society as a whole, is that such values should be derived in a manner that is independent of any particular system of belief or community tradition. Consequently, the concern ought not to be for a Christian ethic but for a universal ethic independently derived.[3]

In a societal context of increasing plurality the attractions of a universal and independently derived ethic should be obvious.[4] Without shared values society cannot function. Values which are imposed upon society by any single dominant community are not truly shared. Besides which, to impose those values would seem, at least in some sense, to undermine those values: how can values be imposed unless coercion, for the sake of the common good, is perceived to be itself good and right? If values are truly to be shared within society they surely must be derived in a manner that is accessible to all without prejudice to the traditions and beliefs of any particular community.

Our awareness of the need for a universally accessible ethic has undoubtedly been heightened by the staggering advances in medical science that occurred as the twentieth century progressed. Even if it were appropriate for Christians to treat Scripture as a book of rules one would not expect to find biblical rules, written two thousand years ago, that can be applied straightforwardly to contemporary medical dilemmas. And even if, through a process of extreme special pleading, one could isolate rules that were relevant to modern medical decision making, on what basis could one expect those rules to be compelling to those who do not share a Christian faith? In debates about genetics, life support systems, embryo research, and abortion, the desirability of a religiously neutral and

[handwritten margin note: Perhaps we might be surprised]

---

[3] '... for many the idea of trying to do Christian ethics has become a doubtful enterprise. Philosophical, theological, and sociological reasons have come together to make problematic the idea that Christian ethics is anything distinct from ethics': Stanley Hauerwas, *Vision and Virtue: Essays in Christian Ethical Reflection* (Notre Dame: University of Notre Dame Press, 1981), p. 1.

[4] Within this book the term 'plurality' will be used to describe the fact that contemporary Western society is comprised of various traditions and communities. The term 'pluralism' will be reserved for the notion that every belief system and tradition is of similar value. That this notion is incoherent will be argued in chapter three. For a fuller description of the distinction between the two terms see Ian S. Markham, *Plurality and Christian Ethics* (Cambridge: Cambridge University Press, 1994).

commonly accessible basis for discovering what is right
and good is overwhelming.

But it is not just in our contemporary era, with its
distinctive moral dilemmas, that this need has been
apparent. Questions of freedom and law, of peace and
conflict, of truthfulness and confidentiality, of sexuality and
faithfulness, all have persistently prompted the quest for a
universally accessible basis for moral decision making. And
perhaps, in an age when such issues may have appeared
less complex, and in societies that were certainly more
homogeneous than our own, proposals for such neutral
ethical foundations may have seemed more convincing.[5]

From the seventeenth century onwards one did not need
overtly to be reacting against the supposed religious and
intellectual tyranny of the medieval period, nor did one
need to adopt a Deist rejection of every form of revelation,
to be persuaded concerning the desirability and viability
of a rational basis for morality. The age that we term
the Enlightenment was characterized by a breathtaking
optimism concerning the mechanical orderliness of the
universe and the potentiality both of human rationality and
of human moral development. Both the rationalism of René
Descartes (1596–1650) and the empiricism of David Hume
(1711–1776) – if not of John Locke – effectively relegated the
possibility of revelation to the periphery of thought and
thereby established a categorical disjunction between reason
and faith, fact and value. Divine revelation and human
religion were not necessarily denied, they were simply
consigned to the sphere of unverifiable personal opinion.[6] In
an ordered universe human enquiry alone should be sufficient to establish the norms of moral rightness, and the
human spirit should be sufficient to fulfil those norms.

[5] I am not, of course, suggesting that these issues were any less complex
but rather that they may have appeared to be so. The relative cultural and
religious homogeneity of societies provided a context in which issues
could be commonly described and therefore appeared to be less complex.
[6] For thorough discussions of this outcome of Enlightenment thought
see Colin E. Gunton, *Enlightenment and Alienation: An Essay towards a
Trinitarian Theology* (Basingstoke: Marshall Morgan & Scott, 1985) and
Lesslie Newbigin, *The Gospel in a Pluralist Society* (London: SPCK, 1989).

Before beginning to respond critically to this unbounded optimism one should note that it did not issue in immediate agreement concerning any independent and rational foundation for moral rightness.[7] Jeremy Bentham (1748–1832)[8] and George Edward Moore (1873–1958) may be united in the view that the consequences of an act determine its rightness or wrongness, but the manner in which they define the goal of acting, as happiness or, with more sophistication, as a matter of aesthetics, renders their ideas as distinct as they are similar.[9]

However, notwithstanding the obvious difficulties involved in calculating consequences – and the tangential complication of the relation between intentionality and foreseeable consequences – teleological approaches are experimentally and theologically over-optimistic. None of us is able to calculate consequences in neutral detachment. None of us exists in neutral detachment. We exist as the people we have become, with our distinctive history, traditions, beliefs and prejudices, and it is as such that we

[7] It should be noted, however, that the distinction between teleological and deontological approaches to ethical decision making is less than absolute; there may be a closer correspondence between these approaches than their designations suggest. Teleological approaches, which seek to identify right action by considering the consequences of that action, in their more extreme form of 'strict act' utilitarianism, require that every moral decision should be determined by a calculation of consequences specific to the particular situation (also referred to as 'unrestricted utilitarianism'). But even in this extreme form, once consequences have been calculated, to act in a manner appropriate to those consequences carries the force of a moral duty. Moreover, in the more nuanced form advocated by John Stuart Mill (1806–1873) – referred to either as 'restricted utilitarianism' or as 'act-rule' utilitarianism – teleological approaches become virtually indistinguishable from deontological approaches in their recognition of the duty of the agent to act in specific ways in certain types of situations because such actions in such situations generally issue in equivalent and predictable consequences: John Stuart Mill, *Utilitarianism*, 1863 (London: Longmans, Green & Co., 1891).
[8] Jeremy Bentham, *An Introduction to the Principles of Morals and Legislation*, ed. J. H. Burns and H. L. A. Hart (London: Methuen, 1982).
[9] Though Moore still claims 'that "right" does and can mean nothing but "cause of a good result," and is thus identified with "useful" ' the manner in which he assesses that 'good result' differs considerably from that suggested by Bentham: G. E. Moore, *Principia Ethica*, p. 146: quoted in Joseph Fletcher, *Situation Ethics: The New Morality* (London: SCM Press, 1966), p. 5.

perceive consequences and attempt to calculate them. My notion of the greatest good for the greatest number of people is distinctively mine; it is a notion formed by my own history and the traditions and perceptions of the community in which I share.

The point can be illustrated with reference to Joseph Fletcher's account of 'situation ethics'. Notwithstanding the notoriety of this 'situationist' approach in evangelical circles, Fletcher should be criticized, not primarily because he relates moral rightness to specific agents in specific situations, but rather because his account represents an extreme form of consequentialism. According to Fletcher, only love is always good and, consequently, love must be identified as the only ethical norm, and – and this is the key issue – love justifies its means. In this respect Fletcher's account exemplifies the tendency to allow secular and liberal approaches to ethics to determine the manner of Christian ethics. But, in other respects, Fletcher's account also exemplifies the incongruity of the liberal ideal of detachment. Though Fletcher is commonly criticized for doing so inadequately (not least because the Christian story and tradition cannot so simply be reduced to a single motive)[10] he does attempt to define love in relation to Christ. He demonstrates no desire to detach himself entirely from a received tradition. Fletcher's notion of the greatest good for the greatest number of people is informed, albeit inadequately, by the tradition he inhabits.

By definition we are concerned to calculate the consequences of an action only if that action in some manner, no matter how remotely, concerns us. We calculate consequences because, to some degree, we are agents involved in the action. As agents, no matter how sincere and serious our commitment to be altruistic, we cannot avoid assessing the consequences of an action from our own perspective, according to our own prejudices, beliefs and, perhaps,

---

[10] Cf. Stanley Hauerwas, 'Situation Ethics, Moral Notions, and Moral Theology' in *Vision and Virtue: Essays in Christian Ethical Reflection* (Indiana: University of Notre Dame, 1981), pp. 11–29, and 'Love's Not All You Need' *ibid.*, pp. 111–26.

even our own self-interest. To conclude that Utilitarianism, through this lack of neutral detachment, inevitably lapses into Hedonism, may appear cynical but it is not wholly without foundation.[11] In particular it is not without theological foundation: since the gospel defines me as a sinner I ought never to minimize the degree of my self-interest, even if I am not always immediately conscious of that self-interest. This is not, of course, to deny the significance of a consideration of consequences in assessing the rightness or wrongness of an action, but it is to plead that all such assessment should be realistic.

However, the realism that takes due account of self-interest, whether for experimental or theological reasons, undermines the very objectivity and universal accessibility that are foundational for every form of Utilitarianism. Consequently, the Rationalism that underlies Utilitarianism inevitably degenerates into an unconvincing Idealism. By our definition as subjects we lack absolute objectivity. We simply cannot be entirely and convincingly altruistic.

It is for this reason that deontological approaches, seeking to determine the rightness of an action in itself, may appear more promising as a foundation for a universally accessible morality. But the appearance of promise is delusory for similar reasons. By reference to a 'universal law' the categorical imperative suggested by Immanuel Kant (1724–1804) would seem to offer the prospect of an objective criterion for moral rightness.[12] But the formula depends upon my ability to assess that an action could be considered a universal law and, once again I can only make this assessment as the person that I am. How can I make such an assessment without some consideration of

---

[11] Nor is this restricted to matters of personal ethics: it is not uncommon, nor even self-consciously cynical, to hear foreign policy described in terms of 'interests' rather than 'allies' and 'commitments'.

[12] Generally Kant's categorical imperative is presented thus: 'Act only on that maxim through which you can at the same time will that it should become a universal law': Immanuel Kant, *Groundwork of the Metaphysic of Morals*, trans. H. Paton (New York: Harper & Row, 1947); *The Metaphysics of Ethics* (Edinburgh: T&T Clark, 1886); cf. Keith Ward, *The Development of Kant's View of Ethics* (Oxford: Blackwell, 1972).

the consequences of that action, with all the concurrent difficulties and delusions already discussed? And how can I confidently ascribe to an action the authority of a universal law when I cannot possibly conceive of every agent and of every situation and circumstance that could be involved in such an action? Kant's underlying assumption of some universally normative rationality or, rather, some universally normative perception is, once again, unrealistically optimistic.[13] Indeed, Kant's proposal would seem to be even further removed from reality than consequentialist approaches: it may just be possible to correct Utilitarianism realistically by taking due cognizance of the disposition of the particular agent, whereas the categorical imperative is, by definition, dependent upon the delusion of a universal rationality or perception.

Every attempt to locate a universally accessible foundation for moral rightness in independent rationality is doomed to failure. It fails because no human rationality is truly independent and, consequently, no human rationality can be universally accessible. Rationality is inherently particular. The disjunction assumed by modernity between fact and value, reason and faith, is incoherent in practice. The assumed possibility of detached objectivity is delusory. My notion of moral rightness is consequent upon my own history and the history and traditions of the community in which I participate. Since communities and traditions are various, perceptions of moral rightness are similarly various. It is for this reason that Alasdair MacIntyre argues that concepts of justice and the rationalities to which they correspond develop within particular communities and can only be evaluated in the light of the traditions of those particular communities.[14] And this recognition that our

[13] In the course of his excellent introduction to Christian theology Trevor Hart similarly criticizes Kant for his view that fixed points of reference are 'given to all humans in and with the structure of their minds, thereby supplying a universal uniformity to the structure and orientation of rational activity': Trevor Hart, *Faith Thinking: The Dynamics of Christian Theology* (London: SPCK, 1995), p. 60.
[14] Alasdair MacIntyre, *After Virtue: A Study in Moral Theory* (London: Duckworth, 1985²).

perceptions are formed by our particular history and traditions conflicts, as MacIntyre later observes, with the central tenet of modernism since the 'belief in its ability to understand everything from human culture and history, no matter how apparently alien, is itself one of the defining beliefs of the culture of modernity'.[15]

Despite this practical incoherence the influence of these supposedly independent approaches to the assessing of moral rightness has been staggering. The demands of liberal modernism that every matter should be considered in rational detachment have thoroughly beguiled the Church, or at least the Protestant churches, as is evidenced by the manner and content of courses in moral theology in most theological colleges and Protestant university faculties.[16] The substantive 'theology' generally lacks all substance within such courses; a consideration of morality has been divorced from a consideration of doctrine; Christian ethics has been effectively reduced to 'liberal' ethics without sufficiently searching questions being asked concerning the validity of the foundation for such an enterprise. This capitulation, of course, is not due entirely to the totalitarian intimidation of modernism – Protestant theology, as will be argued in chapter three, has left itself vulnerable to intimidation through its own lack of any

---

[15] Alasdair MacIntyre, *Whose Justice? Which Rationality?* (London: Duckworth, 1988), p. 385. This same point, which is central to MacIntyre's argument, is made earlier: '... the standpoint of traditions is necessarily at odds with one of the central characteristics of cosmopolitan modernity: the confident belief that all cultural phenomena must be potentially translucent to understanding, that all texts must be capable of being translated into the language which the adherents of modernity speak to each other' (p. 327).

[16] 'The assumption that it is more intellectually honest to doubt than to believe or commit oneself to something which one cannot be absolutely sure of; the unrelenting appeal to "reason" as an independent authority to be set advantageously over against both scripture and tradition; the suggestion that the most responsible thing to do with theological tradition, therefore, is initially to rebel against its authority, to test its worth, and only to afford it respect when one can establish the truth of its offerings on other independent grounds, and thereby commend its truth to those who do not belong to the tradition; these are the now familiar characteristics of the liberal theological tradition' (Trevor Hart, *Faith Thinking*, p. 168).

consistent and coherent basis for ethical reflection – but the totalitarian claims of modernism are ubiquitous and nothing is more illiberal than liberalism.

Probably the most influential form of an attempt to ground morality in an independently derived and universally accessible perception is the pervasive appeal to human rights. With its roots in the political philosophy of John Locke (1632–1704)[17] and its formative expression in the revolutionary tracts of Thomas Paine (1737–1809) and the French Rationalists, Montesquieu (1689–1755), Voltaire (1694–1778) and Rousseau (1712–1778), the notion of rationally inherent or 'self-evident' human rights has become foundational for ethical reflection in contemporary society. While it would be churlish not to acknowledge the positive influence of this approach to social justice it must simultaneously be acknowledged that the recognition of a right is effective morally only if it is accompanied by a corresponding recognition of a duty. Accordingly an appeal to rights is implicitly deontological: by acknowledging your right I am, by implication, acknowledging my duty, or someone's duty, or society's duty, towards you in respect of that right.[18]

The most obvious difficulty of an ethic based on 'rights', as with any appeal to human freedom, is that, on occasions, my perceived 'right' or 'freedom' will conflict with your perceived 'right' or 'freedom'. It is difficult, therefore, to see quite how a 'right' or 'freedom' can be deemed to be

---

[17] Simply put, Locke identifies four 'inalienable rights': the right to life; the right to liberty; the right to property; the right to rebel against unjust rulers and laws.

[18] The common failure to recognize that a right implies a corresponding duty, and the concurrent failure to identify the one owing this corresponding duty, is noted by Lesslie Newbigin: '... if the right of every person to life, liberty, and the pursuit of happiness is asserted, one has to ask, "Who is under obligation to honor the claim?" ... the quest for happiness is infinite. Who, then, has the infinite duty to honor the infinite claims of every person to the pursuit of happiness? The answer of the eighteenth century, and of those who have followed, is familiar: it is the nation-state. The nation-state replaces the holy church and the holy empire as the centerpiece in the post-Enlightenment ordering of society ... And since the pursuit of happiness is endless, the demands upon the state are without limit': Lesslie Newbigin, *Foolishness to the Greeks: The Gospel and Western Culture* (London: SPCK, 1986), p. 27.

absolute. Your right to smoke may conflict with my right to breathe clean air. A mother's rights concerning her own body may conflict with the rights of a foetus to continue to develop in the womb. To a degree the issues at stake in such conflicts can be clarified by identifying the series of obligations implicit in the claim to a right: what obligations does society have – and, in particular, what obligations does the medical profession have – to the mother and to the foetus? But one would have to be naïve in the extreme not to recognize that, partly through their own involvement in the dynamic but even more profoundly through the presuppositions formed by tradition and background, the various parties involved will perceive their obligations differently. Whether one thinks primarily in terms of 'rights' or whether one thinks primarily in terms of 'obligations', it is difficult to maintain an absolute claim in either case, not only because of the inevitability of conflicting claims, but also because of this diversity of perception.

Moreover, where the relationship between a right and an obligation is not explicitly affirmed, an appeal to rights can easily degenerate into the converse of a moral principle, a concern not with that which is due from me to you but rather with that which I perceive to be due from you to me and which I consequently demand; an issue of my rights rather than the rights I acknowledge in respect of my neighbour. Some form of this topsy-turvy corruption of morality is trumpeted by the media on an almost daily basis and constitutes depressing evidence of the rampant self-interest that undermines the false optimism of modernism.

When members of the Orange Order in Ulster claim an 'unalienable right' to march triumphalistically through Catholic districts, they demonstrate not only the manner in which an ethical principle can be inverted in favour of self- · interest but also the manner in which a supposedly 'Christian' culture can abandon any discernible relatedness to Christ as the foundation for its character and action. In the first place, it is difficult to see how such a right can be 'unalienable' when it so clearly conflicts with the perceived rights of others. Moreover, to claim such an 'unalienable right' implies that the wider community has an obligation to indulge such triumphalist demonstrations. But, at a far deeper level, for such a community to claim such a right in such circumstances represents a convenient strategy for avoiding the claims of a more overtly Christian ethic that might express itself in terms of peacableness, humility, mercy and love.

But, notwithstanding this distortion of moral principle by blatant self-interest, attempts to define human rights have proved surprisingly effective as an approach to morality. The element of surprise in this acknowledgement arises as a consequence of the common appeal to that which is self-evident as the basis for discerning these human rights.[19] It ought to be unnecessary to point out that an appeal to the self-evident raises methodological difficulties identical to those encountered when considering other teleological and deontological arguments: it assumes a detached objectivity and universality and, as has been argued already, such an assumption is inherently incoherent. I really do not know what this phrase 'self-evident' means. If a matter is evident it is evident to someone, for a matter to be known requires a knowing subject as well as a knowable object, and knowing subjects are distinctive and particular. That which may be evident to one person, in the light of their particular history and community tradition, may not be evident at all to someone whose background, experience and assumptions are entirely different. Truth and goodness, like beauty, at least appear to be, in this respect, 'in the eye of the beholder'. An appeal to self-evident human rights assumes a universality and commonality that radically conflicts with the apparent diversity of traditions and communities.

So how are we to account for the remarkable degree of influence that this appeal to self-evident human rights has exerted?[20]

---

[19] 'We hold these truths to be self-evident, that all men are created equal, that they are endowed by their Creator with certain unalienable Rights, that among these are Life, Liberty and the Pursuit of Happiness': Declaration of Independence (4 July 1776).
[20] I am concerned not to appear beguiled by the false optimism I oppose. The century that has witnessed the most consistent appeal to human

My concern in this first chapter is to challenge the assumptions of moral foundationalism, to dispute every claim to a universally accessible account of moral rightness that is independent of particular commitments and identities. But without too explicitly anticipating the conclusion of this chapter, the conclusion of chapter two, and an argument that will be resumed again in the concluding section of this book, the denial of any detached basis for commonality is not necessarily the denial of commonality. That there is an authentic, though not detached, basis for commonality will be defended subsequently. Let it suffice at this point to suggest that, if there is an authentic basis for commonality, appeals to self-evident human rights, together with the more simple and apparently instinctive sense of 'right' and 'wrong', could be considered as attempts to account for that commonality which is properly to be accounted for in some other manner.

But before this possibility can be pursued it is necessary to consider a distinct and older tradition which appears to give an account of moral rightness without an immediate and direct appeal to religious belief and identity.

It is understandable, and perhaps inevitable, that ideas of natural law should be inextricably linked to the thought of Thomas Aquinas. Alongside the interpretation of canon law, discussions of natural law have become the cornerstone of Roman Catholic moral theology and discussions of natural law almost invariably begin with discussions of the *Summa Theologica*.[21] This association may be less than fair. Thomas's account of natural law is subordinate to his

---

rights has also witnessed the abuse of those perceived rights on, perhaps, an unprecedented scale. On occasions, as has been suggested in the text, that abuse has actually been perpetrated in defence of rights perceived through the veil of self-interest. But it is in the light of this abuse and the conflicts of self-interest that underlie it that the continuing appeal to self-evident human rights is so remarkable.

[21] St. Thomas Aquinas, *Summa Theologica*, trans. by Fathers of the English Dominican Province (Westminster, Maryland: Christian Classics, 1981), hereafter referred to as *ST*.

account of the virtues.[22] His primary concern is to describe
the moral agent rather than the moral action, to give an
account of moral goodness before an account of moral
rightness. But, more fundamentally, it could be argued that
Thomas Aquinas is as hostile to the idea of any form of
'natural' theology as is Karl Barth. His stated aim in the first
question of the *Summa* is not to expound some independently derived 'natural' or 'philosophical' theology but to
expound 'sacred doctrine'.[23] He is writing for those already
within the community of faith, for those who share his
commitment and identity, for those who, through the
Spirit, have received grace. This 'evangelical' interpretation
of Thomas is ably presented by Eugene Rogers in his
surprising, but persuasive, comparison of Thomas with
Barth. Rogers pursues this possibility of comparison by
interpreting the *Summa* in the light of its first question[24] and
also in the light of Thomas's *Commentaries* (especially that
on Romans), which he holds should take priority.[25]

---

[22] '... Aquinas did not discuss natural law in order to supply an
"objective" account of natural morality, but rather because he needed a
principle of interpretation that would allow him to distinguish the
various kinds of precepts found in scripture ... the "Treatise on Law"
must be placed within Aquinas' attempt to develop an account of human
activity as formed by the virtues. Natural law, like grace, is but the
"external principle" of the more fundamental question of man's proper
end and activity': Stanley Hauerwas with Richard Bondi and David B.
Burrell, *Truthfulness and Tragedy: Further Investigations in Christian Ethics*
(Notre Dame: University of Notre Dame Press, 1977), p. 61.
[23] 'Sacred doctrine derives its principles not from any human
knowledge, but from the divine knowledge, through which, as through
the highest wisdom, all our knowledge is set in order ... the knowledge
proper to this science comes through revelation and not through natural
reason' (*ST* I 1 6).
[24] 'To place our purpose within proper limits, we first endeavor to investigate the nature and extent of this sacred doctrine' (*ST* I 1).
[25] 'As a contribution to *Protestant* theology the essay interprets Thomas
in the direction of Karl Barth. Barth objected to natural theology, but he
did not regard Anselm as doing it, and he deployed Anselm in his
struggle to get beyond the Enlightenment. But Thomas, despite the Five
Ways, also objected to what he called *theologia naturalis*. This essay
attempts to show that Barth might have applied his positive reading of
Anselm also to Thomas; he might have found in Thomas, too, resources
for getting beyond the Enlightenment': Eugene F. Rogers, Jnr., *Thomas
Aquinas and Karl Barth: Sacred Doctrine and the Natural Knowledge of God*
(Notre Dame: University of Notre Dame Press, 1995), p. 3.

Whether this attempt to interpret Thomas in an 'evangelical' direction is successful is for scholars of Thomas to judge. What is at least interesting for Protestant theology, and for students of Barth in particular, is that such an attempt (and consequent comparison) can be made at all. With all this in view it may be more fair to associate a focus on natural law with Thomism rather than with the thought of Thomas himself.[26]

Notwithstanding this more 'evangelical' interpretation of Thomas, the 'natural law' tradition, as it developed over subsequent centuries, does seem to represent another form of that over-optimistic view of commonality already discussed. Central to the theological thought of Thomas Aquinas and his successors is the recognition that all things are ordered to an end, that nothing exists without a 'final cause' or proper goal for its existence. While this recognition is a development of Aristotle's definition of cause it is, nonetheless, an appropriately Christian notion. In contradistinction to any static or cyclic view of reality it is the recognition that reality is historical, that we are 'storied' people, that our existence can only truly be understood eschatologically, in the light of the future. It is the denial, particularly by David Hume, of this 'storied' nature of reality, or indeed of any form of connectedness, that underlies the Enlightenment tendency to ignore ideas of natural law and to pursue other independently rational foundations for morality.[27] The problem within Thomas's

---

[26] Thomas's account of the virtues will be considered positively within the central chapters of this book.

[27] Hume argues that volition rather than reason must determine morality since an obligation cannot be derived from the mere existence of something. This disjunction between obligation and existence is, in the first instance, a further outworking of Hume's denial that cause and effect can be established rationally or empirically; an aspect of the more general denial that the connectedness of reality can be established by reason or by empirical observation. But, in a sense, Hume is correct in bringing this objection. For Thomas, if not always for some of his successors, the 'final cause' or 'goal' of creaturely existence is established by revelation; it is not ultimately to be discovered other than in the context of sacred doctrine: 'Hence all things that exist in whatsoever manner are necessarily directed by God towards some end (ST I 22 2); cf. '... this is clear from a consideration of Divine goodness, which, as we have said ... was the cause of the

account is not the stress he lays on the concept of final cause
– this, as will be argued later, must be crucial to any distinctively Christian account of ethics – the problem is rather
the suggestion, on the part of Thomas's theological heirs
rather than on the part of Thomas himself, that, at least in
some instances, this goal or final cause can be perceived
'naturally'.[28]

It may be no great overstatement to identify almost
every distinction between Roman and Reformed theology
as an implication of differing understandings of the terms
'nature' and 'grace'. To unravel these differing understandings may not be to abolish every distinction but it is
certainly to define the distinctions rightly and to
undermine mutual caricatures. The differing understandings of the term 'grace' within these two traditions, a
difference which underlies differing understandings of the
Church, its ministry, and its sacraments, will be considered
in Part Three of this book with reference to the dynamic of
Christian character. The differing understandings of the
term 'nature' which, like those concerning 'grace', take us
to the heart of Trinitarian theology and the relatedness of
God to the world, identify that which is problematic in the
development of theories of natural law.

If by the term 'nature' is intended the universe as it is; as
it is created, sustained and indwelt by the God who is
Father, Son and Spirit; as it is knowable to me inasmuch as
it is given to me by this triune God to know – then it may
be proper, in this strict sense, to speak validly of a 'natural'
revelation and a 'natural' law. But if by the term 'nature' is
intended some independently attained and 'purely

---

production of things in existence. For as *it belongs to the best to produce the
best*, it is not fitting that the supreme goodness of God should produce
things without giving them their perfection. Now a thing's ultimate
perfection consists in the attainment of its end. Therefore it belongs to the
Divine goodness, as it brought things into existence, so to lead them to
their end: and this is to govern' (*ST* I 103 1).

[28] ' . . . in Thomas Aquinas's exposition, to which, in some degree, all
subsequent Natural Law thinking refers back, the "first principles" are
(like the axioms of propositional proofs) *per se nota*, "self-evident" ': Oliver
O'Donovan, *Resurrection and the Moral Order: An Outline for Evangelical
Ethics* (Leicester: IVP, 1986), pp. 85f.; cf. *ST* II–1 94 2.

objective' knowledge of the universe – then the term 'natural revelation' should be recognized as an oxymoron and the possibility of discerning a 'natural law' should be recognized as delusory. This is the problem of the term 'nature' as it has generally been used in Roman Catholic theology and, it has to be admitted, as it came to be used within Liberal Protestantism.

Certainly the concept of nature within the thought of Thomas Aquinas should be clearly distinguished from that which arises in the context of the Enlightenment. There is no place here for any mechanistic view of the universe, no place here for any view of the world effectively existing without reference to God and independently of God's presence and providence.[29] For Thomas, God, who is the first cause of creation and of every particular within creation, is also the final cause of creation; God orders creation, and every particular within it, towards its final end. Nature is not independent: it is wholly dependent upon God and ordered by God. Indeed, it is for this reason initially that Thomas can be optimistic concerning the possibilities for discerning God's requirements from nature: nature is grounded in God and ordered by God; nature consequently is a valid external means of discerning this divine ordering.[30]

However, one needs no detailed acquaintance with Roman Catholic moral theology to guess that, quite quickly, differing perceptions of nature and of its implications might arise to undermine the effectiveness of an appeal to natural law as universally persuasive. Here, once again, too little account is taken of the differing perceptions that may

---

[29] 'Thomas never uses the phrase "natural theology" to describe what he is up to in the Romans commentary or the *Summa*. He thinks of both as biblical, dogmatic theology, of the sort described in Part I's characterization of sacred doctrine. After Deism, however, one thought that the whole point of natural theology was to be *the same thing* when believers and non-believers practised it (and after Deism it *was* the same thing): one of Thomas's genres had been lost, and Barth rightly rejected it in theology as a category mistake. But Thomas did not make that mistake' (Eugene F. Rogers, Jnr., *Thomas Aquinas and Karl Barth*, p. 131).
[30] See Stanley Hauerwas's essay entitled 'On Doctrine and Ethics' for a good historical survey of how 'ethics' came to be viewed as a distinct discipline from 'doctrine'. Cf. Stanley Hauerwas, *Sanctify Them in the Truth: Holiness Exemplified* (Edinburgh: T&T Clark, 1998), pp. 19–36.

characterize even those who inhabit the same tradition.
Indeed when, in the course of his discussion of 'sodomy',
Thomas simply concurs with Augustine that homosexual
acts are 'against nature' one is left wondering whether dogs
in parks have changed their habits over the centuries.[31]

Moreover, as such an instance may illustrate, a notion of
natural law might too easily presuppose that nature is now
indicative, and is now perceptibly indicative, of how God
intends it to be. It has already been noted that David
Hume's exposure of this 'naturalistic fallacy' rests upon a
radical rejection of any form of connectedness but, in its
more crude and basic form – that one cannot derive an
'ought' from an 'is' – the exposure of this naturalistic
fallacy is persuasive. Overwhelmingly the Christian
tradition has recognized that the universe as it presently
exists is not as it is ultimately intended to be. A doctrine of
the Fall, like the doctrine of Redemption, is cosmic in its
scope. Only by ignoring, or by minimalizing, the 'not yet'
character of the present universe can an 'ought' be derived
directly from an 'is', can 'nature' as presently perceived be
a valid and sufficient foundation for ethical judgement.
And if this qualification must be applied to the universe as
perceived it must similarly be applied to us as the
perceivers. Humankind also is qualified by the 'not yet' of
the Fall and of Redemption. Men and women are not now
in a position, unaided, to perceive the universe accurately
and draw valid ethical conclusions from that perception.
As the apostle Paul comments: 'their thinking became
futile and their foolish hearts were darkened' (Rom. 1.21).

This much Thomas, in his commentary on Romans,
clearly recognizes and it is this recognition that distinguishes him radically from his less cautious successors and
from the rationalistic optimism of the Enlightenment.[32]

[31] *ST* II–II 154 12.
[32] 'The natural recognition of God without the (implicit or explicit) grace
of the Mediator is therefore not a present possibility for anyone of whom
the text speaks' (Eugene F. Rogers, Jnr., *Thomas Aquinas and Karl Barth*, p.
144). Rogers is commenting on 116 of the Romans Commentary: 'In that
way God manifested it to them either interiorly infusing light or exteriorly
tendering visible created things, in which, as in some book, the cognition
of God might be read.'

According to Eugene Rogers (stressing the past tense of *'manifestavit ... legeretur'* as used by Thomas in his *Commentary on Romans*), such knowledge was only possible in Eden.[33] Thomas of course, in practice, interprets natural law within the context of the Christian tradition and, specifically, within the context of the official teaching of the Church. By the very context of the *Summa* and by the assumption of a 'Spirit-given' knowledge, albeit a knowledge given by the Spirit through the offices and traditions of the Church, Thomas preserves himself from this later, rationalistic, delusion. But one might have wished that his entire work, from its beginning, had been more explicitly Trinitarian in its focus, description and method.[34]

If some amongst Thomas's theological heirs fell into the trap of holding natural law to be universally and independently accessible it is probably because, like their Liberal Protestant counterparts, they were beguiled by the optimistic rationalism of the Enlightenment. But this optimism is a delusion. Every attempt to locate a foundation for morality that is universally accessible on the grounds that it is established by detached reason is doomed to failure. There is no detached reason. There could be no detached reason. There is no detached 'reasoner'. In this respect reason implies faith; it operates in the context of the perceptions and presuppositions of the 'reasoner'.[35]

In many senses we are witnessing the collapse of this modernist consensus and, as the next chapter will suggest, contemporary society has a consequent feel of rootlessness. At the most minimal level, this collapse of modernism removes the major root of the Church's feeling of

[33] Eugene F. Rogers, Jnr., *Thomas Aquinas and Karl Barth*, p. 238; cf. *ST* I 94 2–3.
[34] In fairness to Thomas, it has to be admitted that a similar sentiment could be expressed in relation to most Western theologians; Thomas is, in this respect, a faithful representative of an unfortunate tradition.
[35] 'Far [from] being a poor cousin or a shabby alternative to reason, therefore, faith actually furnishes the conditions under which reason must operate, and without which it can achieve nothing. Thus a realm in which reason is exalted is also, in truth, inevitably a realm in which faith is alive and active. Likewise, where faith acts, it does so precisely together with and not apart from an activity of reason' (Trevor Hart, *Faith Thinking*, p. 21).

intimidation. The Church can let her voice be heard again, albeit as part of the cacophony of other post-modern voices, without being disqualified for holding an 'opinion', having a distinct 'perspective', and confessing a 'faith'. But, as has already been noted, to deny any false, because independently rationalistic, foundation need not imply the denial of any foundation at all. The purpose of this book is to attempt to identify the essence of a distinctively Christian ethic and, were it to be seen as the sustained exposition of a single text, then that text would have to be '... no one can lay any foundation other than the one already laid, which is Jesus Christ' (1 Cor. 3.11).[36]

---

[36] Or, in the words of Colin Gunton: 'What, then, is wrong with foundationalism? It is not that it seeks a common basis for rationality, but that it seeks the wrong one and in the wrong way. It seeks the wrong basis, because it seeks one that is merely secular: something inherent within human reason and experience. It thus expects human reason to ground itself. It seeks it in the wrong way, because it believes that it can find what it wants apart from revelation. Another way of putting the matter would be to say that it is intellectually Pelagian' (Colin E. Gunton, *A Brief Theology of Revelation*, p. 50).

2
Morality and Post-Modernism

Defining post-modernism, not to mention trying to identify its beginnings, is far from straightforward not least because, notwithstanding the implication of the prefix 'post-', modernism persists. Appeals to the 'self-evident', together with the regular, if incoherent, belittling of community values in favour of an 'objective' and rationally based morality, has not noticeably abated, at least according to the evidence of the British media. Indeed, maybe the very phenomenon of post-modernism is evidence of this persistence since, as seems so often to be the case when the prefix 'post-' is added, the reference is not so much to that which succeeds that which has gone before as it is to that which reacts to a continuing phenomenon.

In this sense post-modernism is parasitic on modernism: it is evidence of modernism's sickness rather than a viable cure.[1] David Lodge observes that '[t]here is considerable disagreement among critics and aestheticians as to whether postmodernism is a really significant and distinctive kind of art, or whether, being an essentially rule-breaking activity, it must always be a minority mode, dependent on a majority of artists trying to keep the rules'.[2] The recognition of post-modernism as 'an essentially rule-breaking activity' is a helpful identification of one of the defining characteristics both of post-modernism itself and

[1] '... when language is not the basis of the communication that shapes our being – the only outcome can be fragmentation. In that sense, postmodernism is modernity come home to roost': Colin E. Gunton, *The One, The Three and the Many: God, Creation and the Culture of Modernity: The Bampton Lectures 1992* (Cambridge: Cambridge University Press, 1993), p. 124.

[2] David Lodge, *Working with Structuralism: Essays and Reviews on Nineteenth- and Twentieth-Century Literature* (London: Routledge, 1981), p. 15. Lodge later notes that Ihab Hassan views post-modernism 'as a change or development within modernism rather than a decisive break with it', *ibid.*, p. 68; cf. Ihab Hassan, 'POSTmodernISM: A Paracritical Bibliography', *New Literary History* 3 (1971), p. 7.

of the modernism against which it protests. It is perhaps for this reason that so much post-modern comment exudes an atmosphere of daredevilry, of militant nonconformity; it conveys an impression not dissimilar to that of childhood mischievousness or adolescent rebellion. For notwithstanding the appellation 'liberal', with its connotations of freedom and tolerance, liberal modernism demands adherence to its presupposed rules: nothing is as illiberal as liberalism.

The essence of liberal modernism is the assumption that morality should be grounded in human rationality itself and that a rationally grounded morality should be 'value-free' and therefore entirely accessible to any thinking person. Modernity presumes a radical disjunction of fact and value: facts are knowable to all through reason and experience whereas values are inherently personal, matters of individual belief and opinion. In 'un-enlightened' days, the values of a dominant community determined the moral norms that were demanded from everyone else. Enlightened liberalism has brought this imperious imposition to an end by exposing the 'value-laden' – and therefore 'sub-rational' – basis of this coercive morality. Rather, what is moral must be determined by what can be reasoned or experienced without the distorting encumbrance of personal opinions and beliefs. Any moral demand that cannot be demonstrated to be grounded purely in detached reason or experience must be marginalized as secondary, as a matter of personal opinion and preference. Only those practices which can be shown to be desirable purely through reason or experience are to be demanded.

But they are *to be demanded*. By such means liberal modernism claims for itself the moral high ground, a prerogative above every community tradition since it is derived without such distorting values: and to this prerogative every community tradition must comply. For if the moral norms of liberal modernism are universally accessible to reason and experience, without prejudice to individual values, then every reasonable person should be expected to adhere to those norms over and above their personal values or the traditions of their respective communities. Failure so to comply is irrational, an irrationality that must be addressed through a liberal education purged of the distorting influences of distinctive community traditions and beliefs. A more coercive programme it would be difficult to imagine. As Stanley Hauerwas has commented:

> ... the attempt to secure peace through founding morality on rationality itself, or some other 'inherent' human characteristic, ironically underwrites coercion. If others refuse to accept my account of 'rationality,' it seems within my bounds to force them to be true to their 'true' selves.[3]

It is unsurprising that any coercive agenda such as that described should be met with some resistance, but the resistance of post-modernism is even less surprising when considered against the background of the palpable failures, just in the course of the twentieth century, of liberal modernism. The century that witnessed unprecedented environmental damage in the name of progress, together with the horrors of the trenches in Flanders, the nauseating racial arrogance implicit in the Holocaust, the blanket bombing of urban areas of civilian population, the development, deployment and use of nuclear weapons, not to mention the rise and collapse of communism, is hardly the most persuasive advertisement for the effectiveness of the liberal agenda. Not least is this the case when it is considered that at least some of the moral disasters cited could be construed as being directly the outcome of that agenda. The protests of Bishop George Bell and others against the blanket bombing of German cities, protests rooted in a Christian tradition of just war, were ignored in

---

[3] Stanley Hauerwas, *The Peaceable Kingdom*, p. 12; cf. the following comment by Alasdair MacIntyre: 'Thus liberalism, while initially rejecting the claims of any overriding theory of the good, does in fact come to embody just such a theory. Moreover, liberalism can provide no compelling arguments in favour of its conception of the human good except by appeal to premises which collectively already presuppose that theory' (Alasdair MacIntyre, *Whose Justice? Which Rationality?*, p. 345).

favour of purely consequentialist arguments for shortening the war and demoralizing the German people. Similar consequentialist arguments were considered to justify the dropping of nuclear bombs on Nagasaki and Hiroshima. But, even more eloquently, the grinding greyness of Eastern European communism is testimony to the inherent totalitarianism of any system founded on the disavowal and suppression of community traditions and values. That collapsing communism should give way to the resurgence of inter-community strife is evidence, albeit depressing evidence, of the resilience of communities and their traditions. But what is just as depressing is the supposition of Western liberalism that such conflicts can be transcended by an appeal to higher 'objective' values: one form of rationalistic imperialism is to be replaced by another.

The necessarily diverse phenomenon of post-modernism does society the service of exposing the inherent contradiction of supposedly 'objective values'. My values are my own. My reasoning is my own. My experience is my own. Inevitably I filter every event and circumstance through the lens of my own history and influences. Liberal modernism, by alienating me from that history and those influences, creates the delusion of objectivity. But it is a delusion. Every appeal to 'objective values' is, in reality, my attempt to impose my individualistic values on others. Moreover, the radical individualism consequent upon the assumption that I can stand apart from my history and influences issues in values ultimately less persuasive than the community traditions they supposedly supersede since they fail to acknowledge their true grounding. In this respect post-modernism is not the counterpart to modernism; it is the exposure of modernism's underlying delusory reality.[4]

---

[4] The radical individualism underlying this process is exposed by Alasdair MacIntyre: 'My thesis is not that the procedures of the public realm of liberal individualism were the cause and the psychology of the liberal individual effect nor vice versa. What I am claiming is that each required the other and that in coming together they defined a new social and cultural artefact, "the individual." In Aristotelian practical reasoning it is the individual *qua* citizen who reasons; in Thomistic practical

There can be no such thing as a 'value-free' morality, an identification of rightness and goodness that is grounded in a universally accessible rationality without prejudice to individual or community traditions. A 'value-free' morality is a contradiction in terms. It is both delusory and deluding. Indeed, the delusion of 'pure objectivity' is itself the coercive means by which the community values of those in the ascendancy are claimed to be justly imposed throughout a society. The exposure of this delusory justification for arrogant totalitarianism is long overdue. Claims to 'pure objectivity' are epistemologically incoherent and, in this respect, post-modernism is not the opposite of modernism, less still is it its antidote; it is modernism itself with the virtue of a degree of honesty concerning its own lack of credible foundation.

In an unpublished paper read by David Hilborn at a postgraduate seminar I came across a helpful illustration of this epistemological delusion. The illustration assumes a knowledge of baseball and, since I can claim no understanding of baseball (and in particular of what does or does not constitute a 'strike') and am unaware of the origin of the illustration, I take the liberty of relocating it in the game of cricket.[5] Three different Umpires are explaining their

---

reasoning it is the individual *qua* enquirer into his or her good and the good of his or her community; in Humean practical reasoning it is the individual *qua* propertied or unpropertied participant in a society of a particular kind of mutuality and reciprocity; but in the practical reasoning of liberal modernity it is the individual *qua* individual who reasons' (Alasdair MacIntyre, *Whose Justice? Which Rationality?*, p. 339).

[5] The necessity for such a relocation for a primarily English readership is itself a further illustration of the dynamic being illustrated since the game of cricket is largely incomprehensible to anyone who does not, to some degree, inhabit the community and tradition of the game. Stanley Hauerwas (a Texan) uses the following quotation as the epigraph for a book: 'The aesthetics of cricket demand first that you master the game, and, preferably, have played it, if not well, at least in good company. And that is not the easy acquisition outsiders think it to be.' Commenting on the quotation in a footnote, Hauerwas says: 'On finishing the book, I ruefully have to admit that ... I do not understand cricket (and thus the book) but I better understand why I cannot understand cricket': Stanley Hauerwas, *In Good Company: The Church as Polis* (Notre Dame: University of Notre Dame Press, 1995), pp. 7, 219: quoting C. L. R. James, *Beyond a Boundary* (Durham, North Carolina: Duke University Press, 1993), p. 206.

attitude to the 'leg before wicket' (LBW) law.[6] The first claims that if a batsman is out 'lbw' he gives him out. The second claims that if a batsman seems to him to be out 'lbw' he gives him out. The third claims that if he gives a batsman out 'lbw' he is out.

The first Umpire stands as a typical modernist, believing not only in the 'pure objectivity' of the batsman being out 'lbw' but, with typically modernist delusion, apparently believing in his own infallible access to that 'pure objectivity'. The advent of television cameras, slow-motion replays, and 'expert' commentary, on the one hand, may have served to undermine this claim to infallible access. On the other hand, however, these same innovations may appear to give credence to the possibility of 'pure objectivity' by raising the question of whether or not the batsman 'was *really* out'. However, the 'lbw' law is so complex, and so overtly dependent upon matters of individual judgement, that arguments in the commentary box (not to mention the arguments between me and my son watching the recording on a television screen) undermine the delusion of pure objectivity. But, more fundamentally, the first Umpire clearly has forgotten the Laws of Cricket, according to which the probable path of the ball is explicitly a matter of the Umpire's 'opinion'.[7]

---

[6] It may be helpful to quote the law in full: 'The Striker is out 'Leg before wicket' – If with any part of his person except his hand, which is in a straight line between wicket and wicket, even though the point of impact be above the level of the bails, he intercepts a ball which has not first touched his bat or hand, and which, in the opinion of the Umpire, shall have, or would have, pitched on a straight line from the Bowler's wicket to the Striker's wicket, or shall have pitched on the off-side of the Striker's wicket, provided always that the ball would have hit the wicket.' Additionally, under the experimental Law 39, a batsman may be out 'lbw' if the following conditions are fulfilled: '(1) The ball lands on the pitch outside the off-stump. (2) The batsman intercepts the ball with some part of the body which is also outside of the line of the off-stump at the point of contact. (3) The batsman makes no genuine attempt to play the ball with the bat. (4) The ball would have bowled the wicket down if not intercepted by the batsman's body.'

[7] The 'experimental' Law concerning a ball pitching outside the line of the off-stump makes the additional demand upon the Umpire to judge whether or not a batsman makes 'a genuine attempt to play the ball with the bat'.

The second Umpire appears as both more humble and more balanced (maybe he has been intimidated by television commentary). The third Umpire, in his own way, appears as arrogant as the first (and could, perhaps, be perceived to be the extreme post-modernist, displacing any claim to objectivity in favour of his own personal opinion) but it is this third Umpire, rather than the second, who, according to the Laws of Cricket, is 'correct'. Umpires (together with Scorers) are included with Players in the Laws of Cricket and, to this degree, are part of the game – and the Umpire's decision is 'final'. This, of course, need not entirely invalidate discussion of whether an Umpire's decision was 'good' or 'bad', but such discussions do not alter the decision: the batsman was out because the Umpire said he was out; no matter how passionate the discussion in the commentary box, or the discussion between father and son, we are not part of the game – the Umpire is.[8]

It is the recognition of the importance of 'being part of the game' that distinguishes post-modern theories of knowledge and communication from indeterminate relativism or pluralism. *Communication*, as the term itself suggests, occurs within *communities*. The event of seeing, hearing, or reading does not occur in a vacuum of isolation, it occurs in a given context of meaning and understanding. It is for this reason that a text cannot mean just anything, not because it is accessible in some detached or objective manner – a text is a text inasmuch as it is read by someone – but because the someone reading the text already participates in some community of understanding. The point is made effectively in an article by Stanley Fish:

> The answer ... is that communication occurs within situations and that to be in a situation is already to be in possession of (or to be possessed by) a structure of assumptions, of practices understood to be relevant in relation to purposes and goals that are already in place; and it is within the assumption of these

---

[8] I can only ask readers to forgive this decline to gender-specific language enshrined in the Laws of Cricket.

purposes and goals that any utterance is *immediately* heard.
... while relativism is a position one can entertain, it is not a position one can occupy. No one can *be* a relativist, because no one can achieve the distance from his own beliefs and assumptions which would result in their being no more authoritative *for him* than the beliefs and assumptions held by others, or, for that matter, the beliefs and assumptions he himself used to hold.[9]

This book began by asking the question of whether there could be a distinctive approach to ethics that derives from Christian commitment and Christian identity. In some ways we have already arrived at a provisional answer (though the shape of that ethic remains to be demonstrated). No ethic can possibly be formed in a vacuum of detached objectivity; such a vacuum simply doesn't exist. Whether in a manner that is acknowledged or unacknowledged, whether consciously or subconsciously, moral values and practices are formed within specific communities and are shaped by the history and traditions of those communities. Post-modernism, notwithstanding the problematic diversity which is the outcome of that which it denies, at least has the merit of acknowledging this and celebrating it. That is to say, post-modernism is to be welcomed in respect of the detached objectivity which it denies and the communal context of communication which

---

[9] Stanley Fish, *Is There a Text in This Class? The Authority of Interpretive Communities* (Cambridge, Massachusetts: Harvard University Press, 1980), pp. 318f. In a separate essay included in the same volume Fish notes that 'we are never without canons of acceptability ... But the fact ... that readings once considered ridiculous are now respectable and even orthodox, is evidence that the canons of acceptability can change' (*ibid.*, p. 349). Stanley Hauerwas concludes a chapter in which he responds to Fish's arguments thus: 'God certainly uses Scripture to call the Church to faithfulness, but such a call always comes in the form of some in the Church reminding others in the Church how to live as Christians – no "text" can be substituted for the people of God': Stanley Hauerwas, 'Stanley Fish, the Pope, and the Bible' in *Unleashing the Scripture: Freeing the Bible from Captivity to America* (Nashville: Abingdon Press, 1993), pp. 19–28 (p. 28).

MORALITY AND POST-MODERNISM

it affirms even though the manner both of its denial and of its affirmations reinstates, albeit inversely, the very same incoherence it has previously exposed.

Whatever shape a Christian ethic may take, and by whatever means the authenticity of its claim to be distinctively 'Christian' may be tested, it receives that shape in living communities with their distinctive stories and traditions. Christian values, in reality, are not the outcome of abstracted theorizing on the implications of Christian belief, they are formed within the life of distinct communities. I derive my understanding of goodness and rightness not just from the stories that I have heard but from the context in which I heard them, from the lives of those who have been with me as we heard those stories together, from our collective living as much as from our collective thinking and hearing.[10] Consequently, if today we are confronted by rival claims to an authentically Christian ethic this is directly an outcome of the diversity of the Christian communities in which those understandings of goodness and rightness have been formed. For this reason, any attempt to investigate those factors which may constitute an ethic as authentically 'Christian' is, by definition, simultaneously an attempt to investigate the nature of catholicity.

It is the purpose of the central sections of this book to enquire concerning those factors that may validly identify a Christian ethic as 'Christian' and, consequently, to explore the practical (rather than theoretical) nature of catholicity, but no such attempt could be ventured without an initial acknowledgement of its inherent difficulties: we

---

[10] 'The Christian's character is not the result of a strict deduction from basic belief to act. This is not only often a logically doubtful procedure, but it also over-intellectualizes the nature of the Christian life. The "way of being Christian" comes rather from the historical experience of a particular people. The relation of their beliefs and practices is not formed by logical deduction, but by historical experience. Christians are simply those people who engage and do not engage in certain practices because they have found them appropriate or inappropriate to their way of life ...': Stanley Hauerwas, *Character and the Christian Life: A Study in Theological Ethics* (Notre Dame: University of Notre Dame Press, 1994; originally published San Antonio: Trinity University Press, 1975), p. 210.

are confronted with a bewildering array of claims to authentic Christianity and authentic Christian living arising from depressingly diverse expressions of Christian identity and community. Indeed, so marked is the diversity between various claimed expressions of Christian identity that one sometimes is strained to trace any vestige of commonality at all. Different aspects of the Christian story have been related in such different ways, alongside such different 'complementary' stories, within such different communities, that diverse systems of language have developed: it is difficult to identify that which is common between the communities in order for communication to happen effectively.

But if this is the case within and amongst those communities and traditions that can be identified as Christian it is even more markedly the case beyond these barely traceable boundaries. Post-modernism's exposure of the delusion of rationalistic foundationalism has issued in the confusion of Babel. This misplaced confidence in a rationalistic basis for commonality has been dethroned in favour of post-modernism's admission (and even glorification) of a lack of commonality. We seem no longer to be able to talk with one another. Evidence of this breakdown of communication is ubiquitous. Admittedly, that which it is deemed makes for 'good television' – that is the deliberate and manipulative bringing together of radically opposing viewpoints – may exaggerate this gap in understanding but underlying this artificiality there exists a genuine chasm. It is not merely that we can no longer agree with one another: we can no longer understand one another. The common foundation for discussion has been eroded. We no longer share agreed assumptions. Commenting on this phenomenon Alasdair MacIntyre opines that it is not just that no rational debate between traditions can occur, it also appears 'that each tradition must develop its own scheme in a way which is liable to preclude even translation from one tradition to another'.[11] This collapse of understanding isn't eased by focusing on

---

[11] Alasdair MacIntyre, *Whose Justice? Which Rationality?*, p. 348.

practical, rather than theoretical issues since, as Alasdair
MacIntyre earlier observes, '... each theory of practical
reasoning is, among other things, a theory as to how
examples are to be described, and how we describe any
particular example will depend, therefore, upon which
theory we have adopted'.[12]

As has already been intimated, post-modernism in its
various guises not only admits this lack of commonality
and consequent lack of communication, it celebrates it. The
totalitarian claims of an ethical foundation derived from
a supposedly universal rationality have been exposed
and jettisoned but this has issued, not in a quest for a
valid foundation, but in foundation-less existence that,
ultimately, is every bit as delusory and destructive as
the inauthentic foundation it has disowned. Moreover,
inasmuch as the phenomenon of post-modernism, while
rejecting modernism's foundationalism, continues to share
the liberal and individualistic assumptions of modernism,
rather than a positive reaffirmation of communities of
communication and the social context of perception,
post-modernism tends towards an individualism which is
even more radical because it is admitted and self-
conscious. Here then is the most destructive and extreme
form of alienation: I am imprisoned within the boundaries
of my own individual perceptions and values; cut off
from any sustainable community of knowing; cut off from
any assurance that my perceptions and values have any
validity beyond their personalized utility – their apparent
sustaining of my individual but delusory happiness. There
can be no basis for claiming that the perceptions and values
of any individual, or of any individual community, are
more valid than another's.

> In those days Israel had no king; everyone did as they
> saw fit. (Judges 21.25)

All knowledge is a dynamic of relatedness between the
knowing subject and the object known. If the delusion of

---

[12] Alasdair MacIntyre, *Whose Justice? Which Rationality?*, p. 333.

modernism derives from a belittling of the subjectivity of the subject (that is to say, the assumption that each subject can attain to some form of immediate and objective knowledge) then the parallel delusion of post-modernism derives from a belittling of the objectivity of the object.[13] Or, to put the matter more precisely, both modernism and post-modernism assume that all knowledge is 'immediate' to the individual knower, they differ only with respect to the universality of individual perception. This is what Colin Gunton means when he refers to foundationalism as 'intellectually Pelagian';[14] but the charge can similarly be extended to 'anti-foundationalism'. Both assume a radical independency of knowing. Neither contemplates the possibility that knowledge is a 'gift' or, again to put the matter more precisely, a 'being givenness' in which we remain entirely dependent.[15]

It is this rejection of any independent or 'Pelagian' account of our knowing that underlies Berkeley's response to Locke. John Locke suggested that, while the 'primary qualities' of objects exist in the objects themselves, their

---

[13] The point is well-made by Trevor Hart: 'Relativism refuses to admit the possibility of making genuine contact with reality, or of ever knowing that we or others have done so. It frees itself thereby to wander at will, footloose and fancy-free, from one point of view to the next without ever having to commit itself to anything; or, staying at home, it confines itself to polishing and protecting what it has inherited, untroubled by any external demands for revision, development or integration. Objectivism, meanwhile, creates its own reality. Convinced that what it sees and touches and tastes is "the facts", it feels no need to look any further, to consider any alternative points of view. Blindly confusing its particular perspective with "the way things actually are", it renders itself invulnerable to the claims of a reality which remains distinct from that perspective. The fact of epistemological crises pulls both these approaches up short. For here, occasionally, something intrudes into the familiar and accepted and disturbs us, something which refuses to fit into the ready-made categories furnished by our traditions, something which as yet finds no place in them. That something is reality, quietly reminding us of its presence in such a way that we can neither pretend we are ignorant of it, nor that we already have it neatly pinned down' (Trevor Hart, *Faith Thinking*, p. 227).

[14] Colin E. Gunton, *A Brief Theology of Revelation*, p. 50.

[15] 'The doctrine of revelation tells us that we cannot discover certain things unless we are taught them' (Colin E. Gunton, *A Brief Theology of Revelation*, pp. 58f.).

'secondary qualities' produce ideas in our minds. George Berkeley (1685–1753) disputed the 'ability' of a substance to 'cause' sensations in the mind, arguing contrarily that objects only exist inasmuch as they are perceived (*Esse est percipi*) or, to be precise, inasmuch as they are perceived by God; that we perceive anything is dependent upon (and a participation in) this foundational divine perception: 'God perceives everything, including our perceiving minds, and thus assures their existence.'[16] That Berkeley is generally heralded as the father of Idealism is itself an outcome of the 'mechanical' worldview that characterized the Enlightenment and a corresponding definition of God in terms of his absolute otherness to creation, a view which simply cannot comprehend a universe whose reality remains continually dependent upon God. Berkeley's doctrine is not Idealism, it is Realism grounded in God, or, in Berkeley's own words: '[i]f any man thinks this detracts from the existence or reality of things, he is very far from understanding what hath been premised in the plainest terms I could think of.'[17]

In his grounding of the reality of the universe in the knowledge of God, Berkeley is merely reaffirming the mainstream of the Christian tradition. Thomas Aquinas affirms that 'it is manifest that God causes things by His intellect, since His being is His act of understanding; and hence His knowledge must be the cause of things, in so far as His will is joined to it'.[18] That Berkeley's arguments were

---

[16] George Berkeley, *The Principles of Human Knowledge*, in *Works* II, ed. T. E. Jessup and A. A. Luce (London: Thomas Nelson & Sons, 1948ff.), pp. 19–113 (p. 49).

[17] *Ibid.* p. 36. In this respect Colin Gunton comments that '[t]he aim of Berkeley's polemic against atheism and scepticism was in part to establish the concreteness of the particular. Things are as they are perceived to be because God sees to it that they are. The fact that Berkeley's theory of particulars was taken, for example by the foolish Dr Johnson, to be the opposite of what it set out to be is in large measure the fault of the terminology of *idea* that he inherited from the tradition of Descartes and Locke. The concrete particulars appear to be unstable and merely occasional moments of perception rather than the substantial entities that Berkeley intended' (Colin E. Gunton, *The One, The Three and the Many*, p. 199).

[18] *ST* I 14 8. I am grateful to Colin Gunton for raising the question of whether the concept of perception is sufficiently active as a means

viewed as radical and novel only demonstrates the degree
to which a God-centred view of reality had been
abandoned.[19] But if Berkeley represents a reaffirmation of
the tradition he similarly represents a continuance of the
weakness of that tradition, or at least of the tradition of
Western theology. Colin Gunton observes that Berkeley's
'unitary traditional theism' makes it difficult for him to
maintain both the otherness of the world and substantiality.[20] Notwithstanding the prominence given to
the doctrine of the Trinity in Thomas's *Summa Theologica*
there is here, in subsequent Thomism, and overwhelmingly throughout the Western tradition, an insufficiently
Trinitarian account, both of the world, and of the manner
in which we apprehend it. What is lacking in Berkeley is
the explicit recognition that the Father's knowledge of the
universe, that gives the universe its reality, is *through*
the Son and the Spirit, and that our knowledge of the
universe, like our knowledge of the Father, is similarly
mediated by the Spirit through the Son.

Jonathan Edwards (1703–1757), a contemporary of
George Berkeley who similarly responded to the theories
of John Locke, comes closer to a more explicitly Trinitarian
account of reality and of our knowledge of it. Like
Berkeley, Edwards holds that our perceptions are
communicated to us by God.[21] Like Berkeley also, Edwards

---

of expressing God's creative act. In response – and following this
quoatation from the *Summa* – I can only refer to the notion of divine
simplicity: perception may be a 'passive' concept for us but this cannot be
so for God whose being *is* his act of understanding which *is* his will;
perception may not be causative with us but it is certainly so with God.
[19] Murray Rae indicates a similar God-centred reaffirmation in
Kierkegaard inasmuch as Kierkegaard is showing the importance of 'a
relational epistemology ... an epistemology, in other words, which finds
the condition for learning the Truth, not within the self, but in that which
is given by God': Murray Rae, *Kierkegaard's Vision of the Incarnation, by
Faith Transformed* (Oxford: Oxford University Press, 1997), p. 147. I am
grateful to my son-in-law, Tim Rose, for drawing my attention to this
reference.
[20] Colin E. Gunton, *The One, The Three and the Many*, p. 199.
[21] Jonathan Edwards, *Notes on the Mind*, in *Works of Jonathan Edwards*,
gen. ed. John E. Smith, vol. 6, *Scientific and Philosophical Writings*, ed.
Wallace E. Anderson (New Haven: Yale University Press, 1980), p. 339. I

understands created reality to be grounded in the active knowing of God, though, moving beyond Berkeley, Edwards holds that this eternal act of knowing, which is God's upholding of the created order, is 'equivalent to an *immediate production out of nothing*, at each moment, because its existence at this moment is not merely in part from God, but wholly from him, and not in any part, or degree, from its antecedent existence'.[22] But, unlike Berkeley, Edwards considers reality to be grounded not just in the knowledge of God but also in the love of God and, hence, reality is grounded in a Trinitarian manner. God knows and loves the universe as the One that he is, as Father, Son and Spirit: our knowledge of the universe is a participation in this Trinitarian knowledge.[23]

---

am grateful to my colleague, Stephen Holmes, for drawing my attention to these quotations, and I am also grateful for many conversations in which our mutual grasp of the contributions of Edwards and Berkeley have been deepened. Cf. *God of Grace and God of Glory: An Account of the Theology of Jonathan Edwards* (Edinburgh: T&T Clark, 2000). An interesting line of enquiry would be to compare this earlier theistically rooted epistemology with the more recent ideas of Alvin Plantinga in *Warrant and Proper Function* (New York: Oxford University Press, 1993). Paul Helm, for instance, comments that '... Plantinga is attempting not merely to argue for this or that Christian doctrine, not even the doctrine that there is a God, but to place epistemology, the account of all human knowledge, on supernaturalist foundations': Paul Helm, *Faith and Understanding* (Edinburgh: Edinburgh University Press, 1997), p. 203.

[22] Jonathan Edwards, *Original Sin*, in *Works of Jonathan Edwards*, gen. ed. John E. Smith, vol. 3, ed. Clyde A. Holbrook (New Haven: Yale University Press, 1980), p. 402. I share with Stephen Holmes a puzzlement concerning the objections to this theory: if the knowledge of God is the sole ground for reality then it is the *sole* ground for the continuance and connectedness of that reality. In this respect David Hume is justified in questioning the empirical grounds of connectedness (cause and effect): the connectedness of reality, like the reality of reality, is grounded in the knowledge of God *and nowhere else*. Edwards's notion is outlined and discussed by Paul Helm, *Faith and Understanding*, pp. 152ff.

[23] 'As to God's excellence, it is evident it consists in the love of himself. For he was as excellent before he created the universe as he is now. But if the excellence of spirits consists in their disposition and action, God could be excellent no other way at that time, for all the exertions of himself towards himself. But he exerts himself towards himself no other way than in infinitely loving and delighting in himself, in the mutual love of the Father and the Son. This makes the third, the personal Holy Spirit or the holiness of God, which is his infinite beauty, and this is God's infinite consent to being in general. And his love to the creature is his excellence, or the communication of himself, his complacency in them, according as

That which underlies the optimism of the Enlightenment, just as it underlies the development of Thomist theology after Thomas, is an assumption of 'pure objectivity' or, at least, an assumption of a universally normative and independent perception. A more thoroughly Trinitarian account of knowledge than, even optimistically, can be discovered in Thomas recognizes that all knowledge is a gift.[24] It is not just that I am dependent upon the Spirit if I am to know God, it is also that – and at this point something radically different to Thomas is being said – I am dependent upon the Spirit if I am to know anything at all. That the doctrine of the Fall defines the context in which we are now dependent upon the Spirit for an appropriate knowing of anything identifies the implicit Pelagianism of any optimistic assessment of independent human perception. But a recognition of the Trinitarian structure of all human knowledge identifies that, without prejudice to human fallenness, any claim to independent and objective perception is 'intellectually Pelagian'. It is this intellectual Pelagianism that underlies every attempt to identify some religiously neutral foundation for defining moral goodness and moral rightness. But, as Colin Gunton also recognizes, to reject 'foundationalism' is not necessarily to deny the possibility of a valid foundation for rationality.[25]

---

they partake of more or less of excellence and beauty; that is, of holiness, which consists in love; that is, according as he communicates more or less of his Holy Spirit' (Jonathan Edwards, *Notes on the Mind*, p. 364). I am not arguing that this could be considered an adequately Trinitarian account of reality and of our knowledge of it – it still assumes a predominately Augustinian, rather than Cappadocian, account of the Trinity – but I am suggesting that it is indicative of a manner in which Berkeley's account can be 'corrected'.

[24] It is interesting to observe the degree to which Thomas, in his 'Treatise on Man' (*ST* I 75–102), roots his arguments in Aristotle and Augustine, whereas the immediately preceding Questions, the 'Treatise on the work of the six days' (*ST* I 65–74), are answered more overtly in relation to Scripture and with more general reference to the Fathers. Thomas's treatment of human knowledge lacks any overt reference to a Trinitarian structure and dynamic for the act of human knowing, indeed, one needs to be generous to recognize this section of the *Summa* as being theocentric in any sense.

[25] Colin E. Gunton, *A Brief Theology of Revelation*, p. 50.

*cf. John Colwell and
my comment on
Abraham*

Inasmuch as so many 'post-liberal' theologians acknowledge their indebtedness to Karl Barth it is hardly surprising to discover, in his well-known rejection of the Liberal Protestantism of the nineteenth century (not to mention his equally well-known rejection of any form of *analogia entis*), an underlying rejection of any foundation for our knowledge of God independent of God's making himself known to us.[26] It is similarly hardly surprising, therefore, that attempts should be made to interpret Barth in a 'post-modern direction':

> Christian theology does have a 'center' or 'foundation' it wishes to know and to proclaim, for it believes in the living God. Nevertheless, this God cannot be reduced to a foundation located in human experience or tradition or anywhere else. In one sense God alone is the foundation of theology; but God is never reducible to a simple 'given' or 'presence.' Rather than proclaiming the absence of a 'center,' therefore, Barthian theology insists that it is the divine center *itself* that infuses the postmodern intellectual task with all its instability and risk.[27]

Without commenting on the use of the word 'Barthian' in this passage, this seems as good a place as any to offer my own comments on Johnson's interpretation of Barth. It seems to this reader that Johnson is so eager to make his case by (rightly) stressing Barth's understanding of the mystery of God that he takes insufficient account of the significance of Barth's stress on the divine promise

---

[26] William Stacy Johnson introduces his study of Barth with this acknowledgement: 'Lest it be thought the contemporary term "nonfoundational" is either misplaced or anachronistic in reference to Barth, one should note that long before the issue of whether "to have or not to have foundations" became intellectually fashionable, Karl Barth erupted on the European scene with his claim that there can be no "ground" or "givenness" (*Fundament, Gegeben*) to theological reflection': William Stacy Johnson, *The Mystery of God: Karl Barth and the Postmodern Foundations of Theology* (Louisville: Westminster John Knox Press, 1997), p. 3.
[27] William Stacy Johnson, *The Mystery of God*, pp. 184f.

(deriving from divine constancy).[28] As is instanced in the above quotation, Johnson knows that Barth's God is not arbitrary, but he doesn't seem sufficiently to acknowledge the implications of this. The intention of the previous paragraphs has been to indicate the possibility of a God-centred foundation for the dynamic of knowing, a foundation that defines us as dependent rather than independent in this act, a foundation that is dynamic – a 'being-givenness' rather than a 'givenness' – since it is mediated by the living Spirit. Certainly, as dependent rather than independent, such a foundation could not be substantiated by other rational or empirical means. Certainly, as dependent upon this God who is free in his love, this foundation 'is never reducible to a simple "given" or "presence"'. But to conclude, therefore, that the task of knowing is infused with 'instability' effectively denies the faithfulness of this God, the lovingness of his freedom in relation to the created universe.

But what would a Trinitarian dynamic of knowing imply for the manner in which the Church might continue to communicate with the world (or, for that matter, the manner in which differing traditions of the Church might communicate with one another)?[29] Jean-François Lyotard identifies postmodernity as 'incredulity towards metanarratives'.[30] Certainly the Church, in most of its manifestations and throughout most of its history, has proclaimed the gospel in the form of a 'metanarrative' with all of the characteristics implied by Lyotard – as an over-arching story that makes totalitarian and coercive claims, that seeks

[28] 'I have labored in these pages to be loyal to Barth by attempting to see what Barth saw, and in that way to "see beyond Barth." What I have tried to present in this study is a "useable" Barth, a more "open-ended" Barth who may still speak with power to a postmodern age' (William Stacy Johnson, *The Mystery of God*, p. 190).
[29] The provisional response indicated here will be expounded as the theme for the final section of this book.
[30] 'Simplifying to the extreme, I define *postmodern* as incredulity towards metanarratives': Jean-François Lyotard, *The Postmodern Condition: A Report on Knowledge*, trans. G. Bennington and B. Massumi (Minneapolis: University of Minnesota Press, 1984), p. xxiv. (The French word used is *grands reçits*.)

to control and exclude. But need it be so? Is not such a presentation of the Christian story, and of its implications for our knowing of reality, itself a denial of that story's character and of the God it seeks to narrate? It will be the intention of the final section of this book (partly following Barth's use of the word *Urgeschichte*) to examine the possibilities for thinking, living, and proclaiming the Christian story as 'sub-narrative', as that which underlies and offers possibilities for coherence. But before that task can be attempted the nature of the Christian story itself must be re-examined. And before that task can be attempted the signal unpreparedness of Protestantism for such a task needs to be confessed.

3
Morality and Protestantism

It would be both foolish and arrogant to attempt, in the space of a single chapter, a comprehensive account of Protestant approaches to ethics from the time of the Reformation until now. The theme is not just too vast; it is too diverse. Protestantism is no single or simple entity: the rift that initiated its distinct identity issued in countless subsequent rifts – not least because (though it was far from the intention of the first Reformers) the rejection of the authority of Rome blended with the radical individualism of the Enlightenment. One infallible Pope could now be replaced by as many infallible popes as there were (and are) Protestant Christians.[1] There are, then, a range of distinct (and often conflicting) approaches to ethics within Protestantism and an exhaustive description or detailed analysis of their origins would be well beyond the scope of this book (or the expertise of its author). This chapter, after all, like the previous two chapters of this section, is intended as introductory; its aim is to offer a personal view of the context for our living and thinking as Christians. Specifically its aim is to ponder the possible roots of Protestantism's apparent unpreparedness to speak and act coherently within the context outlined in the previous two chapters. Consequently, rather than any detailed analysis or summary, what is offered here is merely a personal enquiry concerning the possible roots of this unpreparedness, relating those possibilities (at least to some degree) to the positive proposals that constitute the remaining three sections of this book. My contention is that Protestantism, generally and to a significant degree, has lost confidence in its authority to speak and act within the world in a manner that coheres with the gospel and that

---

[1] For a provocative response to the contemporary North American form of this phenomenon see the article by Stanley Hauerwas that was mentioned in the previous chapter: 'Stanley Fish, the Pope, and the Bible', in Stanley Hauerwas, *Unleashing the Scripture*, pp. 19–28.

this loss of confidence is deeply rooted in aspects of its origin and early development, namely in misappropriations of the Reformation doctrines of *sola fide*, *sola Scriptura* and *sola gratia*.

Since this pretends to be no more than a personal response to a phenomenon (albeit a response conditioned by my own indwelling of the Christian community) let me begin with a personal anecdote, which is also a personal confession. Some few years ago I was engaged as a member of the pastoral team serving in a church in southeast London that, in fact, consisted of two churches that had just been brought together. Bringing two churches together was easy: almost immediately new friendships were established and it was difficult for visitors or newcomers to 'see the join'. Bringing the leaderships of two churches together, however, was entirely a different matter. After several months of increasing difficulty and tension we invited a friend, removed from the specific situation, to meet with us and advise us. Wisely, he spent time listening to each member of the leadership team, trying to discern the reasons underlying our ineffectiveness. In the course of his conversation with me I admitted my propensity (as another 'friend' put it) to 'pour oil on troubled waters and then drop a lighted match'. 'You see', I confessed, 'it's just my nature: in certain situations I "lose my rag".' I'm grateful now for his response (though I'm not sure that I was too grateful at the time). Graciously, but firmly, he reminded me that actually this was not 'my nature'; that I had received a new nature in Christ, and that I shouldn't make excuses for sin.

We really are quite expert at making excuses for our sinfulness, at claiming that we 'can't help it', and that 'it's just my nature'. But, when we do so, we betray the poverty and inadequacy of our doctrine of sanctification. I (along with many others) would suggest that this inadequacy is deeply rooted in the early development of Protestantism and, specifically, in a misappropriation of Luther's emphasis on 'justification by faith alone'. I say 'misappropriation' since, as is the case in relation to so many formative figures in Christian history, the fault would appear to be rooted in a caricature of Luther's teaching rather than in any careful reading of his own contribution.

Certainly Luther remained constant in his rejection of 'works righteousness' and of any notion that our standing before God might in any way be based on merit. But to portray Luther as uninterested in the practical holiness that derives from faith is a grave distortion of his position. In speaking of 'Two Kinds of Righteousness' (1519) Luther identifies the second, not as the false righteousness that is opposed to the righteousness that comes by faith, but as 'our proper righteousness' in which 'we work with that first and alien righteousness'.[2] Similarly, in the 'Treatise on Good Works' (1520), which comprises an extended exposition and application of the Decalogue, Luther argues that the truly righteous man 'draws his life out of his faith' and that true faith 'fulfils all commandments and makes all its works righteous, since no one is justified unless he does all the commandments of God'.[3] Indeed, it is hard to conceive of why Luther should lay such stress on the Decalogue, both here and elsewhere, if he had no interest in Christian behaviour.[4] Here, rather than being opposed

---

[2] 'The second kind of righteousness is our proper righteousness, not because we alone work it, but because we work with that first and alien righteousness. This is that manner of life spent profitably in good works, in the first place, in slaying the flesh and crucifying the desires with respect to the self ... In the second place, this righteousness consists in love to one's neighbor, and in the third place, in meekness and fear toward God': Martin Luther, 'Two Kinds of Righteousness', trans. Lowell J. Satre, in *Luther's Works* vol. 31, *Career of the Reformer I*, ed. Harold J. Grimm; gen. ed. Helmut T. Lehmann (Philadelphia: Muhlenberg Press, 1957) pp. 297–306 (p. 299).

[3] Martin Luther, 'Treatise on Good Works' (1520) trans. W. A. Lambert, revised. James Atkinson, in *Luther's Works* vol. 47, *The Christian in Society IV*, ed. James Atkinson; gen. ed. Helmut T. Lehmann (Philadelphia: Muhlenberg Press, 1966), pp. 21–114 (p. 31).

[4] 'There is just no better mirror in which to see your need than the Ten Commandments, in which you will find what you lack and what you should seek. Therefore, where you find in yourself a weak faith, feeble hope, and little love toward God; where you find that you do not praise and honor God but love your own honor and fame, think much more of the favor of men, do not gladly hear mass and sermon, are too lazy to pray (in which matters there is no one who has not sinned), then you must pay more heed to these infirmities than to all physical harm to goods, honor and life, and believe that they are worse than death and all mortal

to 'works', true faith 'goes out into works and through works comes back to itself again ...'.[5] Again, in the course of his letter 'Against the Antinomians' (1539), a piece primarily concerned with the preparatory place of law in preaching the gospel, Luther draws attention to the stress laid upon the catechism in all his writings.[6]

However, notwithstanding this underlying emphasis throughout Luther's writings on the character that derives from faith, his conviction that the Christian remains *simul iustus et peccator* appears to have been misappropriated even in his own lifetime. Commenting on Caspar Schwenckfeld's rejection of this *simul*, George Williams opines that 'it had been the palpable failure of Lutheranism to change the moral life of its proponents, especially among the simple parishioners, that had pushed Schwenckfeld, as a practical reformer, along the path that he called the royal way' (this 'royal way' represents Schwenckfeld's belief that 'the regenerate man was able to achieve sanctification').[7] There can be little doubt that this unease with Luther's *simul* was one of the factors underlying the Anabaptist emphasis on the obedience of

---

sickness. You should earnestly lay these [infirmities] before God, lament and ask for help, and with all confidence expect help, believing that you are heard and that you will receive help and mercy' (*ibid.*, p. 63). In an article comparing Luther's use of the Decalogue with that of Thomas Aquinas, Stanley Hauerwas focuses on the use of the Decalogue in *The Large Catechism* 'partly to avoid the criticism that the Treatise is early, thereby implying that what Luther says there about the Decalogue cannot be viewed as reflective of his mature position'. Hauerwas also draws attention to the observation by George Lindbeck that 'Luther never calls the Decalogue "law" but "instruction or teaching (*doctrina*) of the type which can variously be termed *praeceptum Gebot*, and *mandatum*" ': Stanley Hauerwas, 'The Truth about God: The Decalogue as Condition for Truthful Speech' in *Sanctify Them in the Truth*, pp. 37–59, p. 50; referring to George Lindbeck, 'Martin Luther and the Rabbinic Mind', in *Understanding the Rabbinic Mind: Essays on the Hermeneutic of Max Kadushin*, ed. Peter Ochs (Atlanta: Scholars Press, 1990), p. 151.

[5] Martin Luther, 'Treatise on Good Works', p. 79.

[6] Martin Luther, 'Against the Antinomians' (1539), trans. Martin H. Bertram in *Luther's Works* vol. 47 *The Christian in Society IV*, ed. Franklin Sherman; gen. ed. Helmut T. Lehmann (Philadelphia: Muhlenberg Press, 1971), pp. 107–19 (p. 112).

[7] George H. Williams, *The Radical Reformation* (Philadelphia: Westminster Press, 1962), pp. 109f.

discipleship.[8] Wrenched from its context of cheerful confidence in God's mercy, Luther's advice to Philip Melanchthon to 'sin boldly' is quickly misconstrued as counsel for carelessness.

The Lutheran emphasis on justification by faith alone is seen by Stanley Hauerwas to be the root of the tendency in both Karl Barth and Rudolf Bultmann 'to associate the very concept of ethics with man's attempt to justify himself before God'.[9] Commenting on Bultmann's essay 'Christ the End of the Law', Professor Hauerwas suggests:

> This understanding of ethics is Bultmann's attempt to carry through in a radical manner the Protestant principle of justification by faith. It assumes that all human activity is basically an attempt to secure the self from the demand of God. Man is a creature who is bent on justifying himself. This is the reason that even when man wills the good in a relative sense he wills evil, as he is actually willing the establishment of his own righteousness.[10]

While Hauerwas goes on to distinguish Barth from Bultmann on the basis of the former's understanding that 'the man himself has been created a new being',[11] and while he acknowledges at the beginning of his analysis that Barth's objections (like Bultmann's) are to an 'independent' or 'general conception' of ethics, there is no evading the strength of Barth's language in defining all 'general' ethics as 'sin':[12]

---

[8] 'Mere faith alone is not sufficient for salvation ... mere faith is like a green fig tree without fruit, like a cistern without water, like a cloud without rain ... mere faith does not deserve to be called faith, for a true faith can never exist without deeds of love': Balthasar Hubmaier, 'Apologia' (1528) in *Balthasar Hubmaier: Theologian of Anabaptism*, trans. and ed. H. Wayne Pipkin and John H. Yoder (Scottdale: Herald Press, 1989), pp. 524–62 (pp. 526f.).

[9] Stanley Hauerwas, *Character and the Christian Life*, p. 131.

[10] Stanley Hauerwas, *Character and the Christian Life*, p. 133, commenting on Rudolf Bultmann, *Essays: Philosophical and Theological*, trans. C. G. Greig (London: SCM Press, 1955), p. 51.

[11] Stanley Hauerwas, *Character and the Christian Life*, p. 141.

[12] *CD* II/2, p. 518.

Man cannot begin to answer the ethical question in actual life. He can only continue to recognize that he is wholly incapable of commanding an answer. The conception of the moral objective offers us only a sense of what the Bible describes as the *fall* of man, which precedes and determines all history.[13]

Certainly we must remember that Barth's objections are to a 'general ethic'. The adequacy of his account of the Christian life, together with the questions raised by Hauerwas concerning whether 'Barth's theological affirmations have a corresponding empirical reality', will be addressed later in this book,[14] but, to anticipate that discussion, the notion that Barth has little interest in an ethic rooted in the gospel would be difficult to sustain in the light of the considerable space he devotes to the theme within the *Church Dogmatics*.[15] Karl Barth, like Thomas Aquinas before him, held that to become a Christian implied a change of knowing that constituted a change of being.[16] It is this expectation for change that was undermined by an

[13] Karl Barth, 'The Problem of Ethics Today' in *The Word of God and the Word of Man*, trans. Douglas Horton (London: Hodder & Stoughton, 1928), pp. 136–82 (p. 166). For a summary of the traditional criticisms of Barth's approach to ethics see Nigel Biggar, *The Hastening that Waits: Karl Barth's Ethics* (Oxford: Clarendon Press, 1993), pp. 19–25. Biggar notes that those who would want to defend the mature Barth from such criticisms must reckon with the fact that even in 1953, in the first part-volume of the *Church Dogmatics* dealing with the doctrine of reconciliation, Barth still relates ethics to the fall (Nigel Biggar, p. 7, cf. *CD* IV/1, p. 448; cf. James M. Gustafson, *Protestant and Roman Catholic Ethics: Prospects for Rapprochement* (Chicago: University of Chicago Press, 1978): note that, even though he limits his analysis to 'moderate' Protestant theologians, Gustafson seems to have great difficulty in identifying a coherent entity (pp. 32ff.).
[14] Stanley Hauerwas, *Character and the Christian Life*, p. 146.
[15] One must remember that it was an issue of morality (his response to reading the signatories of the Kaiser's war policy) that contributed to Barth's change of theological direction (cf. Nigel Biggar, 'Hearing God's Command and Thinking about What's Right: With and Beyond Barth' in *Reckoning with Barth: Essays in Commemoration of the Centenary of Karl Barth's Birth*, ed. Nigel Biggar (London: Mowbray, 1988), pp. 101–18 (p. 101).
[16] This interpretation of Barth is outlined later in this chapter. See also Francis Selman's comment that '[f]or St Thomas grace is a reality, a *res*. This helps us see that theology is about *realities*. Grace does not just mean

interpretation, if not by the intention, of Luther's *simul*, together with his overwhelmingly forensic understanding of justification: if I am merely 'accounted' righteous and if, identified as righteous in this manner, I remain 'wholly sinful at the same time' (*simul totus peccator*), then it is difficult to sustain any lively expectation for the development of character in coherence with the gospel.

Sadly, the evidence for this lack of expectation is ubiquitous: it occurs, not just in the more blatant forms of antinomianism that have occasionally arisen within Protestantism, but in the assumptions that underlie many forms of British and North American evangelicalism. Evangelistic programmes informing 'converts' that they have 'become Christians' by virtue of having come to the front of a meeting in response to an appeal, repeated 'the sinner's prayer', or signed a 'decision card', are merely the more blatant instances of the assumption that becoming a Christian is merely a cerebral process, a matter of intellectual assent to a series of propositions. By contrast, more recent evangelistic programmes that focus on a defining experience, feeling or generated atmosphere, not only tend to lack significant intellectual content, they also tend to detach Christian 'experiences' from the rigours of daily discipleship. It is hardly surprising that many of those who are 'added' to the Church by such means experience (and demonstrate) little change that distinguishes them from wider society or from their own previous history – they expect none; they are given no grounds to expect otherwise. Indeed, the expectation that too often is instilled in such converts is that they will not change; that God has pronounced them righteous, not in a manner that may effect any change in them, but solely on the basis of the substitutionary righteousness of Christ; that they are 'justified' but still 'sinners'; that normal Christian experience is a cycle of continuing sin and

---

the way God looks on us or divine acceptance, as justification in Luther means that God does not count our sins against us, but it makes a *real* difference to us since it has positive effects, recreating and transforming us. St Thomas calls justification a change (*transmutatio*), by which we are ordered within to God': Francis Selman, *Saint Thomas Aquinas: Teacher of Truth* (Edinburgh: T&T Clark, 1994), p. 80; cf. *ST* I–II 113, 2.

continual confession; that God has forgiven them and will continue to forgive them. There is small wonder, then, that churches grounded on such pessimistic prospects have little credibility under the scrutiny of a critical society. Here then is one possible basis for a loss of ethical confidence within some elements of contemporary Protestantism: confidence to speak and live in a manner that is ethically distinctive is absent simply because the ethical essence of faith is denied; through a misappropriation of the doctrines of *sola fide* and *sola gratia* the language of ethics is dismissed as a symptom of self-justification and the possibility of practical ethical coherence is minimized or repudiated.

The distortion or misappropriation of a truth is always more dangerous than a blatant lie; it is beguiling simply because the underlying truth, though twisted, remains present. It is certainly not my intention to deny what I understand to be the Reformation doctrines of *sola fide* and *sola gratia*, or even to deny what I suspect Luther intended by his definition of the Christian as *simul iustus et simul peccator*: we are saved through God's mercy, not in respect of any merit on our part; and there will never come a time, at least in this life, when our dependence upon that mercy will cease or even diminish. But to interpret faith merely in terms of intellectual assent, to interpret justification merely in terms of judicial pronouncement (effectively severing it from any doctrine of sanctification), and to interpret grace merely in terms of mercy, represents (what at least this reader considers to be) a grave distortion both of the teaching of the Reformers and the teaching of Scripture.[17] Karl Barth has sometimes been criticized for implying that the Christian is distinguished from the non-Christian merely on the basis of that which the Christian knows,[18]

[17] Whether the Greek term δικαιοσύνη, as it is used in the New Testament, should ever be interpreted in this forensic sense will be considered in chapter eight of this book.
[18] 'The Holy Spirit is the awakening power in which Jesus Christ summons a sinful man to His community and therefore as a Christian to believe in Him: to acknowledge and know and confess Him as the Lord who for him became a servant' (*CD* IV/1, p. 740): the German words used here are *anerkennen, erkennen und bekennen*.

but, as was mentioned previously and as I have argued at length elsewhere,[19] this change of knowing constitutes a change of being.[20] For Barth, 'baptism in the Spirit' constitutes a genuine and actual change in the identity and life of the Christian.[21] Within the *Church Dogmatics* Barth uses cognates of the verb 'to know' with the same force and implications as they tend to bear in Scripture generally, and specifically bear in the Johanine corpus:

> ... you will know the truth, and the truth will set you free. (John 8.32)[22]

Here is a personal knowledge, an intimate knowledge, a transforming knowledge: the 'truth' that is known is not

[19] John Colwell, *Actuality and Provisionality: Eternity and Election in the Theology of Karl Barth* (Edinburgh: Rutherford House Books, 1989). Discussions of Barth's understanding of the Christian's knowledge occur especially on pages 260ff. and 285ff. Note in particular my arguments (on pages 298ff.) against the conclusion of Philip J. Rosato, S.J. in his book *The Spirit as Lord: The Pneumatology of Karl Barth* (Edinburgh: T&T Clark, 1981). Despite earlier recognizing that, for Barth, the Holy Spirit is 'the divine Noetic which has all the force of a divine Ontic' (p. 126), Rosato arrives at the amazingly contradictory conclusion that the Spirit in Barth's writing possesses 'a purely noetic function' (p. 161).

[20] Barth 'can refer to the work of the Holy Spirit in the "calling" of the elect as "the objective difference" (*die objektive Unterscheidung*) which "corresponds objectively" (*entspricht objektiv*) to the distinction which is peculiar to the elect': John E. Colwell, *Actuality and Provisionality*, p. 285; referring to *CD* II/2, p. 345 (*Die Kirkliche Dogmatik* II 2 (Zürich: Evangelischer Verlag, 1942), p. 380. Similarly, 'The work of the Holy Spirit in the sanctification of man is certainly to be described as the giving and receiving of a direction but this new direction radically alters man's actual existence, it does not just consist of a new possibility but the new actuality in which man is genuinely liberated from the bondage of his sinful being' (John E. Colwell, *Actuality and Provisionality*, pp. 291f.; referring to *CD* IV/2, pp. 522ff.).

[21] 'Baptism with the Spirit is effective, causative, even creative action on man and in man. It is, indeed, divinely effective, divinely causative, divinely creative. Here, if anywhere, one might speak of a sacramental happening' (*CD* IV/4, p. 34).

[22] Both the word γινώσκω, used here, and the cognate ἐπιγινώσκω can be used in a more general sense (though the idea of a 'detached' knowing of anything is probably foreign to Scripture) but, like the Hebrew word יָדַע they often are used to express a knowledge that is specifically personal or intimate.

a series of propositions but Jesus himself; he is known, not
in detachment, but personally in a manner mediated by the
Spirit; and this relational knowledge of the one who is
the truth does not merely inform, it transforms and
liberates the knower. Karl Barth, like the writer of the
Fourth Gospel, would be baffled (if not horrified) by a
'decision card' mentality. And, in this respect at least, Barth
is at one, not just with the Reformers, but also with Thomas
Aquinas and the mainstream of the Catholic tradition (and,
in fairness, not a few contemporary Evangelicals). The
Christian, by virtue of becoming a Christian, is a new
creation, has been re-born, has been re-made. The appropriate response to the gospel is not to come to the front and
sign a decision card, it is to 'repent and be baptized' (Acts
2.38). Baptism in water is not merely a demonstration of
belief and commitment, it is the promise and sign of the re-
birth which is baptism in the Spirit.[23] We are saved through
faith alone, but true faith, precisely because it is not mere
intellectual assent, does not remain alone. We are saved by
grace alone, but grace, though it accepts us as we are,
precisely because it is more than just mercy, does not leave
us as we are.
    Even if, especially with regard to his later writings,
there may be some grounds for dispute concerning the
coherence of Luther's account of the Christian life and his
all-pervading emphasis on *sola fide*, there need be no such
equivocation with respect to Calvin.[24] Both in his writing
and in his practice at Geneva, John Calvin is pre-
eminently focused on the continuing work of the Spirit in
the life of the believer and its outcome in practical

---

[23] For a response to Barth's later questioning of the sacramental significance of baptism see my article 'Baptism, conscience and the resurrection:
a reappraisal of 1 Peter 3:21' in *Baptism, the New Testament and the Church:
Historical and Contemporary Studies in Honour of R. E. O. White*, ed. S. E.
Porter and A. R. Cross (Sheffield: Sheffield Academic Press, 1999), pp.
210–27.
[24] François Wendel goes so far as to comment that 'The author of the
Institutes finds himself here in reaction against the unilateral accentuation
of justification that one meets with in Luther and his disciples': François
Wendel, *Calvin: The Origins and Development of His Religious Thought*, trans.
Philip Mairet (London: Collins, 1963), p. 257.

52   LIVING THE CHRISTIAN STORY

holiness.[25] Throughout his discussion of 'the way we receive the grace of Christ' he resolutely refuses to separate justification from sanctification:

> ... Christ justifies no one whom he does not at the same time sanctify. These benefits are joined together by an everlasting and indissoluble bond, so that those whom he illumines by his wisdom, he redeems; those whom he redeems, he justifies; those whom he justifies, he sanctifies.[26]

For Calvin, to divide justification from sanctification would be tantamount to dividing Christ: to be a Christian is to participate in Christ and his benefits through the Spirit. By receiving Christ we are both reconciled to the Father 'through Christ's blamelessness' and sanctified by the Spirit in order that we 'may cultivate blamelessness and purity of life'.[27] At the very beginning of the *Institutes*, in his discussion of 'the Knowledge of God the Creator', Calvin argues that there can be no true knowledge of God without accompanying piety.[28] Similarly, Calvin refuses to separate faith, as the knowledge of Christ, from 'a devout disposition' since 'Christ cannot be known apart from the sanctification of his Spirit'.[29] Indeed, at certain key points in the *Institutes* Calvin appears to use the word 'right-eousness' (*iustitia*) in a manner that embraces both the idea of forensic justification (as in Luther) and the active

[25] In relation to the order of Calvin's treatment of the themes of regeneration and justification in the final version of the *Institutes*, T. H. L. Parker comments that 'Calvin had laid himself open to attack from Lutherans as suggesting that good works, although produced by faith, can at least be considered before justification ...': *Calvin: An Introduction to His Thought* (London: Geoffrey Chapman, 1995), p. 95.
[26] *Institutes* III xvi 1.
[27] *Institutes* III xi 1. In the course of his response to Osiander, Calvin similarly comments that '... as Christ cannot be torn into parts, so these two which we perceive in him together and conjointly are inseparable – namely, righteousness and sanctification' (*Institutes* III xi 6).
[28] *Institutes* I ii 1: 'I call "piety" that reverence joined with love of God which the knowledge of his benefits induces'.
[29] *Institutes* III ii 8.

righteousness which is the outcome of regeneration and has as its goal the restoration of the image of God.[30]

Certainly Calvin does not believe that this restoration is completed in an instant – 'there remains in a regenerate man a smoldering cinder of evil'[31] – but the Christian, by virtue of this regeneration through the Spirit, has a new nature and therefore a new series of possibilities.[32] The Christian, then, though in this wholly new situation, is involved nonetheless in a lifetime of struggle:

> ... this restoration does not take place in one moment or one day or one year; but through continual and sometimes even slow advances God wipes out in his elect the corruptions of the flesh, cleanses them from guilt, consecrates them to himself as temples renewing all their minds to true purity that they may practice repentance throughout their lives and know that this warfare will end only at death.[33]

It is in relation to this continuing struggle that the law, according to Calvin, is 'useful' to the Christian. Like Luther and others before him, Calvin understands the law to have been given to lead us to Christ,[34] and to restrain unbelieving sinners.[35] But that which I have suggested to be implicit in Luther's use of the Decalogue is made explicit by Calvin, namely that the law is also 'useful' in the practice of Christian living:

---

[30] '... we are restored by this regeneration through the benefit of Christ into the righteousness of God; from which we had fallen through Adam' (*Institutes* III iii 9).

[31] *Institutes* III iii 10.

[32] François Wendel comments that 'the death of the old man in us and the new birth are certainly no mere imaginations: on the contrary, they are expressions of a reality. But this reality has its existence solely in Christ – at least as regards its attainment, and so long as we are living on earth. We attain to and participate in it only in the same measure as we are united with Christ. We continue to be sinners even while we are being progressively sanctified' (Wendel, *Calvin*, p. 243).

[33] *Institutes* III iii 9.

[34] *Institutes* II vii 1–9.

[35] *Institutes* II vii 10–11.

> The third and principal use, which pertains more
> closely to the proper purpose of the law, finds its place
> among believers in whose hearts the Spirit of God
> already lives and reigns. For even though they have
> the law written and engraved upon their hearts by the
> finger of God ... that is, have been so moved and
> quickened through the directing of the Spirit that they
> long to obey God, they still profit by the law ...[36]

Note that, for Calvin, it is this that constitutes the
'principal' use of the law. Certainly the law has been
abrogated for the Christian inasmuch as it is no longer 'a
power to bind their consciences with a curse'.[37] Certainly
the ceremonial law has been abrogated inasmuch as it has
been fulfilled through Christ's sacrifice.[38] But the law
remains useful inasmuch as, through it, the Christian may
'learn more thoroughly each day the nature of the Lord's
will' and, through 'frequent meditation' upon it, the
Christian may 'be aroused to obedience, be strengthened
in it, and be drawn back from the slippery path of
transgression'.[39]

Here again, while it would be difficult to dispute the
manner in which Calvin speaks of the law's utility in these
passages, the manner in which this proposal was received
and interpreted is another matter entirely. For Calvin, the
essence of sanctification is our participation in Christ by
the Spirit and growing conformity in his image. By the
Spirit, God's ultimate law – which is his perfect will – has
been 'written on our hearts'. The law previously written on
tablets of stone, then, remains 'useful' to us as a provisional
(and partial) expression and guide for our progress in
holiness: it does not, therefore, comprise the essence of
holiness itself. But what, for Calvin, remained a matter
of secondary utility all too easily became the primary
concern and focus amongst his theological heirs and

---

[36] *Institutes* II vii 12.
[37] *Institutes* II vii 14.
[38] *Institutes* II vii 16.
[39] *Institutes* II vii 12.

interpreters: biblical law itself came to be seen as the measure of holy living.[40] The matter is illustrated by the issue of sabbatarianism. For Calvin, as for Luther before him, the growing phenomenon of sabbatarianism was to be resisted; the sabbath law was to be recognized as part of the cultic law that had been fulfilled by Christ.[41] Yet on the evidence of his Presbyterian heirs one would never suspect that this was Calvin's teaching concerning the Sabbath. In this as in every other respect one quickly gains the impression of inhabiting legalistic territory where the Pharisees who opposed Jesus would feel entirely at home.

This focus on biblical law as an 'objective' standard of holiness was considerably compounded by the misappropriation of another facet of Calvin's thought. Within the *Institutes* the doctrine of predestination serves the pastoral purpose of reassuring believers that their salvation is rooted in God and not in themselves: they are saved because they are chosen. At no point does Calvin encourage any form of personal introspection in order to discern the 'fruits' of election; any 'testimony of works' in the life of the believer is merely an *adminiculum inferius*; only by looking at Christ can the believer be assured of the Father's love and mercy. Nor indeed does Calvin

---

[40] While it would be far from the intention of its author, this subtle change of focus is amply illustrated in Ernest Kevan's thoroughly sympathetic study of Puritan moral theology: Ernest F. Kevan, *The Grace of Law: A Study in Puritan Theology* (London: Carey Kingsgate Press, 1964) – 'The Law which is obligatory on the believer is the same in substance as the Law of Moses' (p. 158). The same point is made in the following quotation from William Pemble: 'The righteousness of the Law, and of the Gospell, are not two severall kindes of righteousnesse; but the same in regard of the matter and substance thereof' (p. 216), quoting William Pemble, *Vindiciae Fidei: A Treatise of Justification by Faith* (Oxford, 1625), p. 3; and again with reference to John Flavel: 'The fact of identity between the original Law and the newly-written Law is in John Flavel's mind when he speaks of God's action as a reviving of the knowledge of the Law in the heart of man and a trimming of the lamp of reason' (p. 226); referring to John Flavel, *The Reasonableness of Personal Reformation and the Necessity of Conversion* (London, 1691), p. 3.

[41] *Institutes* II viii 28–34; cf. Martin Luther, *Against the Sabbatarians: Letter to a Good Friend*, in *Luther's Works* vol. 47, ed. Franklin Sherman; gen. ed. (vols. 31–55) Helmut T. Lehmann (Philadelphia: Muhlenberg Press, 1971), pp. 65–98.

encourage any unhealthy preoccupation with the doctrine itself but rather warns his readers against such folly.[42] The point is similarly made in a separate work, published in 1552, to refute ideas of free will proposed by the Roman Catholic theologian Albert Pighius.[43] Here again the believer is discouraged from any form of introspection; assurance of salvation is located in Christ himself who is 'for us the bright mirror of the eternal and hidden election of God, and also the earnest and pledge':[44]

> If Pighius asks how I know I am elect, I answer that Christ is more than a thousand testimonies to me. For when we find ourselves in His body, our salvation rests in a secure and tranquil place, as though already located in heaven.[45]

But, as Karl Barth was later to point out, it is difficult to see how he could expect believers to be content to fix their assurance in Christ when Calvin had previously defined election in terms of a hidden decree of election and reprobation.[46] If my salvation is determined, not in Christ, but in a hidden decree of the Father before the world's foundation, how can I be content to see in Christ the mirror

---

[42] 'First, then, let them remember that when they inquire into predestination they are penetrating the sacred precincts of divine wisdom. If anyone with carefree assurance breaks into this place, he will not succeed in satisfying his curiosity and he will enter a labyrinth from which he can find no exit. For it is not right for a man unrestrainedly to search out things that the Lord has willed to be hid in himself, and to unfold from eternity itself the sublimest wisdom, which he would have us revere but not understand that through this also he should fill us with wonder. He has set forth by his Word the secrets of his will that he has decided to reveal to us. These he decided to reveal in so far as he foresaw that they would concern us and benefit us' (*Institutes* III xxi 1).

[43] John Calvin, *Concerning the Eternal Predestination of God*, trans. J. K. S. Reid (London: James Clarke, 1961). The work is, in fact, a re-working of an earlier book (*De libero Arbitrio*, 1543).

[44] John Calvin, *Concerning the Eternal Predestination of God*, p. 127.

[45] John Calvin, *Concerning the Eternal Predestination of God*, p. 130.

[46] 'We call predestination God's eternal decree, by which he compacted with himself what he willed to become of each man. For all are not created in equal condition; rather, eternal life is foreordained for some, eternal damnation for others' (*Institutes* III xxi 5).

of my election?[47] What alternative do I have, if the decision whereby I am saved is hidden from me, but to seek evidence of my election in myself? The Puritan *syllogismus practicus* is the inevitable outcome of such reasoning: God's elect produce the fruits of election; I produce the fruits of election; therefore I am among God's elect. Here, then, is a most effective way of smuggling a 'works righteousness' (as Luther would have termed it) through the back door of Reformed theology. Inevitably the outcome of this 'reflexive' assurance is either despair or arrogant presumption and both responses are amply illustrated in the course of Reformed ecclesiology: on the one hand we find despair worse than that of the tax collector since, failing to find sufficient evidence of election in one's life, one must conclude that one is amongst the reprobate and therefore beyond God's mercy; and on the other hand we find self-satisfied complacency that far outstrips the Pharisee's confident praying (Luke 18.9–14). And, of course, in such a context an 'objective' means of assessing the fruit of election in my life is crucial. It is hardly surprising that biblical law assumed such prominence for the Puritans.[48]

---

[47] '... can we really expect this man ... to hold primarily to Christ? If Christ is only the means of grace of the God who secretly elects or rejects, then how can He be the crown witness for his election? If he himself is the one elected by the hidden God, why cannot he himself rather be the crown witness, and the *consideratio operum* be no mere *adminiculum inferius*, but the first and decisive stage of election' (*CD* II/2, p. 338).

[48] For a helpful and lucid overview of this 'domestication of grace' by the heirs of the Reformers see William C. Placher, *The Domestication of Transcendence: How Modern Thinking about God Went Wrong* (Louisville: Westminster John Knox Press, 1996), esp. pp. 88–107. Thorough accounts of the development of Puritan theology are presented by M. Charles Bell, *Calvin and Scottish Theology: The Doctrine of Assurance* (Edinburgh: Handsel Press, 1985) and R. T. Kendall, *Calvin and English Calvinism to 1649* (Oxford: Oxford University Press, 1979). It should be observed, however, that there were notable exceptions to these trends that retained a Christ-focused basis for assurance and resisted any confidence in a 'testimony of works'. So, for instance, the following extract from Richard Sibbes: 'Christ was chosen before all worlds to be the head of the elect. He was predestinate and ordained by God. As we are ordained to salvation, so Christ is ordained to be the head of all that shall be saved. He was chosen eternally, and chosen in time. He was singled out to the work of God; and all others that are chosen are chosen in him. There had been no choosing of men but

This descent into legalism – a descent which, in fact, lost sight of both grace and mercy – was, of course, not without its protests, but the protests generally were dismissed by the mainstream of the Reformed movement as dangerous instances of antinomianism (though a detailed inspection of the teaching of those so dismissed usually reveals their ideas to have been closer to those of Calvin than were those of their supposedly 'orthodox' detractors).[49] Notwithstanding his self-declared 'Arminianism', John Wesley's teaching on holiness similarly can be interpreted as an attempt to reinstate sanctification as a gracious work of the Spirit (just as his rejection of predestination, in the only form in which he had encountered it, can be interpreted as an attempt to reassert a Christ-centred assurance).[50] Certainly the 'Keswick' movement of the late nineteenth and early twentieth centuries – itself, at least in part, an heir of Wesley's teaching – was a clear attempt to identify sanctification as a work of grace rather than as an outcome of mere human effort.[51] However, that both Wesley and Keswick viewed sanctification as a separate and subsequent work of the Spirit demonstrates the degree to which expectations of initial Christian conversion had been minimalized. And that the distinctive emphases of the early Keswick movement seem to have been qualified (or even repudiated) as the twentieth century progressed only serves as evidence of the enduring allure of legalism.[52]

---

in him; for God saw us so defiled, lying in our filth, that he could not look upon us but in his Son He chose him, and us in him': Richard Sibbes, 'A Description of Christ' (1639) in *Works of Richard Sibbes*, vol. 1, ed. Alexander B. Grosart (Edinburgh: Banner of Truth Trust, 1973), pp. 1–31 (p. 9).

[49] M. Charles Bell, *Calvin and Scottish Theology*, is particularly good at pointing this out.

[50] For an analysis along these lines of Wesley's contribution (particularly in comparison with John Calvin, John Owen and Richard Baxter) see Alan C. Clifford, *Atonement and Justification: English Evangelical Theology 1640–1790 An Evaluation* (Oxford: Clarendon Press, 1990).

[51] Both the teaching of Wesley and of the early Keswick movement will be considered in greater depth in the course of chapter seven of the book.

[52] For a full and authoritative discussion of these developments see Ian M. Randall, *Evangelical Experiences: A Study in the Spirituality of English Evangelicalism 1918–1939* (Carlisle: Paternoster Press, 1999).

This allure of legalism ought not, perhaps, to be so surprising. To codify behavioural demands is to simplify those demands and, hence, to render them (apparently) more accessible. If holiness can be reduced to a series of prescriptions and proscriptions then I have 'objective' criteria for assessing my own progress and that of my Christian associates. A similar disposition towards legalism can be observed in the development of the Mennonite strand of Anabaptism, a development that is probably best considered in distinction rather than response to Lutheranism or Calvinism. To listen to any modern-day Mennonite repudiating the taking of an oath leaves this listener, at least, with the feeling that, once again, we are inhabiting a context where camels are regularly swallowed with ease and gnats are removed from the menu (Matt. 23. 24).

If the previously observed weakness of Protestantism seemed to relate to a misappropriation of the doctrines of *sola fide* and *sola gratia* then, in relation to this tendency towards legalism, we would seem to have a misappropriation of *sola Scriptura*. Here faith and grace appear to have been marginalized while Scripture has been appropriated as if it were a 'book of rules'. William Placher is surely right to identify this as a 'domestication' of grace and of God himself, but it also represents a domestication of Scripture.[53] It is certainly not my intention to deny the *sola Scriptura* of the Reformation, any more than it was previously my intention to deny the *sola fide* or *sola gratia*, but we accord Scripture poor honour if we press it to a service for which it was not intended and for which it is so poorly suited. Proposals for a more faithful reading of Scripture will be the focus of the next section of this book but, at this point, we need merely to notice the monumental impracticality of this strategy.[54]

---

[53] William Placher, *The Domestication of Transcendence.*
[54] It is not just, or even primarily, that I find such literalist readings of Scripture unpersuasive (though, of course, I do), it is more that I consider them to be 'unfaithful'. By implying that we are dealing here with 'objective' facts (or rules), accessible to independent reason, such strategies undermine the actual authority of Scripture that is dependent upon

Any attempt to read the Bible as if it were intended to provide a blueprint for behaviour fails, as Stanley Hauerwas points out in relation to any rule-based ethic, to take account of the complexity of moral life,[55] but it also fails to take sufficient account of Scripture's radical particularity. This is not a series of detached and 'time-free' texts but of narratives rooted in specific time and space. Where the text does take the form of a rule it does so within the context of a temporally and spatially specific narrative. Consequently, even apparently 'timeless' rules concerning killing and stealing are rooted in a narrative context: the command not to kill – rightly translated by the more specific, 'You shall not murder' – is immediately hedged by contextually specific qualifications concerning what does and what does not constitute legitimate killing; similarly the command, 'You shall not steal', is related particularly to the economic and social conditions of ancient Israel (Exod. 20.13, 15).[56] This, of course, is not to claim that such laws have no relevance whatsoever for contemporary Christian behaviour, but it is to acknowledge the difficulties of any straightforward transposition: we ought not to assume that what constituted legitimate or illegitimate killing in ancient Israel will necessarily be determinative for the complex dilemmas deriving from modern medical science; nor should we assume that the economic and social structures of ancient Israel are necessarily a sufficient basis for contemporary business ethics. The manner in

---

the Spirit and accessed within the life and worship of the Church. For an interesting and lively discussion of these issues see particularly the first two chapters of Helmut Thielicke's *Between Heaven and Earth: Conversations with American Christians*, trans. and ed. John W. Doberstein (London: James Clarke, 1967).

[55] 'The problem of legalism is not only that it is religiously faulty as an attempt to domesticate God's will; but it is morally faulty, for the man who observes only the external norm cannot be trusted to act faithfully in view of the complexity of most of our action' (Stanley Hauerwas, *Character and the Christian Life*, p. 208).

[56] Those who would hear these commands as 'time-free' must reckon with the appropriateness of stoning a girl to death if she cannot produce 'proof' of her virginity on her wedding night and, similarly, with the avoidance of any and every form of usury (which, according to the Torah, is counted as theft).

which, for instance, texts concerning God's presence and purposes in the beginnings of human life are pressed into service of the abortion debate is not just a misuse of those texts, it is also deeply unconvincing.[57]

I am suggesting that this ever-widening gap between the possible references of Scripture, treated as a 'book of rules', and the complexities of contemporary life represents a further basis for Protestantism's loss of ethical confidence; a loss of confidence which, in this respect, tends to manifest itself in a retreat to the specifically non-biblical and modernistic approaches to ethical decision making considered in chapter one of this book. As was noted then, the disproportionate emphasis on consequentialist and 'rights' based approaches to ethics in so many Protestant theological courses is testimony to this loss of confidence.

Of course, this loss of confidence in a rule-based ethic derived from a particular reading of Scripture is not ubiquitous. In its most sinister form, it survives in the total-itarian claims of 'Reconstructionism' with its millennialist expectations of a Christian majority and the consequent imposition of biblical law on secular society.[58] More generally, it survives, and even thrives, in fundamentalist circles where its lack of credibility or persuasiveness is almost perceived to be an advantage, making visible the absolute distinction between the Christian community and the world. However, the assumption of this absolute distinction – the assumption that the world will not be able to comprehend the ethical life and claims of the Church – is not confined to Fundamentalism and may rather derive from another deeply rooted tendency of Protestant thought.

[57] This misappropriation of Scripture is rooted, not just in the sinful desire for codified self-justification, it is also a symptom of the funda-mentalist tendency to force Scripture into a modernist strait-jacket by treating it as if it were a scientific textbook. It is ironic that, in their rigorous opposition to modernism, these literalist approaches rest on explicitly modernist assumptions.

[58] For an example '. . . civil law cannot be separated from Biblical law, for the Biblical doctrine of law includes all law, civil, ecclesiastical, societal, familial, and all other forms of law. The social order which despises God's law places itself on death row: it is marked for judgment': Rousas John Rushdoony, *The Institutes of Biblical Law* (Nutley, NJ: The Presbyterian and Reformed Publishing Company, 1973), p. 4.

That Abraham stands before God pleading for Sodom on the basis of God's justice implies both that divine justice is not arbitrary and also that, while Abraham may have an inadequate conception of justice and while divine justice may not be subject to independent rational definition, divine justice is at least coherent within a created context.[59] Abraham's assumptions are not universally shared. In Plato's *Euthyphro* we encounter the question of whether something is right in itself or whether it is right simply because God commands it (and, if the former, why we should need God to command it at all).[60] Socrates' distinction may be rendered meaningless once it is acknowledged that the universe (which is the only context we have in which to discern rightness) is itself the creation of God who is absolutely righteous, and that our knowledge of rightness (as our knowledge of anything) is mediated and dependent rather than immediate and independent. However, the question receives a novel and disastrous twist once the absolute goodness of God is undermined by a suspicion of arbitrariness. When Calvin argues that 'God's will is so much the highest rule of right-eousness that whatever he wills, by the very fact that he wills it, must be considered righteous' this may be taken as an affirmation of the utter goodness of God and (in conse-quence both of our mortality and our fallenness) our dependence upon him to know what is right.[61] It could also, however, be taken as implying that what is right, for God himself, is arbitrary.[62]

59 'Will not the Judge of all the earth do right?' (Gen. 18.25) translates לֹא יַעֲשֶׂה מִשְׁפָּט הֲשֹׁפֵט כָּל־הָאָרֶץ. Note that, in this story, God's justice exceeds Abraham's hopes: though he finds less than ten righteous in the city, and though he consequently destroys the city, he first rescues the righteous that he does find.
60 Plato, *Euthyphron or 'On Holiness'* in *The Works of Plato* vol. 1, trans. Henry Cary (London: G. Bell & Sons, 1915), pp. 458–76 (pp. 467ff.).
61 *Institutes* III xxiii 2.
62 This may be a convenient strategy for coping with the moral diffi-culties of divinely sanctioned genocide in Joshua and Judges but it is an exegetical convenience bought at far too high a price. It is a blasphemous strategy. A god whose goodness is arbitrary could not be identified as the God of the gospel. An alternative exegetical strategy will be suggested in chapter ten of this book.

If we entertain the possibility of interpreting Calvin in the latter sense it is partly through a recognition of the dominance of nominalism in the era immediately preceding the Reformation. Certainly Luther, if not Calvin, was influenced by the nominalism propounded by William of Ockham which, by denying that 'forms' of justice or goodness exist even for God, established divine arbitrariness and in the words of Colin Gunton, '... because it subverted the rationality of theology, thus severing *any* link between revelation and reason, ... in practice achieved the opposite of what it required'.[63] It is difficult to see how ethical coherence can be maintained once nominalist assumptions are admitted. As Oliver O'Donovan has observed, '... hatred of God and other sins are evil merely circumstantially, by virtue of being performed by someone who has been forbidden by God to perform them ... If they were commanded by God, they would be meritorious'.[64] The outcome of nominalism is ethical gnosticism: knowledge of the good is not just mediated and dependent; it is irrational and incoherent.

But, as Colin Gunton has also observed, the roots of divine arbitrariness are even more deeply embedded in the tendency of Western theology to define God primarily in terms of his will rather than his love.[65] Whether or not Calvin is influenced by the nominalism of Ockham, the spectre of divine arbitrariness lurks beneath his account of

---

[63] Colin E. Gunton, *A Brief Theology of Revelation*, p. 47. Note also Professor Gunton's earlier comment that 'Ockham abolished particularity by asserting the existence only of particulars while simultaneously denying that there are real relations between them. Ockhamism is thus a doctrine of the Platonic abstract particular deprived of the support of the forms, which at least has the merit of conceiving a form of relatedness between things' (Colin E. Gunton, *The One, The Three and the Many*, pp. 56f.).

[64] Oliver O'Donovan, *Resurrection and the Moral Order*, pp. 134f.

[65] '... it comes to be that the theme of love becomes subordinate to that of will. If not in Augustine, certainly in those who learned from him, creation becomes very much the product of pure, unmotivated and therefore arbitrary will, a will that operates equally arbitrarily in the theology of double predestination that became after him so much a mark of the Western tradition' (Colin E. Gunton, *The One, The Three and the Many*, pp. 120f.).

the 'hidden decree'.[66] The deeper theological issue underlying the philosophical debate between nominalism and
realism is the doctrine of God and the thoroughness in
which God is perceived to have defined himself in the
gospel. Indeed, the more general tendency of Western
theology to define God other than in terms of the gospel
paves the way for the nominalism of Ockham.[67] It is at this
point that we should recognize the cruciality of Barth's
definition of God as 'the One who Loves in Freedom',[68] and
his consequent insistence that God's freedom is in no sense
arbitrary or indeterminate but is specifically his freedom to
be this God, the one who loves, the one who is loving as

[66] In this respect note Jeremy Begbie's comments on the development
of Dutch Neo-Calvinism: '... the Neo-Calvinist concept of God is
insufficiently shaped by the self-disclosure of the Trinity in the history
of Jesus Christ. God is portrayed fundamentally as the powerful Law-
giver, whose absolute and sovereign will is enacted in the establishment of precepts which we are summoned to obey; his love is a
secondary attribute, reserved for the elect': Jeremy Begbie, *Voicing
Creation's Praise: Towards a Theology of the Arts* (Edinburgh: T&T Clark,
1991), pp. 158f.
[67] This may be a convenient point to comment on (what could be
conceived as) the 'inverse' of nominalism that is a consequence of
defining God as necessary being and which, by effectively eliminating the
volitional essence of God's goodness, forfeits his freedom and
personhood. The tendency is illustrated in the following quotation from
Keith Ward: 'We must conceive "God", then as a necessary being – a
being which could not be non-existent – and which necessarily has the
general nature it has. If there is a physical universe (as, of course, there is)
the moral claims which exist in it will be necessarily determined to be
what they are by the being of God. And it will be appropriate for moral
agents in this universe to speak of the being of God, as apprehended by
them, as an objective teleology of the world, morally binding on them;
that is, in the language of "Divine intention". It is in this highly qualified
sense that the being of God, even as expressed in moral experience alone,
can be properly spoken of as personal and also as incomprehensibly far
beyond personal categories; and it seems to me that sustained analysis of
any moral objectivism will disclose such a theistic view as the most
adequate basis of the moral life': Keith Ward, *Ethics and Christianity* (New
York: George Allen & Unwin, 1970), p. 120.
[68] 'God is who He is in the act of His revelation. God seeks and creates
fellowship between Himself and us, and therefore He loves us. But He is
this loving God without us as Father, Son and Holy Spirit, in the freedom
of the Lord, who has His life from Himself' (*CD* II/1, p. 257). Barth
develops the significance of this definition throughout the rest of II/1 and
it remains his 'working definition' for the remaining volumes of the
Dogmatics.

Father, Son and Spirit.[69] Commenting on the question raised in Plato's *Euthyphro*, William Stacy Johnson observes that

> from Barth's point of view, this Socratic query, by means of its implicit separation between God and the good, insinuates a false dilemma. For Barth, God alone is good, and goodness is identical with who God is and what God is doing. On the one hand, the good is defined by God; but, on the other hand, God's definition is not arbitrary. For what God does is always circumscribed by God's overarching election to be 'for' and 'with' humanity in Jesus Christ. Thus, God's commands are always in accordance with the good which is already inherent in God's character. Yet what this good is in a given situation cannot be known apart from the immediate context. This means that while God alone is the 'foundation' of the good, we are speaking of a 'foundation' that, strangely, has neither made itself fully available to reason, nor yet established itself empirically in the world. For the command of God has yet to be enacted *by us*; the Reign of God has yet to become fully present *in us*.[70]

While the 'not yet' element at the conclusion of the above quotation could not be gainsaid one may be left with the suspicion that it is overstated, if not by Johnson (as was intimated in the previous chapter), then by Barth himself. If Barth is guilty of such an overstatement it relates partly to a possible inadequacy in his account of the empirical reality of the Church and partly to a less contestable lingering weakness (notwithstanding his best attempts to the contrary) in the manner in which he relates creation and redemption. Each of these weaknesses will be investigated later in this book – what is pertinent at this point is

---

[69] It is this of course, that should banish any lingering suspicion of nominalism in Barth's thought; cf. Nigel Biggar, *The Hastening that Waits*, p. 24.

[70] William Stacy Johnson, *The Mystery of God*, p. 160.

merely to note the manner in which any such hesitation might compound a lack of confidence in the coherence of the Church's ethical speaking and living.

This section of the argument began with reference to the story of Abraham pleading on behalf of Sodom – a story that implies both that God is unequivocally good and that his goodness, though it cannot be established by independent reason, is nonetheless rationally coherent. Whether the coherence of God's goodness is undermined by resorting to nominalistic arbitrariness or by belittling the relatedness of creation and redemption the outcome is a loss of confidence in the Church's ability to speak and live within the world – for whichever of these reasons, or for a combination of the two of them, we have lost confidence in the resonance of our message and lifestyle. Every instance of 'ghetto mentality', of the Church retreating from the world and from public ethical debate, demonstrates this third loss of confidence – a loss of confidence that the grace of this unequivocally good God will resonate beyond the boundaries of the Church.

The intention of the remaining sections of this book is to address this threefold loss of confidence, firstly by exploring the possibilities for a more faithful reading of Scripture, then by exploring the possibilities for the empirical coherence of Christian living, and finally by exploring the basis on which, even in a post-modern context, the Church's speaking and living might resonate beyond its boundaries.

Part Two
GOSPEL AND LAW

4

The Gospel as Story

*'All that I desire to point out is the general principle that
Life imitates Art far more than Art imitates Life'*

Oscar Wilde[1]

Sermon Class was the peril of my student years. A friend
has since described it as a 'blood sport' (though there
were few, in those days, who would dare to protest and
intervene on behalf of the sacrificial victim). It was humil-
iating enough that one's carefully prepared sermon was
pitilessly savaged by the baying hounds of students and
faculty, but sometimes one's conduct of worship was
similarly mauled. There was one occasion when a student
took exception to the preacher's choice of hymn:

> God has given us a book full of stories,
> Which was made for His people of old,
> It begins with the tale of a garden,
> And ends with the city of gold.[2]

'It's not a "book full of stories",' he protested, 'it's a book
full of factual accounts.' Now one has to admit that this
was not a particularly notable hymn and it is hardly
surprising that it has been omitted from most more recent
collections: frankly, it is naïve (both theologically and
poetically); it is strong on sentiment, weak on wonder,
and lacking in any obvious worshipful intent. But it is not
erroneous and, in this respect, its rabid critic exposed
himself as espousing the modernist assumptions that, in
other contexts, he would have repudiated. The Bible is
precisely a 'book full of stories'. Indeed, one could go
further in the defence of the hymn. As a 'book full of

---

[1] Oscar Wilde, 'The Decay of Lying' in *Intentions* (London: James R.
Osgood, McIlvaine & Co, 1891).
[2] Maria Penstone (1859–1910) in *Baptist Praise and Worship* (Oxford:
Oxford University Press for Psalms and Hymns Trust, 1991), No. 200.

stories' the Bible has a clear beginning, a clear end, a clear centre, and an intended utility in relation to each phase of human life.[3] It is not an account of 'bare facts' – as if such an enterprise were either possible or desirable – it is self-confessedly interpretative of 'facts'. It is prophetic and proclamatory narrative. It is story.[4]

My preliminary purpose in identifying the Bible as a 'book full of stories' is twofold: firstly to recognize its non-detached and interpretative character – that is to say, it is not merely a book full of 'factual accounts' – and secondly to recognize that propositions and rules occurring in the course of these narratives are narratively rooted and that the narratives remain primary. I am, of course, aware that there is today an identifiable 'narrative theology movement'.[5] Whether or not I am to be identified as aligned with that 'movement' is for others to judge – past mistakes have taught me not to be favourably disposed to movements or fashions of any kind and I certainly have no

---

[3] For those unfamiliar with the hymn it may be appropriate to quote its remaining verses in full:

But the best is the story of Jesus,
Of the babe with the ox in the stall,
Of the song that was sung by the angels,
The most beautiful story of all.

There are stories for parents and children,
For the old who are ready to rest,
But for all who can read them or listen,
The story of Jesus is best.

For it tells how He came from the Father,
His far-away children to call,
To bring the lost sheep to their Shepherd –
The most beautiful story of all.

[4] In affirming that the Bible has a 'clear centre' I am assuming that the Gospel accounts of Christ form this centre within the Christian Scriptures as received by the Church. Throughout this book 'Gospel' (capitalized) is used to refer specifically to Matthew, Mark, Luke or John, whereas 'gospel' (not capitalized) is used to refer more generally to the overall message of the Christian Scriptures as focused on Christ and interpreted through this focus.

[5] For a general comment on the variety of uses of this focus on narrative in recent thought, and the differences of significance deriving from this diversity, see the introduction to *Why Narrative? Readings in Narrative Theology*, ed. Stanley Hauerwas and L. Gregory Jones (Grand Rapids: Eerdmans, 1989), p. 2.

intention of jumping onto this latest 'band-wagon'. My point is simply descriptive. The Bible is a 'book full of stories'. It may be possible to read it in some other way but it is not easy to do so. It may be possible to read the Bible as a 'code-book' – gnosticism, in one form or another, remains depressingly persistent – but this is far from a straightforward strategy. It may be possible to read the Bible as a book of 'rules' and 'propositions' – rules and propositions are certainly included within its text – but overwhelmingly they occur in a narrative context and tend to be misappropriated when they are extracted from that context. Indeed, even the apparently 'context-less' sayings of Proverbs or Ecclesiastes are contextually located within the Old Testament canon and therefore within the storied relatedness of God and his people.

The notion of a purely 'factual account', I would argue, is a contradiction in terms: if we are dealing with an 'account' of events, that 'account', by virtue of being an *account* cannot be purely 'factual'. An occurrence is recalled or recorded only if it has some degree of significance, and, having such significance, it simply is not possible for that significance not to colour the manner in which it is recalled or recorded. That this interpretative process of recording is generally an 'unconscious' activity may beguile us concerning the nature of the process in which we are engaged. More seriously, the fact that in certain contexts we may have a special concern to present 'bare facts' may delude us into thinking that this is what we are achieving. But, inevitably and necessarily, our account of events is precisely that – *our account* of events. Consequently, every account, by virtue of being an account, is itself creative; it is art rather than pure science – indeed, the recognition of this creative dynamic of description blurs the supposed distinction between science and art that is a fundamental assumption of modernism. In particular, the recognition of this creative character of any form of account undermines the modernist notion of positivist historical science. This is not to deny the scientific nature of historical research but it is to recognize that any historical account is artistic and creative as well as scientific. Consequently, while there is, of course, a distinction between an historical textbook and an historical novel, that distinction is not absolute: both are concerned with historical factuality and both are creative. Here again a post-modern critique of modernism is simply a matter of integrity – it promotes the honesty that admits the artistic and creative character of true science.

This lack of integrity concerning the creative and interpretative element of description, that is rooted in the modernist disjunction between fact and value, objectivity and subjectivity, is generally foreign to ancient texts and is certainly foreign to Scripture. The Bible, consistently and explicitly, offers itself as interpreting events rather than merely describing them; it makes no claim to neutral detachment; it is never concerned merely with the relating of 'bare events'. To some degree this universal interpretative concern of Scripture has been undermined in our thinking through modernist assumptions promoting too clear-cut distinctions between the various literary genres of biblical literature. To distinguish between poetry and wisdom, prophecy and history, Epistle and Gospel, obscures the reality that each genre is interpretative and creative and encourages the modernist tendency to favour the supposedly 'factual'. Contrastingly, it could be argued that quite the reverse priority should pertain, as is instanced in the following comment by Kevin Vanhoozer:

> When philosophers refuse to take metaphor or poetic language seriously, they reinforce the prejudice that the only adequate relation between language and reality is the literal and that reality itself is limited to the actual and the manipulable. Literal or descriptive language alone ultimately diminishes human being because it is unable to articulate those fundamental values that orient our lives.[6]

Even the common distinction between poetry and prose can be misappropriated as implying that the latter is

---

[6]   Kevin J. Vanhoozer, *Biblical Narrative in the Philosophy of Paul Ricoeur: A Study in Hermeneutics and Theology* (Cambridge: Cambridge University Press, 1990), pp. 60f.

'factual' in a manner that the former is not, whereas the poetic sections of the Old Testament are grounded in the events of God's history with his people or with individuals and the prose sections of the Old Testament are explicitly interpretative and emotive. In the Masoretic canon of the Old Testament the books of the 'prophets' begin, not with Isaiah, but with Joshua and proceed through Judges and the books of Samuel and Kings: the concern of the text is not merely to describe events but to interpret them and proclaim them. Similarly, though Luke states his aim as being 'to write an orderly account' for Theophilus (Luke 1.3), the resulting Gospel is overtly interpretative, proclamatory and 'artistic'. It is in this sense that Scripture is 'theological', not that it ever attempts to itemize a watertight and comprehensive system of belief,[7] but that it relates its stories for explicitly theological purpose; its goal concerns the nature and identity of God and the nature and identity of his people.[8]

Consequently, quests for the 'historical Jesus' are not merely futile, they are unfaithful. They are futile inasmuch as any reconstruction of a Jesus underlying the text is

[7] 'The Bible is full of theology, but it is not theology in the sense that later came to be understood, of a systematic attempt to formulate the rationality and truth of Christianity as a unity' (Colin E. Gunton, *The One, The Three and the Many*, p. 22).

[8] It would be tangential to the purposes of this book to enter into long discussions of authorial intention or theories of reader response. I am, of course, aware that there is considerable and important debate here but it is not my purpose (at least in this context) to enter that debate. For the purposes of this present argument I am assuming that we have no other access to authorial intention than the text itself – here I agree with Francis Watson that '... authorial intention is to be seen as primarily embodied in the words the author wrote ...' – and that the text of the Christian Scriptures only 'exists' as it has been received and heard within the Christian community. Or, to quote Francis Watson again: 'A determinate communicative intention is embedded in the text; it is not to be found "behind the text" in an authorial psychology or an "original" historical context. Interpretation *may* therefore concern itself with the appropriate reception of the communicative intention constituted by the text; and, if interpretation occurs within a communal context in which the text possesses some kind of normative significance, interpretation *must* concern itself with this issue': Francis Watson, *Text and Truth: Redefining Biblical Theology* (Edinburgh: T&T Clark, 1997), p. 11 (the previous quotation occurs on page 118).

precisely that, a *reconstruction*, a re-telling of the story from the perspective of the critic that is every bit as interpretative and creative as the Gospel sources upon which that reconstruction is based though entirely lacking their 'authority'.[9] But, far more seriously, such attempted reconstructions, by giving priority to that which lies behind the text of the Gospels, fail to be formed by the Gospels themselves, assuming (once again in modernist fashion) that content can be extricated from form, bare 'fact' from interpretation. The authority of the Gospels for the Church (as with every other text of Christian Scripture) concerns not merely the underlying 'facts' they relate but the manner in which they relate those 'facts'; their interpretation of those 'facts' is no less determinative for the Church than the 'facts' they interpret. All this, it should be noted, is not to deny that the factuality underlying the Gospels is crucial – 'if Christ has not been raised, your faith is futile' (1 Cor. 15.17): the significance of Jesus as attested by the Gospels is dependent upon his factuality.[10] This, of course, is not true of every Scriptural story – the significance of Job or Jonah may not be similarly dependent upon their factuality and the significance of Genesis ch. 1 is certainly not dependent upon its being read as if it represented the assured conclusions of natural science – but it is most certainly true of the Gospel narratives; here significance is

---

[9] 'As Martin Kähler sagely observed almost one hundred years ago, the critic who reconstructs a "historical Jesus" inevitably becomes a "fifth evangelist," cutting and pasting the tradition so as to articulate a new vision of Jesus for his or her own time': Richard B. Hays, *The Moral Vision of the New Testament: A Contemporary Introduction to New Testament Ethics* (Edinburgh: T&T Clark, 1996), p. 159.

[10] 'Having said all that, however, it must be acknowledged that the question about the Jesus of history will not go away, because the question of truth looms. If the canonical accounts of Jesus were in fundamental conflict with what actually happened, if they were sheer fabrications of religious fanaticism or wishful thinking, then Christians would be, in Paul's words, of all people most to be pitied' (Richard B. Hays, *The Moral Vision of the New Testament*, p. 160). Francis Watson offers a similar comment: 'The gospels cease to be gospel if they merely preserve scattered traces of a historical reality qualitatively different from its narrative rendering, or if they merely render an intratextual character whose extratextual existence is a matter of indifference' (Francis Watson, *Text and Truth*, p. 9).

explicitly dependent upon factuality. But significance is more than mere factuality; the Gospels do not pretend to be detached or dispassionate and, for this reason, 'story' is an appropriate description of their form.

It is because the Bible is a 'book full of stories', self-confessedly interpreting and responding to events rather than merely describing them, that it includes 'propositional' statements. Such propositions, as Colin Gunton has indicated, may not themselves be revelation, 'but they may in a derivative sense be revelatory'.[11] Once it is conceded, following Karl Barth, that the subject of revelation is God himself rather than mere information about him, it must be recognized that revelation necessarily is an event and, accordingly, no mere statement could possibly be revelation itself. Events in which God makes himself known are narrated in Scripture, and propositions, in a variety of forms, occur in the context of those narratives and in response to those events – but the propositions derive from the narratives, and the narratives, in and of themselves, are not identical with the events they narrate. The failure to acknowledge this derivatory and secondary character of biblical propositions is disastrous: the statement 'God is love' identifies a truth that is general in the sense of being universal and eternal, but it is not general in the sense of being non-specific or indeterminate – the significance of the statement is itself identified in the Johanine account of the gospel story – 'This is love: not that we loved God, but that he loved us and sent his Son as an atoning sacrifice for our sins' (1 John 4.10).[12]

However, at least inasmuch as propositional statements are derivative they are themselves revelatory. Indeed, the matter can be pressed further (and will be pressed yet

[11] Colin E. Gunton, *A Brief Theology of Revelation*, p. 105.
[12] A more blatant example of the distortions consequent on the abstracting of biblical propositions occurs in Malachi 3.6: 'I the LORD do not change' – a text which occurs in the context of God's constancy and covenant faithfulness, but which, when abstracted from its context could be taken as concurring with abstract concepts of immutability and impassibility, a notion of God which Barth dismisses as implying an immobility that would prohibit his freedom to be related to that which is distinct from himself (*CD* II/1, pp. 493f.).

further still towards the conclusion of this chapter): inasmuch as propositional statements are intrinsic to the biblical narratives they are themselves an integral element of the biblical witness to God's self-revelation; they represent summary statements responding to the narratives to which they relate; they demonstrate the inferential relationship of the narratives to the events narrated. The statement 'God is love' must be understood in its relatedness to the gospel story, but, as such, it stands as the consummate inference to be drawn from that story.

While all this is true of Scripture in general it is particularly pertinent to the Gospels themselves. Though it may be inappropriate to compare the Gospels to the contemporary genre of biography, they each are concerned, albeit in differing ways, not just with the things that Jesus said and did, but with Jesus himself.[13] There is, of course, the danger, as Stanley Hauerwas indicates, that we might focus on the theological significance of Jesus in a manner that effectively ignores the details of his life and teaching,[14] but particularly in a modernist context the opposite danger predominated: the theological significance of Jesus was

[13] However, note the conclusions of Richard A. Burridge (following Graham Stanton) that the Gospels conform to the Graeco-Roman genre of βίοι (biography). The case is established in great detail in his *What are the Gospels? A Comparison with Graeco-Roman Biography* (Cambridge: Cambridge University Press, 1992) but underlies his *Four Gospels, One Jesus? A Symbolic Reading* (London: SPCK, 1994) where it is summarized thus: 'The gospels, then, are a form of ancient biography. When we study them, we walk through an ancient portrait gallery; the gospels are hung in the same hall as other ancient biographies – and we must study them with the same concentration upon their subject, to see the particular way each author tries to portray his understanding of Jesus. The gospels are Christology in narrative form, or less technically, the story of Jesus. This is why the methods of literary criticism are so vital for gospel studies. We need to learn how they were written, what they contain and how their narratives function' (p. 8).
[14] '... Christian ethics has tended to make "Christology" rather than Jesus its starting point. His relevance is seen as resting in more substantive claims about the incarnation. Christian ethics then often begins with some broadly drawn theological claims about the significance of God becoming man, but the life of the man whom God made his representative is ignored or used selectively' (Stanley Hauerwas, *The Peaceable Kingdom*, p. 72).

effectively ignored while elements of his teaching were
abstracted from their narrative and theological context and
appropriated as enunciations of general moral insights.
Neither strategy is faithful to the text. The recorded
teachings of Jesus can no more be abstracted from the
Gospels' proclamations of his person than the significance
of his person, as proclaimed in the Gospels, can be
abstracted from the narrative context in which those
proclamations occur.[15] The four Gospels, in different but
complementary ways, narrate the story of Jesus, giving
details of his actions and his teaching, with the expressed
aim of identifying him as the Christ, as 'Son of God' and
'Son of Man'. This textual intention may be less overt in the
Synoptics than in the fourth Gospel but it is no less explicit;
it shapes the manner of their beginnings as much as their
endings; each is dominated by the question of Jesus'
identity, and to this end they tell their stories.

That the Church then comes at the Council of Chalcedon
to define Jesus as 'truly God and truly human ... of one
substance with the Father ... and of one substance with us
... ', while it is certainly an elaboration of the witness of the
Gospels, is nonetheless an elaboration that is consistent

---

[15] There were always protests against this modernist strategy of Gospel
interpretation. One such protest recurs throughout Kierkegaard's
theological writings: 'The teacher ... is inseparable from and more
essential than the teaching ... But in our day everything is made abstract
and everything personal is abolished: we take Christ's teaching – and
abolish Christ. This is to abolish Christianity, for Christ is a person and is
the teacher who is more important than the teaching. – Just as Christ's life,
the fact that he has lived, is vastly more important than all the results of
his life ..., so also is Christ infinitely more important than his teaching. It
is true only of a human being that his teaching is more important than he
himself; to apply this to Christ is a blasphemy, inasmuch as it makes him
into only a human being': Søren Kierkegaard, *Practice in Christianity*, ed.
and trans. Howard and Edna Hong (Princeton: Princeton University
Press, 1991), pp. 123f. Tim Rose comments in relation to this quotation
that 'Kierkegaard's Incarnational Christianity stands in sharp contrast to
any claim that there should be a humanistic 'religion of Jesus' in which the
person of Christ is seen to be of passing interest in favour of the 'eternal'
value of his moral teaching. Several years later Kierkegaard was to clarify
this through Anti-Climacus in *Practice in Christianity*': Tim E. F. Rose,
'Paradox and Revelation: the Incarnation and Natural Theology in
Kierkegaard's Religious Thought', PhD dissertation (University of
London, 1998) shortly to be published by Ashgate Press.

and coherent with their witness.[16] And in the light of the conclusions of Chalcedon, together with the earlier conclusions of Nicæa and Constantinople, the Church is defined as the community constituted by the Spirit to hear this story in this manner. An affirmation of the cruciality of Church tradition, enshrined in these ecumenical councils, does not then establish a rival authority alongside Scripture, it rather identifies the manner in which, within this community, Scripture is validly heard.[17] Consequently it is entirely appropriate for Christian theologians to interpret Scripture in the light of the propositional doctrines affirmed at these formative councils – but never in a manner that loses sight of the narratives to which those propositions relate.[18]

To summarize the matter so far: because Scripture is primarily narrative in form it is necessarily and overtly interpretative, and because it is interpretative it includes propositional statements; the Church, as the community constituted by the Spirit to hear and interpret these narratives in a particular manner, responds to the narratives – at

[16] The function of propositions within Christian theology is identified helpfully in the following quotation from Colin Gunton: 'Certainly, revelation does not *consist in*, as is sometimes suggested, the transmission of authoritative propositions. Rather, Christianity is a revealed religion in the sense that essential to its being what it is, is its articulation by means of affirmations and confessions in which are implicit certain claims about what is true of God, the world and human life. These confessions do not aspire to systematic completeness, but to general logical coherence. They do not aspire to watertight coherence with each other, and in some details are found to disagree, but do aspire to intellectual continuity and coherence *necessarily* with what is sometimes called the biblical revelation . . . and *contingently* with the earliest rule of faith and the later decisions of the ecumenical councils' (Colin E. Gunton, *A Brief Theology of Revelation*, p. 17).

[17] For an excellent series of discussions of the relationship between Scripture and Church tradition see the essays collected in *Reclaiming the Bible for the Church*, ed. Carl E. Braaten and Robert W. Jenson (Edinburgh: T&T Clark, 1995).

[18] Though it may be appropriate for Karl Barth, as Nigel Biggar comments, to interpret Scripture by the 'canon' of the 'Christological "story" as narrated by Nicaea and Chalcedon' (Nigel Biggar, *The Hastening that Waits*, p. 122), one may question whether in his treatment of the doctrine of reconciliation, as well as in the rest of the *Church Dogmatics*, Barth pays sufficient attention to the Gospel narratives themselves.

least in part – with its own interpretative propositions; but, because the Church's propositional responses to the narrative are indeed *responses* to the narrative, they can never displace or replace the narrative. The gospel irreducibly is story:

> Christians do not figure out the 'real meaning' of the biblical narratives in some doctrinal formulation and then discard the stories, but doctrines serve as aids for reflection on the biblical narratives.[19]

The temptation to displace the narratives of Scripture with the interpretative propositions of the Church derives from the modernist tendency to view stories as merely illustrative of general truths – the task of the interpreter being to isolate the general truth from the particulars of the story.[20] Indeed, much evangelical expositional preaching falls precisely into this trap, employing the narratives of Scripture as convenient access points for the affirmation of abstracted doctrinal truths. This is a calamitous categorical mistake: God is personal, and as such he cannot be reduced to a series of propositional statements; persons cannot be reduced to propositions. Were I to list a series of

[19] William C. Placher, *Narratives of a Vulnerable God: Christ, Theology, and Scripture* (Louisville, Kentucky: Westminster John Knox Press, 1994), p. 40.
[20] The point again is taken from Stanley Hauerwas: 'Too often we assume the narrative character of Christian convictions is incidental to those convictions. Both believer and unbeliever are under the impression that narrative is a relatively unimportant moral category. Specifically, we tend to think of "stories" as illustrations of some deeper truth that we can and should learn to articulate in a non-narrative mode' (Stanley Hauerwas, *The Peaceable Kingdom*, p. 25). Similarly in his *Christian Existence Today: Essays on Church, World, and Living In Between* (Durham, North Carolina: Labyrinth, 1988), Professor Hauerwas comments on the 'mythical' use we make of stories (p. 25). Colin Gunton relates this belittling of narrative to a more general belittling of particularity: 'According to the much cited scholium to his [Newton's] *Principia Mathematica*, there exists, underlying the space and time of our experience – relative space and time – absolute space and time. The significant feature of the concept is its effective relegation to secondary status of experienced space and time, for it encourages the belief that experienced space and time are in some way not fully real' (Colin E. Gunton, *The One, The Three and the Many*, p. 85).

propositional statements concerning my wife – her height, her colouring, her age, her gentleness, her remarkable tolerance of her husband – these statements, though accurate (from my perspective), would not prove remotely as effective in communicating her character as the relating of stories about her. But, more fundamentally, propositional statements can too easily be abstracted from their particular reference and appropriated as general truths: the statements concerning my wife might well apply to any number of people, whereas stories relating to my wife are necessarily particular. It could therefore be said that Scripture takes narrative form because its purpose is to communicate the character of God and character is most effectively communicated by narrative – this may be the case but it is not primary. Primarily Scripture takes narrative form because God's making himself known has occurred in the particularities of human time and space: the Bible does not bear witness to general and abstract notions concerning a general and abstract deity; it witnesses to the particular events in which this God has made himself known.

However, while Scripture takes narrative form primarily because it responds to the particularities of God's acting and speaking, perhaps it does so also because of the power of stories to affect us by drawing us into the world they narrate.[21] Generally, we are not greatly affected through reading a telephone directory or a mathematics textbook – we may be informed but we are hardly affected. Yet it is difficult to read a story without being engaged by it and engaging with it; stories draw us into the world they narrate; as readers we become part of the narrated story and find ourselves interacting with the characters portrayed in the story and involved with the story's key events. For this reason stories are an appropriate literary form if we are to be changed rather than merely

---

[21] 'Biography is a form of story, and human beings find their identity through stories, which brings a community dimension to interpretation. There is an inevitable triangle of relationships in any communication: the author, the text, and the reader – or the storyteller, the story, and the audience' (Richard A. Burridge, *Four Gospels, One Jesus?*, p. 178).

informed.[22] Kevin Vanhoozer identifies this idea of 'the
world of the text' as the means by which Paul Ricoeur, in
contrast to purely structuralist approaches, maintains an
'extra-linguistic' reference for a text: stories are not self-
contained; they draw us into their world in a manner that
renders our involvement with the text indispensable for
any interpretative strategy.[23] It is not that stories merely
relate events – they recreate those events in a manner that
involves the reader and equips the reader with the means
to view the world in a new way.[24] Or, to repeat the
quotation which headed this chapter: 'Life imitates Art far
more than Art imitates Life.'[25]

The Passover Festival, as it is ordained within the Old
Testament, makes explicit this dynamic whereby the
hearers of a story are drawn into the story itself in a

---

[22] '... stories do not illustrate a meaning, they do not symbolize a
meaning, but rather the meaning is embodied in the form of the story
itself. Put differently, stories are indispensable if we are to know
ourselves; they are not replaceable by some other kind of account'
(Stanley Hauerwas with Richard Bondi and David B. Burrell, *Truthfulness
and Tragedy*, p. 77).

[23] 'Unlike the earlier Romantics, Ricoeur is unable to say that what is
appropriated is the author's intention. But unlike modern structuralists,
Ricoeur is unwilling to abandon his key idea that discourse is *about*
something. The notion of the "world of the text" provides him with a
solution to both problems. The reader, by following the semantic itiner-
aries sketched out in the text, eventually comes to see the text's world, and
himself, in the light of that world' (Kevin J. Vanhoozer, *Biblical Narrative
in the Philosophy of Paul Ricoeur*, p. 89). Note also the following earlier
reference that clarifies Ricoeur's distinction from historical critics, on
the one hand, and structuralists, on the other: 'Ricoeur refuses to follow the
historical critics in their reduction of a text to its constituent traditions or
to confine its meaning to the original situation and its reference to "what
actually happened." At the same time, Ricoeur will not countenance
a purely structuralist or "theology as story" approach which reduces a
text's sense to its immanent relations and cuts it off from any extra-
linguistic reference' (p. 12).

[24] 'Narratives are still about human action, but not in the way of
reference. That is, instead of corresponding to, describing or "imitating"
human action (the pedestrian sense of mimesis), histories and fictions
redescribe or remake it. Histories and fictions become interpretative grids
through which we view human action. The move from reference to refig-
uration is a move from considering human action as it is to human action
as it could be, a move from actuality to possibility' (Kevin J. Vanhoozer,
Biblical Narrative in the Philosophy of Paul Ricoeur, p. 192).

[25] Oscar Wilde, 'The Decay of Lying'.

manner that prompts them to re-envisage their world in the light of the story. The Passover, like the Feast of Tabernacles, is not merely a graphic means of remembering past events; it is a means of entering into them and reliving them; by participating in the Passover the community of hearers is identified with the community that was brought out of Egypt; by participating in the Feast of Tabernacles the community of hearers is identified with the community that experienced God's provision in the desert. The Feasts of Passover and Tabernacles are enacted stories. The same, of course, is overtly true of the Christian sacraments: the Eucharist is not merely a means of remembering the cross of Christ, it is a means through which the Christian community enters into that once-for-all sacrifice in order to be re-assured, sustained and re-envisioned; baptism is not merely a means of drawing attention to one's personal commitment, it is a means through which we identify with the death and resurrection of Christ in expectation of the gift of his recreating Spirit. It is for this reason that, as Sara Maitland observes, the sacraments must occur in the context of the re-telling of the story lest they be reduced to empty ritual:

> With all due respect to Jung, symbols – recognized patterns of meaning – are not ahistorical, transcendent idealist absolutes. They are socially constructed. But they are not abstracts, purified essences of experience or meaning, they are constructed within contexts, and the contexts are *narratives* ... Christians know this of course – it is one reason, however unconscious, why the eucharistic prayer always contains the narrative, the story, of the Last Supper, even though this has created considerable theological confusion. The fact remains that you can't just wave a chunk of not very convincing looking bread about and expect everyone to 'get it' straight off. The bread and the wine, or the water of baptism, or the cross itself for that matter, have no 'pure' meaning; they are given their meaning by the stories which make them, place them, frame them. Which, not incidentally, is why the theory that

signifiers – words – have no connection to the signified
– objects – is wrong. However casual or random the
association may have been originally, usage, history –
that is time in the genuinely creative, poetic (*making*)
sense ... has given them meaning, real meaning, by
placing them within sentences of meaning, placing
these symbols of meaning within narratives which
carry that meaning.[26]

By now the ethical power of narratives ought to be clear.
There may be some readers of this book who, until this
point, have considered this discussion of the narrative
nature of Scripture an unwarranted excursus, a diversion
from an ethical focus. Nothing could be more mistaken.
That which has been argued here concerning the nature of
narratives is pivotal for everything else that will be argued
in the remainder of this book. 'Life imitates Art'; we are
shaped by stories. By virtue of drawing us into their world,
stories re-orientate our lives; they are inevitably ethical in
outcome.[27] The sacraments are not mere remembrances,
they are re-creative. In relation to Scripture, as Stanley
Hauerwas again notes, this re-creating dynamic is as true
for those who formed the narratives as it is for those who
are drawn into them:

> The historical fact that we only learn who Jesus is as he
> is reflected through the eyes of his followers, a fact that
> has driven many to despair because it seems they
> cannot know the real Jesus, in fact is a theological
> necessity. For the 'real Jesus' did not come to leave us
> unchanged, but rather to transform us to be worthy
> members of the community of the new age.[28]

---

[26] Sara Maitland, *A Big-Enough God: Artful Theology* (London: Mowbray, 1995), p. 141.
[27] 'Stories form our values and moral sensibilities in more indirect and complex ways, teaching us how to see the world, what to fear, and what to hope for; stories offer us nuanced models of behavior both wise and foolish, courageous and cowardly, faithful and faithless' (Richard B. Hays, *The Moral Vision of the New Testament*, p. 73).
[28] Stanley Hauerwas, *The Peaceable Kingdom*, p. 73.

A generation that appears to be addicted to television 'soaps' should hardly need to be convinced of the ethical significance of narratives. The stories we choose to indwell shape us for better or for worse.[29] Mention was made earlier of the 'Unionist' movement in Ulster, a movement most overtly shaped, not by historical events themselves (William of Orange had the backing of the Pope in his struggle against James Stuart and the might of Louis XIV), but by the manner in which those events have come to be narrated within a tradition. While, thankfully, there is (and always has been) evidence of other stories being heard, the conflict within Northern Ireland can begin to be comprehended, not merely in the light of its history, but in the light of the manner in which that history has been retold.[30] The underlying tragedy of this conflict therefore, as was indicated earlier, is that for both communities these rival narratives tended to displace the gospel story as the formative narrative for a tradition. Another virtue of postmodernism is its recognition of this formative nature of stories for the communities in which they are re-told and re-heard. But, as medieval church frescos indicate, we are certainly not the first generation to recognize the potential of stories, rather it is the modernist period, with its preoccupation with the 'factual' and propositional, that stands out as anomalous.

However, while this ethical dynamic of stories pertains in general it is realized in a particular and distinctive way

[29] '... there is no ethically neutral narrative. Literature is a vast laboratory in which we experiment with estimations, evaluations and judgments of approval and condemnation through which narrativity serves as a propaedeutic to ethics': Paul Ricoeur, *Oneself As Another* (Chicago: University of Chicago Press, 1992), p. 115.

[30] Alasdair MacIntyre draws attention to the general phenomenon whereby practices are intelligible only in terms of a history of tradition: 'Once again the narrative phenomenon of embedding is crucial: the history of a practice in our time is generally and characteristically embedded in and made intelligible in terms of the larger and longer history of the tradition through which the practice in its present form was conveyed to us; the history of each of our own lives is generally and characteristically embedded in and made intelligible in terms of the larger and longer histories of a number of traditions' (Alasdair MacIntyre, *After Virtue*, p. 222).

in relation to Scripture. As I have already intimated (and as I will argue more thoroughly in the concluding chapters of this book), I would follow Berkeley and Edwards in proposing a 'spiritual' epistemology: we only know anything inasmuch as the Spirit gives us to know, or, to put the matter more precisely, the Spirit enables us to participate – albeit partially and provisionally – in the Father's knowledge of created reality. But if this is generally the case it is so in a particular manner in relation to Scripture. Just as the Enlightenment was characterized by an independent and rationalistic epistemology so it gave rise to an independent and rationalistic view of Scripture's authority and inspiration. Too often the supposed heirs of Calvin, forsaking his understanding of the inner testimony of the Spirit,[31] located the authority of Scripture in its factuality and effectively limited the inspiration of Scripture to an understanding of its origins. Colin Gunton rightly comments that the outcome of this hermeneutical strategy was to render 'redundant the mediating work of the Spirit' by equating inspiration and revelation 'in such a way that the text in some way replaces' that mediating work.[32]

Scripture stands under the promise of Jesus that the Spirit 'will take from what is mine and make it known to you' (John 16.15); it is not a dead text to be apprehended by independent reason – it is 'living and active' inasmuch as the Spirit causes it to be heard (Heb. 4.12). Here then we are not dealing with mere narrative or even mere propositions

---

[31] '... the testimony of the Spirit is more excellent than all reason. For God alone is a fit witness of himself in his Word, so also the Word will not find acceptance in men's hearts before it is sealed by the inward testimony of the Spirit' (*Institutes* I vii 4). Note that Calvin considers supporting arguments for Scripture's authority to be 'secondary aids (*secundaria adminicula*) to our feebleness' (I viii 13). Perhaps it was inevitable that, in an Enlightenment context, these *secundaria adminicula*, as in the case of his doctrine of election, should displace the primary witness.

[32] Colin E. Gunton, *A Brief Theology of Revelation*, p. 66. Note also his further comment two pages later: 'The work of the Spirit is in some way either replaced by human intellectual activity, or centred in subjective human response, on the one hand, or, on the other, made to appear objective in a rather authoritarian manner, for example in the legal judgement of some ecclesiastical body' (p. 68).

since even propositions, through this promised dynamic, can become the means through which we are encountered and transformed by the Spirit. What is in view then is not a general possibility of narrative to draw us into itself and reshape us; we are referring rather to a specific promise that the Spirit will draw us into these narratives and reshape us through them as a community who, by our lives and worship, bear testimony as a living narrative to the person of Jesus.[33]

To recognize this spiritual dynamic of Scripture, then, is to recognize its unique ethical potential deriving from its particular promise. But to recognize the primarily narrative character of Scripture thus mediated is to identify Christian ethics, not as a series of rules or moral code, but as a reorientation of life in coherence with these narratives effected and empowered by the Spirit. Through our communal indwelling of these narratives we are recreated by the Spirit and brought to view the world and ourselves in a new way:

> Christian ethics, therefore, is not first of all concerned with 'Thou shalt' or 'Thou shalt not.' Its first task is to

---

[33] All this implies (as will be substantiated in the third section of this book) a Christian community that, *in reality and in the present*, is genuinely transformed by the Spirit to be a living narrative of the gospel story. The point is made in the following quotation from Edward Irving: 'Within Himself from all eternity there was an image of Himself in the person of the Eternal Son: out of Himself that image is found in man; first in the person of Christ, and then in every one who is renewed after the image of God in righteousness and true holiness': *The Prophetical Works of Edward Irving in Two Volumes*, vol. 2, ed. G. Carlyle (London: Alexander Strahan, 1865), p. 382, quoted in Graham McFarlane, *Christ and the Spirit: The Doctrine of the Incarnation According to Edward Irving* (Carlisle: Paternoster Press, 1996), p. 79. Whether or not this implies some form of 'perfectionism' will be discussed later. It certainly reinforces an understanding of the nature of the Christian life as witness, as is instanced in the following quotation from Stanley Hauerwas: 'What we must understand is that witness is necessary because we are so storied. If the gospel were a truth that could be known in general, then there would be no necessity to witness. All that would be necessary would be to confirm people in what they already know. If the gospel were about general human experience that is unavoidable, then there would be no necessity of being confronted by anyone as odd as a Christian. But because the story we tell of God is the story of the life and death of Jesus of Nazareth, then the only way to know that story is through witness' (Stanley Hauerwas, *After Christendom?* p. 149).

help us rightly envision the world. Christian ethics is specifically formed by a very definite story with determinative content. If we somehow discover the world is not as that story suggests, then we have good grounds for not believing in, or more accurately, not worshipping the God revealed in the life, cross, and resurrection of Jesus. In other words, the enterprise of Christian ethics primarily helps us to see. We can only act within the world we can envision, and we can envision the world rightly only as we are trained to see. We do not come to see merely by looking, but must develop disciplined skills through initiation into that community that attempts to live faithful to the story of God. Furthermore, we cannot see the world rightly unless we are changed, for as sinners we do not desire to see truthfully. Therefore Christian ethics must assert that by learning to be faithful disciples, we are more able to see the world as it is, namely God's creation.[34]

[34] Stanley Hauerwas, *The Peaceable Kingdom*, pp. 29f.

5
The Gospel as Mercy

As I have already acknowledged, there may be some readers of this book who feel that, in the course of the last chapter, it has already lost its way; it began as an enquiry into the distinctive nature of Christian ethics and, at best, it has indulged in an irrelevant digression concerning the nature of narrative. There has been, after all, little so far that would encourage the imaginary librarian, introduced in the Preface, to list this book within the section on ethics; as yet there has been no discussion of dilemmas, no prolonged discussion of the relative merits of deontological or teleological approaches, no identification of distinctive rules or principles that might determine an ethic to be 'Christian'. Would it not have been better, not to say more practically relevant – particularly since one aim of the book is to consider how Christians might still be able to speak ethically within secular society – to have begun with a doctrine of creation and to have drawn from this distinctive views of the sanctity of life and of human responsibilities for the environment?

It is in the light of such objections that the previous chapter must be recognized, not as a digression, but as pivotal for all that follows. My point is simply that it is the Christian story, rather than any principles, rules or moral strategies, that is fundamental to a Christian ethic. Respect for human (and animal) life is by no means the sole prerogative of Christians – indeed, some traditions might be perceived to be more rigorous in these respects – and even the belief that the universe is, in some sense, a creation is certainly not confined to the Christian Church. That which is unique and therefore distinctive for the Christian Church is that the universe is the creation of *this* God, the one who has made himself known in the history of his people, the one who has defined himself in the gospel story as Father, Son and Spirit.[1] The very first doctrinal essay I was asked

---

[1] It is at least possible to interpret the third article of Question Two of the *Summa*, not as offering five independent proofs of the existence of the God

to write as a theological student concerned the distinctive doctrine of the Christian faith. Out of a class of about twenty students there were essays on the Resurrection, the Cross, the authority of Scripture, the nature of conversion, the work of the Spirit, but – as I am now ashamed to admit – there was not one single essay on the person of Christ. It is Christ who is distinctive for Christian faith and living. And who Jesus is, as truly God and truly human, is defined narratively.

Although I had been engaging with Karl Barth's *Church Dogmatics* for several years, it was not until I heard a lecture by Prof. Alasdair Heron that I was awakened to what now seems obvious – that, in his treatment of the doctrine of reconciliation, Barth defines the deity and humanity of Christ *by his movement*: what it means for Christ to be truly God is defined in 'The Way of the Son of God into the Far Country';[2] and what it means for Christ to be truly human is defined in 'The Homecoming of the Son of Man'.[3] Whether Barth is entirely successful in this strategy is open to question (and, though important, is not entirely pertinent to the immediate issue) but the strategy itself may constitute Barth's most innovative and perceptive contribution. A possible criticism of the Chalcedonian definition of Christ's two natures is that it seems to deal in ontological abstractions. Barth is certainly not avoiding ontological categories (statements about the *being* of Christ as truly God and truly human), but he is recognizing that this ontology comes to expression in the Church's reflection (*nachdenkend*) on the gospel *story*, and

---

of the gospel story, but rather as identifying the God of the gospel story (already defined by revelation according to Question One) as the one who *truly* is this first and final cause etc. (*ST* I 2 3). Hence: '... "proofs" serve in Thomas and in Anselm and in Schleiermacher only to elaborate, explicate, unfold the faith, to exploit faith's own reasonableness and world, to exhibit faith's own beauty, and not to "prove" anything as we commonly (mis)understand the word, certainly not by appeal to any foundation in extra-Christian reason or the extra-Christian world': Eugene F. Rogers Jnr., 'Schleiermacher as an Anselmian Theologian: Aesthetics, Dogmatics, Apologetics and Proof' in *SJT* 51 (1998), pp. 342–79 (p. 355).
[2] *CD* IV/1, pp. 157ff.
[3] *CD* IV/2, pp. 20ff.

that, therefore, it should take *narrative* form in the work of dogmatics: the true God is defined precisely in the self-humbling of Christ and true humanity is defined in Christ's exaltation. The ethical significance of this storied definition of humanity will be the theme of the next chapter and, in an underlying sense, the theme of the next section. The concern of this present chapter is with the ethical significance of this storied definition of the true God.

As Barth asserts from the beginning of his *Church Dogmatics*, there can be no law without gospel; law occurs in the context of the gospel; law is a form of the gospel; gospel always takes priority.[4] God's first words to Israel at Mount Sinai were not 'You shall have no other gods before me', they were rather 'I am the LORD your God, who brought you out of Egypt, out of the land of slavery': indicative precedes imperative; gospel comes before law – and gospel is a narrative; it is an account of God's action.[5] Earlier in this particular narrative God makes himself known to Moses, albeit enigmatically, as 'I AM WHO I AM' (or 'I WILL BE WHAT I WILL BE') which, amongst a range of possible meanings, could itself imply that Moses will know God's nature (his 'name') on the basis of what he will do and say. The possibility of this interpretation might be reinforced by the supplementary disclosure that he is 'the LORD, the God of your fathers – the God of Abraham, the God of Isaac and the God of Jacob': God's character is known in the particularities of these stories.

The Gospel accounts of Jesus form the focus of the Christian Scriptures: 'In the past God spoke to our ancestors through the prophets at many times and in various ways, but in these last days he has spoken to us by

---

[4] 'The Law is completely enclosed in the Gospel. It is not a second thing alongside and beyond the Gospel. It is not a foreign element which precedes or only follows it. It is the claim which is addressed to us by the Gospel itself and as such, the Gospel in so far as it has the form of a claim addressed to us, the Gospel which we cannot really hear except we obey it' (*CD* II/2, p. 557; cf. *CD* II/1, p. 349: 'God's revelation is first and last a Gospel').
[5] Exod. 20.1ff.; cf. Deut. 5.6f.

his Son ...' (Heb. 1.1f.). For the Church these narratives are decisive in defining the character of the Triune God: God is truly known through this 'way of the Son of God into the far country'; through this incarnation; through this life; through this death; through this resurrection. The story in which God is ultimately known is a story of weakness, a story of temptation, a story of rejection, a story of one executed on the city rubbish-dump between two robbers, a story of one who forgives his torturers, a story of one who offers the signs of his sacrifice to those who will desert him, deny him, and even betray him. And, in the re-enactment of this narrative at the centre of the Church's worship, this unrepeatable sacrifice is re-presented again and again in mercy for those who are weak, failing and sinful.[6]

In chapter eight of this book some aspects of a Protestant interpretation of the doctrine of justification (in particular the tendency to sever it from a doctrine of sanctification) will be questioned: but what is not in question is the fundamental insight that our acceptability to God is dependent upon him and not upon us; it is a gift rather than a reward; it is not a consequence of our work but of the work of Christ; it is a matter of mercy rather than merit, of God's grace rather than our independent human performance.[7] The argument to be developed at a later stage is that this grace, which receives us as we are, does not leave us as we are; that it constitutes a *real* change of our being in the power of the Spirit; that, by virtue of liberating us in mercy it constitutes a greater, rather than lesser, demand than

---

[6] Having recounted the story of an Amish family and the manner in which they attempted reconciliation rather than prosecution after their child was killed, Stanley Hauerwas speaks of the '... belief in a God who refused to let our sin determine his relation to us' as the only means of making sense of their attitude and action (Stanley Hauerwas, *Christian Existence Today*, p. 85).

[7] 'The morally serious Christian asks in the midst of his concrete responsibilities and opportunities, "What ought I to do?" One answer he hears from theology is, "That is the wrong question. You cannot know what you ought to do, or can do, until you acknowledge what has been done for you and for the world': James M. Gustafson, *Christ and the Moral Life* (Chicago: University of Chicago Press, 1968), p. 12; Gustafson repeats this question throughout the book, offering a series of different responses in the light of the significance of Christ.

mere law.[8] But the issue for the present is that this grace is unequivocal.

Contrary to every 'Dispensationalist' hermeneutical strategy, this unequivocal grace cannot be undermined by playing off the Old Testament against the New Testament: the Christian Church reads the Old Testament as the 'shadow' or anticipation of the New, not as offering an alternative strategy for God's dealings with humankind. God is no less gracious in Genesis than in Romans; judgement is no less a possibility in the Gospels than in the Prophets. In both Testaments gospel precedes law, indicative precedes imperative, judgement is an outworking of grace rather than a distinct divine programme.

It is this latter point which is, perhaps, the most controversial. We have become accustomed to thinking of judgement as the contrary to grace rather than as an outworking of grace. Yet, in some respects, it is within the Old Testament that this ordering of grace and judgement is most clear since, predominantly, judgement occurs in the context of God's covenantal relationship with Israel and is overwhelmingly redemptive in purpose.[9] Even when judgement is directed to the nations beyond Israel it can either be mitigated by the presence of ten righteous persons, as in the case of Sodom and Gomorrah (Gen. 18.16ff.), or, as in the case of Nineveh in the book of Jonah, judgement remains a real but unrealized threat – Jonah's complaint and the reason behind his initial flight towards

---

[8] The insight that only a gracious demand can constitute a realistically absolute demand underlies the following quotation from Eberhard Jüngel (which, inasmuch as it occurs in the course of a discussion of the Barmen Declaration, also testifies to the dangers inherent in any attempt to define a Christian ethic other than Christologically): 'Moralism is indeed for its part a kind of "powerful", even domineering, "demand on our whole life" – only it is not grounded in the "promise of the forgiveness of all our sins". And because of that it is, for a Christian, an absolutely unbearable demand. For only that which *liberates* our whole life may lay claim to our whole life. It is only, indeed, as our whole life is *liberated* that it ever becomes a *whole* life, a *healed* life': Eberhard Jüngel, *Christ, Justice and Peace: Toward a Theology of the State in Dialogue with the Barmen Declaration*, trans. D. Bruce Hamill and Alan J. Torrance (Edinburgh: T&T Clark, 1992), p. 33.

[9] Amos 3.2: 'You only have I chosen of all the families of the earth; therefore I will punish you for all your sins.'

Tarshish was that he knew God to be 'a gracious and compassionate God, slow to anger and abounding in love, a God who relents from sending calamity' (Jonah 4.2). Similarly in the Gospels, the threat of judgement is directed to those who hear the words of Jesus and who stubbornly refuse to respond to them. Judgement, then, is not a separate and independent word or possibility; it is itself an outworking of the gospel, an outworking of grace; it is the form God's love assumes when it is resisted; or, in the words of Karl Barth: 'If the fire of His wrath scorches us, it is because it is the fire of His wrathful love and not His wrathful hate.'[10] Moreover, in the light of the gospel and the cosmic significance of Christ we have every reason to hope that judgement, at least in the heart of God, cannot be a final word since he 'wants all people to be saved and to come to a knowledge of the truth' and, more explicitly, he 'has bound everyone over to disobedience so that he may have mercy on them all' (1 Tim. 2. 4; Rom. 11.32).

The outcome of this universal hope is not so-called universalism. I am no more a universalist than was Karl Barth: with Barth I accept the possibility that God might love an individual enough to allow their rejection of his love to be ultimate, but with Barth I also accept the possibility that he might love them enough *not* to allow that rejection to be ultimate. In either case, however, it is an issue and an outworking of God's love; it is not an issue of any supposed 'loveless' judgement. With Barth we dare not limit the freedom of God's love by presuming some automatic and necessary 'universalism', but neither dare we limit the lovingness of God's freedom by presuming the opposite. We are not in a position to presume. The ultimate salvation of all men and women is that for which we must work, pray and hope (how could we conceivably do the opposite?), but, in the light of the dreadful warnings on the lips of Jesus himself, we may not presume that this hope will necessarily be fulfilled.[11]

---

[10] *CD* III/2, p. 609.
[11] For a succinct statement of Barth's own position see *CD* IV/4, pp. 208f. For a defence of Barth against the charge of 'Universalism' see J. D. Bettis,

One root of an equivocation concerning God's graciousness was identified towards the end of chapter three of this book in the influence of nominalism and the older tendency to consider God's will as indeterminate rather than as explicitly determined in love. That John Owen can think of God's justice as essential and his love as arbitrary is, in part, an instance of this trend but, at least in Owen's case, it is also an outcome of a trend towards penal interpretations of the Atonement.[12]

For Anselm, like Athanasius before him, human sin presents God with a dilemma, not because he is internally divided between a desire to punish and a desire to forgive – for both authors God is unequivocally loving and merciful towards humankind – but because, while it would be unthinkable for God to abandon the creature he loves, it would be equally unthinkable for him to undermine the ordering of the universe he has created.[13] For Athanasius universal order would be undermined if God went back on

---

'Is Karl Barth a Universalist?' *SJT* 20 (1967), pp. 423–36; and John E. Colwell, 'The Contemporaneity of the Divine Decision: Reflections on Barth's Denial of Universalism' in *Universalism and the Doctrine of Hell*, ed. Nigel M. de S. Cameron (Grand Rapids: Baker Book House, 1993), pp. 139–60.

[12] This is particularly plain in Owen's robust defence of 'limited atonement' in *The Death of Death in the Death of Christ*, in *The Works of John Owen*, X, ed. William H. Goold (London: Banner of Truth Trust, 1967), pp. 157–424. Hence, in the first respect: 'That God hath any natural or necessary inclination, by his goodness, or any other property, to do good to us, or any of his creatures, we do deny. Every thing that concerns us is an act of his free will and good pleasure, and not a natural, necessary act of his Deity ...' (p. 227). And in respect of the 'penal' logic of limited atonement consider the following: 'God imposed his wrath due unto, and Christ underwent the pains of hell for, either all the sins of all men, or all the sins of some men, or some sins of all men ... If the last ... then have all men some sins to answer for, and so shall no man be saved ... If the second ... Christ in their stead and room suffered for all the sins of all the elect in the world. If the first, why then, are not all freed from the punishment of all their sins?' (pp. 173f.)

[13] Gustav Aulén in his *Christus Victor: An Historical Study of the Three Main Types of the Idea of the Atonement*, trans. G. Hebert (London: SPCK, 1931), identifies Anselm as representative of a penal view of the Atonement and links Athanasius (rightly, but in a far too general manner) with patristic ideas of the Cross as a victory. This seems to be a misreading of Anselm's explicit argument. Moreover, while it is commonplace to censure Anselm for driving a wedge between the Father and the Son, this too is a difficult criticism to maintain: the Son, in his humanity, offers a perfect satisfaction

his word concerning the consequences of human sin: 'you must not eat from the tree of the knowledge of good and evil, for when you eat of it you will surely die' (Gen. 2.17).[14] For Anselm universal order would be undermined if God did not act to maintain and satisfy his own honour.[15] For neither Athanasius nor Anselm is the cross of Christ, in any sense, a vicarious punishment: for Athanasius the Son, by assuming our humanity, overcomes sin, corruption and death and re-establishes humanity in the divine image; for Anselm the Son, by assuming our humanity, satisfies the Father's honour on our behalf through his perfect obedience. There is a world of difference between Christ doing on our behalf what we have failed to do or are unable to do (the view, albeit in different forms, of both Anselm and Athanasius) and Christ bearing on our behalf the consequences of what we have done.[16]

By the time of the Reformation the notions of satisfaction and of punishment had become confused, in both Protestant and Roman Catholic thinking, in a manner that

to the Father, but this represents the loving purpose of the Father as much as of the Son. In this respect (i.e., in the absence of any division in the nature of God), Anselm stands closer to the earlier tradition than to the 'penal' tradition with which he is wrongly associated. For a thorough discussion of Anselm's contribution see the appropriate chapter in Colin E. Gunton, *The Actuality of Atonement: A Study of Metaphor, Rationality and the Christian Tradition* (Edinburgh: T&T Clark, 1988); see also Trevor A. Hart's excellent article 'Anselm of Canterbury and John McLeod Campbell: Where opposites Meet?', *Evangelical Quarterly 62* (1990), pp. 311–33.

[14] 'It would, of course, have been unthinkable that God should go back upon His word and that man, having transgressed, should not die; but it was equally monstrous that beings which once had shared the nature of the Word should perish and turn back again into non-existence through corruption': *St. Athanasius on the Incarnation: The Treatise De Incarnatione Verbi Dei*, trans. and ed. 'A Religious of C.S.M.V.' (London: G. Bles, 1944), II 6.

[15] 'Nothing is less tolerable in the order of things, than for the creature to take away the honor due to the Creator and not repay what he takes away': Anselm, *Why God became Man*, trans. E. R. Fairweather, in *A Scholastic Miscellany: Anselm to Ockham. Library of Christian Classics X* (London: SCM Press, 1956).

[16] The contrary nature of satisfaction and punishment is clear, for instance, in the following quotation from Anselm: '. . . every sin is necessarily followed either by satisfaction or by punishment' (*Why God became Man*, I 15).

undermined the unequivocal grace of God, since if punishment is perceived as a distinct option for God alongside mercy – in a manner unthinkable for either Athanasius or Anselm – God himself, in some sense, is divided.[17] The consequence of this perceived 'division' in God is that either we ourselves (through the sacrament of penance) in association with Christ, or Christ alone on our behalf (and explicitly in contradistinction to the Father) must 'change' the Father's attitude towards us, turning away his just wrath in order to receive his loving mercy.[18] This undermining of unequivocal grace was further compounded in the developing Reformed tradition by interpretations of the doctrine of predestination, and in particular of Calvin's notion of a 'double decree', that divided humanity categorically as the 'elect' or as the 'reprobate', as those who were objects of God's love or as those who were objects of God's wrath.[19] John Owen's refined account of 'limited atonement' may have the merit of uniting the persons of the Trinity in the work of salvation but it achieves this goal by assuming that same degree of equivocation in the work of the Son as was now assumed to pertain in the attitude of the Father and the work of the Spirit.[20] But that the Son of God *might* have

---

[17] For an instance of this confusion between punishment and satisfaction see the following quotation from Calvin: 'To take away our condemnation, it was not enough for him to suffer any kind of death: to make satisfaction for our redemption a form of death had to be chosen in which he might free us both by transferring our condemnation to himself and by taking our guilt upon himself ... the guilt that held us liable for punishment has been transferred to the head of the Son of God' (*Institutes* II xvi 5).

[18] So, for instance, the following extract from the *Institutes*: '... God's righteous curse bars our access to him, and God in his capacity as judge is angry toward us. Hence, an expiation must intervene in order that Christ as priest may obtain God's favour for us and appease his wrath' (II xv 6).

[19] As was mentioned in chapter three, helpful accounts of these developments can be found in M. Charles Bell's *Calvin and Scottish Theology*, R. T. Kendall's *Calvin and English Calvinism to 1649*, and, more recently, in William C. Placher's *The Domestication of Transcendence*.

[20] Owen's starting point in the work previously quoted is that, since the agent of the work of atonement is 'the whole blessed Trinity', there must exist absolute unity between them in the object and goal of their work (*The Death of Death in the Death of Christ*, p. 163).

loved me and *might* have given himself for me is hardly good news.

While understandings of the sacrament of penance and of the nature of the Atonement may be crucial themes in their own right they are necessarily derivative: the key issue here is the doctrine of God (and, by implication, the doctrine of revelation). To assume that the sacrifice of Christ is valid for some but not for others renders Jesus' words 'This is my body given for you ...' – granted that they were addressed to Judas along with the other disciples – a cruel and specious charade (Luke 22.19).[21] Only by positing a 'god' hidden behind the gospel story, one other than *this* Father, *this* Son and *this* Spirit, can one conclude that mercy and judgement remain in unresolved equilibrium.[22] Karl Barth dismisses the notion of a hidden decree of election and reprobation as implying that the 'book of life' has a 'death-column'.[23] Indeed, the fundamental distinction between Barth's account of election and the doctrine as it developed within the older Reformed tradition is precisely that Barth recognizes Jesus Christ as occupying the place previously taken by this 'hidden decree'.[24] There is no 'god' hidden behind the gospel story; there is no divine word other than this one Word made flesh; there is no divine law, no divine justice, no divine wrath, independent of God's gracious choice of humanity in Christ.[25]

[21] In the light of v. 21 we must accept that Judas was present when these words were spoken, just as, in John 13 he is present when Jesus washes the disciples' feet.

[22] It is this supposed equilibrium, the notion that God is glorified as much by the damnation of the reprobate as by the bliss of the elect, that underlies Jonathan Edwards's graphic adherence to a 'traditional' understanding of hell: see John E. Colwell, 'The Glory of God's Justice and the Glory of God's Grace: Contemporary reflections on the doctrine of Hell in the Teaching of Jonathan Edwards' (Drew Lecture on Immortality, 12 November 1992) published in *Called to One Hope: Perspectives on the Life to Come*, ed. John Colwell (Carlisle: Paternoster Press, 2000), pp. 113–29.

[23] *CD* II/2, p. 16.

[24] *CD* II/2, p. 161.

[25] *CD* II/2, p. 115: 'In the very foreground of our existence in history we can and should cleave wholly and with full assurance to Him because in the eternal background of history, in the beginning with God, the only decree which was passed, the only Word which was spoken and which prevails, was the decision which was executed by Him.'

All this need not imply that God is 'unfree', that it is necessary for him to create us and to love us if he is to be love in himself – as Father, Son and Holy Spirit, God is perfect love and perfect community eternally; he does not need us in order to be the God he is; he does not need us in order to be loving. But it does imply that God's freedom is *his* freedom; it is determinate and not indeterminate; it is not arbitrary; it is his freedom to be for us rather than against us; it is his freedom to create; it is his freedom to redeem.[26] And since God's freedom is positively and determinately the freedom of his love, his justice is an out-working of his grace just as his law is an outworking of the gospel. He is not divided. He is simple.

The point at issue here is that, if God is unequivocally this God, if his character is unequivocally as it is narrated in the gospel story, if he is undivided in mercy and grace, then not only is there no other valid understanding of him, there is also no valid way of understanding ourselves and the world we inhabit other than in the light of who he is as narrated in this story. This and this alone is a true foundation for a distinctively Christian ethic. To live authentically as Christians is to live in response to this God, to live in coherence with this story.[27]

In the Introduction to his analysis of Barth's ethics of reconciliation, John Webster observes that:

> It is arguable that one of the most serious obstacles to the reception of Barth's *magnum opus* is an inadequate

---

[26] Colin Gunton notes that, for Barth, transcendence is not the opposite of immanence; it is precisely God's freedom to be immanent; it is conceived dynamically rather than spatially: Colin E. Gunton, 'Transcendence, Metaphor, and the Knowability of God', *JTS* 31 (1980), pp. 501–16 (p. 512). Hence: 'This dynamic transcendence of God which is actual in Jesus Christ is not dialectically antithetical to His immanence, it is rather the ontological possibility of His immanence; the transcendence of God consists in His specific freedom to be immanent in Jesus Christ' (John E. Colwell, *Actuality and Provisionality*, p. 28).

[27] 'A Christianly successful moral ontology must be a depiction of the world of human action as it is enclosed and governed by the creative, redemptive, and sanctifying work of God in Christ, present in the power of the Holy Spirit': John Webster, *Barth's Ethics of Reconciliation* (Cambridge: Cambridge University Press, 1995), p. 2.

grasp of the fact that the *Church Dogmatics* is a work of moral theology as well as a systematics. More closely, Barth's *Dogmatics* is, amongst other things, a moral ontology – an extensive account of the situation in which human agents act.[28]

It is, indeed, remarkable that, though such a high proportion of the *Church Dogmatics* is expressly devoted to ethics, these sections have attracted proportionately little comment, either from those who have responded to his treatment of doctrine and epistemology or from those more generally concerned with ethical themes. In the case of students of Barth's theology, one may suspect that, sadly, many 'skip' these concluding sections to his treatment of the Doctrine of God, the Doctrine of Creation, and the Doctrine of Reconciliation, considering them to be an intrusion to the dogmatic argument. The more general neglect, however, may derive from the fact that, while Barth addresses many of the concerns commonly raised by ethicists, he does so in such an explicitly theological, and therefore untypical, manner.

The mere location of these ethical sections within the *Dogmatics* identifies their explicitly theological orientation. Indeed, in one sense it is inadequate to view them merely as responses to the dogmatic sections since, though they are certainly responsive in character, they constitute an integrated element of each of these key doctrines:[29] the doctrine of God has not been expounded adequately until we have considered our human identity as his covenant partners in Christ; the doctrine of creation has not been expounded adequately until we have considered the

---

[28] John Webster, *Barth's Ethics of Reconciliation*, p. 1.

[29] 'Theological ethics can be understood only as an integral element of dogmatics': Karl Barth, *The Christian Life: Church Dogmatics IV,4, Lecture Fragments*, trans. Geoffrey W. Bromiley (Edinburgh: T&T Clark, 1981), p. 3. Barth had already established this point in his 'Prolegomena' (*CD* I/2, pp. 782ff.), hence: '... the theme of dogmatics is always the Word of God and nothing else. But the theme of the Word is human existence, human life and volition and action ... neither theology nor dogmatics can be true to itself if it is not genuinely ready at the same time to be ethics ... Dogmatics has no option: it has to be ethics as well' (*CD* I/2, p. 793).

nature of our creatureliness, both in relation to the Creator and to the rest of creation; the doctrine of reconciliation has not been expounded adequately until we have considered what it means to live truthfully and faithfully as those who know that this reconciliation has taken place.[30] For Barth, then, Christian doctrine is inherently ethical and Christian ethics is inherently doctrinal; we pay Barth scant honour if we fail to take seriously his own understanding of the ethical nature and orientation of the dogmatic task.

The responsive character of Christian ethics is clear in each of Barth's explicitly ethical sections: the Word of God which is gospel is itself the command of God and by that command we are identified and established as the human agents called to answer to that command.[31] Consequently, 'As the doctrine of God's command, ethics interprets the Law as the form of the Gospel, i.e., as the sanctification which comes to man through the electing God.'[32] Moreover, this 'one command of the one God who is gracious to man in Jesus Christ is also the command of his Creator and therefore already the sanctification of the creaturely action and abstention of man'.[33] Similarly also ethics 'as a task of the doctrine of reconciliation' concerns the response of one who has been justified, sanctified and called by this gracious and faithful God:

> If we understand the situation of human existence in terms of Christian existence, we infer that the man

[30] The recent fashion of speaking of 'applied theology' is regrettable in this respect: not because such application is illegitimate (though the methodology of what sometimes passes as 'applied theology' is open to question) but because it reinforces the common assumption that theology can ever validly remain 'unapplied'.

[31] 'The metaphor of "answer" catches exactly what Barth wants to say about human morality: it is finite, brought into being by an external summons, and yet as such a real, reciprocal act. In effect, the model of summons and answer rules out both abstract divine monergism and pure human autonomy. More concretely, the human response is a matter of a proper correspondence or conformity between our life-act and the divine action from which it derives' (John Webster, *Barth's Ethics of Reconciliation*, p. 57).

[32] *CD* II/2, p. 509.

[33] *CD* III/4, p. 3.

who is responsible to the gracious God is the man who is affirmed and loved and elected by God. He is so either actually or virtually as a member of the people or community of God. He lives by what God is, by what he is in the word of his grace for this people and therefore also for him. He thus lives by God's eternal mercy, whose power is that God, faithful to his affirmation, love, and election, has in the freedom of his lovingkindness made him also free. To have freed him is to have reconciled him to himself; to have reconciled him is to have justified him so that he can stand before him; to have sanctified him, so that he can live with and for him; and to have called him, so that he can serve him as his witness.[34]

It is perhaps in the final fragments of an ethics of reconciliation that the radically responsive nature of Christian ethics is most clearly demonstrated. As is well known, Barth never completed his *Church Dogmatics*; the fifth volume (on the doctrine of Redemption) was never begun, and the final chapter of the fourth volume ('The Command of God the Reconciler') remained unfinished: the section on baptism was prepared for publication by Barth himself, and the remaining fragments were published separately after his death. Following a general introduction (from which I have already quoted) Barth expounds baptism as 'The Foundation of the Christian Life' and then begins to expound the clauses of the Lord's Prayer. This may not be a common approach to the question of ethics (which Barth himself earlier describes as the question of 'what may be called *good* human action'[35]) but it is a profoundly and distinctively *Christian* approach. The foundation of my being and living as a Christian – my '*good* human action' – is precisely a matter of my 'turning to faithfulness to God', which is his work in me by the Spirit, and of my responding confession of obedience and 'prayer for God's

---

[34] Karl Barth, *The Christian Life*, p. 22.
[35] Karl Barth, *The Christian Life*, p. 3.

grace' in baptism.[36] And my continuing as a Christian is constituted precisely in my praying, in and with Jesus Christ, as the child before the Father, as one seeking his will which is the establishing of his kingdom and his holiness on earth, as one trustfully dependent upon his provision and sustenance, as one continually defined by his forgiveness and therefore called continually to forgive, as one utterly dependent upon God in the face of temptation and evil.[37]

It was Barth's intention to complete this ethics of the doctrine of reconciliation with an exposition of the Lord's Supper – he did not even begin it and, according to Geoffrey Bromiley in his 'Translator's Preface', Barth 'was also not satisfied that he had found the best way to organize his material in the . . . central sections', hesitating between the concepts of 'faithfulness', 'invocation' and 'gratitude'.[38] Be that as it may, each potential organizing concept is responsive. *Christian* ethics cannot be other than

---

[36] The adequacy (or inadequacy) of Barth's final 'non-sacramental' treatment of baptism and the dualism he seemingly reintroduces between divine action and human action will be considered in chapter seven of this book and again in chapter nine. The point at issue at this stage is merely to establish the responsive, and therefore distinctive, nature of Christian ethics. Nonetheless, the discussion can be anticipated by recognizing (with Barth himself) that Christian baptism derives its significance from the narrative of Jesus' baptism.

[37] 'In tying together prayer and ethics, Barth explores a moral ontology and a moral anthropology in which dependence is not diminishment and resolute action is not self-assertion' (John Webster, *Barth's Ethics of Reconciliation*, p. 114). Compare the following comment of Nigel Biggar in relation to an earlier section of the *Dogmatics*: 'Barth proposes prayer as "the primal and basic form" of the Christian ethos and the "archetypal form" of all good acts (CD III/3:89)': Nigel Biggar, 'Hearing God's Command and Thinking about What's Right: With and Beyond Barth' in *Reckoning with Barth: Essays in Commemoration of the Centenary of Karl Barth's Birth*, ed. Nigel Biggar (London: Mowbray, 1988) pp. 101–18 (p. 105).

[38] Geoffrey W. Bromiley, 'Translator's Preface' in Karl Barth, *The Christian Life*, pp. vii–viii, p. vii. In respect of the possibility of a more explicit focus on gratitude, note the wording of the heading with which Barth may have intended to revise these sections (included in the Appendix to *The Christian Life*): 'The Word of God's free grace, effective and revealed in Jesus Christ, is his command to each person and all people in which he calls for the response of their obedience in the thought, speech, and action of their free gratitude' (p. 291).

responsive. What is at issue is no human command but the command of God which is Jesus Christ. *Christian* rationality is not a matter of discernible rights or consequences but of coherence with the gospel story, a coherence that expresses itself in faithfulness and thanksgiving: for the one who has been brought to know this God as narrated in the gospel story, it would be irrational and incoherent *not* to live thankfully and trustfully.[39] And, because *Christian* ethics is responsive to the gospel story, it is precisely in this thankfulness and trustfulness that the authentic distinctiveness of *Christian* ethics is located. Thankfulness may not be commonly recognized as an ethical category within *general* approaches to ethics – which only serves to underline its distinctively *Christian* association. With Thomas Aquinas, of course, we must identify love – as it is defined narratively in the gospel story – as the supreme theological virtue, but faith and hope constitute the remaining theological virtues and, thereby, constitute the other distinctive marks of Christian living.[40] The distinctive character of Christian love will be the theme of the next chapter but, if its true distinctiveness is to be maintained, it must not be considered other than in relation to faith and hope; Christians are being re-formed in love precisely inasmuch as they are learning to live trustfully and hopefully.

In his exposition of the Lord's Prayer within these fragments of an ethics of reconciliation Barth does not seem to have progressed beyond the phrase 'Thy Kingdom come'.[41] But it is the opening address, 'Our Father in

---

[39] Notwithstanding the usual English translations of Romans 12.1 in terms of 'your spiritual act of worship' the Greek text reads τὴν λογικὴν λατρείαν ὑμῶν and, as the *NIV* acknowledges in the margin, could be translated 'your reasonable act of worship'. Christian rationality, then, is a matter of offering ourselves as 'living sacrifices', of not being conformed to 'the pattern of this world', of being 'transformed' by the 'renewing' of our minds, of discerning God's 'good, pleasing and perfect will'.

[40] 'Now, since the three theological virtues look at God as their proper object, it cannot be said that any one of them is greater than another by reason of its having a greater object, but only from the fact that it approaches nearer than another to that object; and in this way charity is greater than the others' (*ST* I–II 66 6).

[41] Karl Barth, *The Christian Life*, pp. 205ff.

heaven', together with the later phrase 'Forgive us our debts', which, conjoined with a beginning in baptism and a conclusion in the Lord's Supper, identify that response which is distinctively coherent with the narration of God's grace and mercy. Joined with Christ in baptism in prayerful expectation of the gift of the Spirit, the Christian has been established as a 'new creation'; yet again and again in the Eucharist the Christian comes confessing continued sinfulness and acknowledging continual and absolute dependence upon the sacrifice of Christ. By the Spirit the Christian has been joined to the Son and, consequently, may address the Father; yet the Christian can do so only as one who always stands in need of forgiveness. The Christian life, which necessarily begins in absolute and conscious dependence upon God's mercy, continues in this manner. Christians know that they 'have no claim on heaven's rewards' but that they stand 'in constant need of heaven's mercy and help'.[42] The Christian can only come before God praying, 'Have mercy on me, a sinner' (Luke 18.13).

In this recognition of our continual dependence upon God's mercy lies the truth (or at least one aspect of the truth) underlying Luther's definition of the Christian as *simul iustus et peccator* – not as a means of excusing sin but as an honest recognition of continuing weakness and dependence. The Christian does not stand before God on the basis of any perceived 'right' or 'claim' but solely on the basis of God's mercy as narrated in the gospel story.[43] I cannot approach this Father or live my life before him other than as one who continues in this confession, as one who is *simul iustus et peccator et penitens*.

[42] 'Invitation to the Table' in *Patterns and Prayers for Christian Worship*, Baptist Union of Great Britain (Oxford: Oxford University Press, 1991), p. 81.
[43] Notwithstanding attempts by Kieran Cronin and others to habilitate a notion of 'rights' within Christian ethics, I must concur with Stanley Hauerwas that '[t]here are, after all, strong Christian presuppositions that at the very least relativize any claim that we might have to rights, if not denying them entirely' (Stanley Hauerwas, *After Christendom?* p. 90); cf. Kieran Cronin, *Rights and Christian Ethics* (Cambridge: Cambridge University Press, 1992).

But if this dependence upon mercy derives from a recognition of our continuing weakness it also derives from a recognition of the 'fallenness' of the context in which we presently live. As will be argued in chapter ten of this book, the universe is not yet as God would ultimately have it to be. Here and now we are confronted with contradiction, opposition, pain and suffering – to such a degree that 'absolute right' (however that might be defined) simply is not always an option for us. There is a sense in which, whatever course of action we take, following our highest and most worthy deliberations, the outcome will always be tinged with some element of regret and inadequacy.[44] The 'best' simply is not presently available to us.

It is in response to this 'tragic' reality that the Roman Catholic debates concerning the 'principle of double effect', together with the more radical (though perhaps more realistic) notion of 'proportionalism', have arisen.[45] A classic instance of the dynamic in question would be the occurrence of an ectopic pregnancy: if no action is taken both mother and baby will die, yet (at present) the only action which can be taken to save the mother's life does so at the expense of the life of the baby; that is to say, a single action done with good intent has both a good and a bad consequence. Proponents of the double effect principle argue that four criteria must be met if any action with this double effect is to be 'rightly' performed: (1) the action should be good in itself, or at least not evil; (2) the intention of the agent performing the act should be

---

[44] The insight that 'whichever choice you make you will regret it' may be a parody of Kierkegaard's argument in *Either/Or* but, inasmuch as this enigmatic work derives, at least in part, from his decision to break his engagement to Regine, it illustrates the frailty and partiality of our moral decision-making, which, indeed, may be Kierkegaard's purpose in writing the book: Søren Kierkegaard, *Either/Or: A Fragment of Life*, vol. 1, trans. David F. Swenson and Lillian Marvin Swenson; *Either/Or*, vol. 2, trans. Walter Lowrie (Princeton: Princeton University Press, 1949).
[45] For a succinct introduction to the debate see Bernard Hoose, *Proportionalism: The American Debate and its European Roots* (Georgetown: Georgetown University Press, 1987), also Peter Knauer, 'The Hermeneutic Function of the Principle of Double Effect' in *Readings in Moral Theology No. 1: Moral Norms and Catholic Tradition*, ed. Charles E. Curran and Richard A. McCormick (New York: Paulist Press, 1979), pp. 1–39.

good;[46] (3) the good effect of the action should not itself be a direct outcome of the evil effect; (4) there should be a proportionate reason for acting in such a manner as produces this double effect. In the case of an ectopic pregnancy, for instance: (1) surgery, since it is done for good effect, should not be considered as mutilation; (2) the reason for acting is to save the life of the mother; (3) the mother's life is saved by the removal of the baby from the Fallopian tube, not by the killing of the baby (though this is a consequence of the removal of the baby); (4) to act in such a circumstance (and save the mother's life) would clearly be better than not to act (and forfeit the lives of both mother and baby). Those who are termed 'proportionalists' (as the label suggests) argue that it is the fourth criterion here which is decisive, even if one or more of the first three criteria may be unfulfilled. Critics of proportionalism generally dismiss the position as a form of consequentialism though this is probably unfair: the entire debate occurs within the broader bounds of natural law theory and is only intelligible in a context where an action is deemed to be good or bad in and of itself (and not just with regard to its consequences).[47]

On the other hand (and predictably), there are those who argue that it can never be right to act against any single 'good'. My difficulty with this latter position is that it is simply unrealistic;[48] the world is not like this; the example of an ectopic pregnancy may be extreme but, in everyday

[46] In this context 'intention' relates to the reason for which the action is performed.
[47] Note, for instance, Bernard Hoose's comment: 'This ... is where proportionalism and situation ethics must part company. Both agree that love (agape), or the lack of it, is the only criterion for moral goodness or badness. Proportionalism, however, if it is to be coherent, cannot accept that love alone makes an action right, although love most certainly demands the pursuit of morally right activity. An action born of love can be wrong, while an action not resulting from love can be right' (Bernard Hoose, *Proportionalism*, p. 63). It must be conceded, however, that this is a clear instance of how, in practice, the boundaries between deontological and teleological approaches to ethical dilemmas become blurred.
[48] Generally, of course, those who seek to maintain such 'conservative' positions tend to invoke other (and more traditional) casuistic strategies to justify acting.

life we are continually confronted with decisions of potentially mixed outcome; whenever I start my car I am acting
proportionately – I am acting (I hope) for the good, but in
the knowledge that this will have some bad effects. The
ubiquity of such 'dilemmas' only reinforces the conclusion
(to be developed in the next chapter) that this entire
approach is unhelpful and (at least in terms of identifying
a distinctively *Christian* ethic) inadequate: the primary
focus for a Christian ethic – in response to the storied
character of Christ – must be the goodness of the agent
rather than the rightness of the action; given the
'fallenness' of the world the latter is simply too confused
and complex to be viable foundationally.

But my other underlying sense of unease with all such
approaches is that they imply a context of self-justification:
the underlying concern is to identify strategies whereby an
action, which has mixed effects, may be deemed to be
'right'. I presume that a consistent 'proportionalist' who, as
a surgeon, performed an operation to terminate an ectopic
pregnancy, would feel no need to raise the matter in the
confessional – the point of proportionalist analysis, after
all, is to determine that the act is 'right'.[49] Under similar
circumstances, I suspect that I would feel the need to
'confess' – I hope I would have acted in the best way that I
could within a fallen world, but because I had acted within
a *fallen* world, and because I would have done no more
than *my best*, I simply could not 'overlook' the mixed
outcome of my action. Nor, in the light of the mercy of God
as narrated in the gospel, would I see the need to overlook
the mixed outcome of the action or to indulge in any form
of casuistic self-justification. It seems to me that any
attempt at self-justification, any attempt to defend an
action as unequivocally 'right', is both unrealistic and
ungrateful: it is unrealistic inasmuch as it takes insufficient
account of the fallenness of the universe and the frailty of

---

[49] James M. Gustafson identifies the sacrament of penance and the
associated need to evaluate the seriousness of sins as providing Roman
Catholic ethics with its distinctive orientation (James M. Gustafson,
Protestant and Roman Catholic Ethics, pp. 1f.).

human agents; it is ungrateful inasmuch as it seeks to circumvent the mercy of God narrated in the gospel. In this present context I am incapable of an action that does not cry out for divine mercy.

When Luther urges Melanchthon to 'sin boldly', while (as we noted previously) this may be unwise phraseology and may be misconstrued as counsel for moral carelessness, his motivation was a grateful trust in the mercy of God and a desire to magnify that mercy. The Christian should certainly be concerned to live coherently with the gospel, but such coherence cannot be reduced to being unequivocally right in every instance, indeed, the claim to be unequivocally right is itself incoherent with the gospel. Knowing ourselves and knowing the nature of the world in which we live we know that we cannot be consistently right. In and of itself this knowledge would be a matter of grief but we do not have this knowledge in and of itself. We only have this knowledge in the light of the gospel and therefore in the context of God's prevenient mercy. It is not merely that we have heard of this mercy: through the Word, through the sacraments and through the living sacrament of the Christian community, we have received this mercy; it has become the fundamental definition of our lives. And in the light of this prevenient mercy, grief is overwhelmed by joy; we cannot but live in unqualified gratitude.[50]

[50] 'So, then, this thought that against God you are always in the wrong is not a truth you are compelled to recognize, not a comfort which assuages your pain, not a compensation for the loss of something better, but it is a joy in which you triumph over yourself and over the world, it is your delight, your anthem of praise, your divine worship, a demonstration that your love is a happy one, as only that love can be wherewith one loves God' (Søren Kierkegaard, *Either/Or*, vol. 2, p. 291).

6
The Gospel as Command

One balmy evening, two summers ago, my wife and I were enjoying a quite excellent barbecue in our friends' garden. Two other friends were present besides our hosts and all six of us were (and are) members of the same Baptist church. In fact, though our family had only just moved back into the area, and re-joined the church, we had all been together within the same church for the best part of thirty years (longer in some cases). Though nostalgia is not what it used to be, reminiscence was inevitable – and a church can change its character significantly in the space of thirty years. Indeed, evangelical spirituality in Britain generally, at least in its outward manifestations, has undergone considerable change since the early sixties. Time was when it was not at all uncommon to see men (and I mean 'men') leaving morning worship and lighting a cigarette on the church steps – but very few would have admitted to enjoying any form of alcoholic drink. It would have taken considerable courage to go to a church service in jeans and a sweater, and none of us would have dreamed of playing football or cricket on a Sunday. My upbringing may have been a little extreme but I can remember being taken as a child to see a documentary film at a cinema with my parents casting furtive glances lest they should be seen exposing themselves – and their child – to such worldliness.

Thirty years ago this particular church had an excellent (and very large) young people's group, although it had been very strict, especially in the matter of alcohol. 'But at least in those days,' one of our friends mused, 'you knew who the Christians were; we were different; we knew something about discipleship.'[1] I should explain that we all have children in their late teens or early twenties; we are

---

[1] I didn't have a tape-recorder at the time and this is not a precise quotation though I hope I am being an accurate interpreter of my friend's concerns.

all only too aware of the rather more lax atmosphere that
pertains in many church youth groups. And in many ways
I share my friend's concerns: years of 'cheap believism'
have undermined Christian distinctiveness in Evangelical
Christianity generally and the church of which we are a
part has inevitably been coloured by this more widespread
trend. But at the time I was somewhat less gracious and
agreeable. We argued. Were not those outward distinctives
merely manifestations of passing prejudice? What possible
basis did they have in the gospel? Could it not be the case
that, at least in some respects, present apparent laxity was
a reaction to that illegitimate legalism?

'But what then should be the distinctives of Christian
living?' was the challenge that my friend not unreasonably
laid down and the challenge to which this book is, at least
in part, an attempted response.

The story of how Jesus' disciples were censured by
the Pharisees for picking and eating ears of corn on the
Sabbath demonstrates how easily a proper concern for
distinctiveness can degenerate into pettiness. Somehow an
appropriate care for Israel's identity as the people of God,
of which the Sabbath provision was a defining mark, had
sunk beneath a mass of rules and regulations. Included
among the range of Jesus' responses in the Gospels'
narration of this incident is the indictment that his
disciples' accusers had forgotten God's demand for 'mercy,
not sacrifice' (Matt. 12.7). The reference is to a verse in
Hosea and the word mercy (ἔλεος) translates the Hebrew
word חֶסֶד: a word that is notoriously difficult to translate –
it has variously been rendered as 'steadfast love',
'lovingkindness', 'covenant love', 'faithfulness' – but
which is probably the Old Testament's most distinctive
word for the character of God (Hos. 6.6).[2] This חֶסֶד, then,
does not refer to any impersonal or indeterminate principle
or abstracted virtue but refers specifically to the character
of this God who has made himself known to Israel.
Moreover, the word does not merely signify God's singular
lovingness; it also signifies God's utter constancy, the

---

[2] כִּי חֶסֶד חָפַצְתִּי וְלֹא־זָבַח וְדַעַת אֱלֹהִים מֵעֹלוֹת

changelessness of his love, the unfailing faithfulness of God's covenant commitment to Israel:

> How can I give you up, Ephraim?
> How can I hand you over, Israel?
> How can I treat you like Admah?
> How can I make you like Zeboiim?
> My heart is changed within me;
> all my compassion is aroused.
> I will not carry out my fierce anger,
> nor will I turn and devastate Ephraim.
> For I am God, and not a human being –
> the Holy One among you.
> I will not come in wrath. (Hosea 11.8f.)

But the Old Testament uses this word חֶסֶד, which specifically identifies the character of God, to speak also of that virtue which, supremely, should characterize his covenant people: Israel is called to live coherently as the people of *this* God; called to reflect God's character; called to live in absolute faithfulness to this covenant; called to 'act justly and to love mercy and to walk humbly' with their God (Micah 6.8).[3] The word Hasidim, used of the forebears of the Pharisees, derives from this word חֶסֶד and identifies those who, during the period of Greek persecution, remained faithful to the covenant. How easily we, like the Pharisees who criticized Jesus' disciples, come to measure faithfulness by outward conformity to established convention.

God's command to Abram was to 'walk before me and be blameless' (Gen. 17.1). The command of the gospel never is and never has been anything less than this command for 'blamelessness' or 'perfection'. We, like Abram, are called to conformity with the character of this God who has apprehended us in mercy; to live in coherence with who this God is and with what this God is doing. The law was given to Israel not to supersede this command to perfect conformity but to specify the outworkings of this command for this particular people in their particular historical and

---

[3] כִּי אִם־עֲשׂוֹת מִשְׁפָּט וְאַהֲבַת חֶסֶד וְהַצְנֵעַ לֶכֶת עִם־אֱלֹהֶיךָ

social context. The details of this law, then, are misappropriated either if they are extracted from their context within the narrative of the covenant or if they are granted an ultimacy that cannot be warranted either from their inherent nature or from their context within the canon. That which is ultimate is the call to 'blamelessness' or 'perfection'; the law could never be other than a provisional indication of this ultimate imperative. The command of the gospel is for conformity with the character of God – character cannot be reduced to rules and regulations any more than it can be reduced to propositions. It is, perhaps, partly for this reason that Jeremiah anticipates the fulfilment of the covenant in terms of God's law being written on people's hearts and minds rather than on tablets of stone: ultimately only character can portray character.

This call to conformity with the character of God is reiterated by Jesus in the context of the 'Sermon on the Mount':

> Be perfect, therefore, as your heavenly Father is perfect. (Matthew 5.48)

The significance of this 'Sermon' is negated if, in Dispensationalist fashion, it is misappropriated as Jesus' ethical challenge to historic Israel (an ethic to be fulfilled only in the premillennial kingdom) or if, as is common more generally in Protestant circles, it is perceived as an idealistic ethic of perfection, intended only to bring us to the conviction of our own inadequacy and to the awareness of our need for divine mercy – Jesus concludes the Sermon with a parable exposing the foolishness of those who hear these words and do not put them into practice (Matt. 7.24ff.). But the Sermon is also misappropriated if Jesus is perceived merely as the giver of a new law – to become as pernickety about oath-taking as the Pharisees were about Sabbath observance is hardly an advance.[4] Jesus' concern

---

[4] While Thomas Aquinas writes of the 'New Law' in contrast to the 'Old Law' he does so in terms of its continuity rather than its discontinuity, or rather, he sees the 'New' as the perfect that fulfils what was lacking in the

here is not so much to give a new law as to reinterpret the
old law, or rather, to indicate that which always was
underlying the law – that we should live in coherence with
the character of God; his concern is with the character that
underlies outward speech and action. Indeed, the Sermon
is at least as concerned with description as with imperative: we are not *commanded to be* 'meek' if we are to be
'blessed' and to 'inherit the earth', we are rather told that it
is those who *are* 'meek' who are 'blessed' and who will
'inherit the earth' (Matt. 5.5).[5] The concern of the Sermon is
to identify the characteristics of those who live in
coherence with the character of this 'Father in heaven' and
who therefore act and speak in consequence of this
identity; its concern for who we are takes precedence over
its concern for what we do.

But even when the Sermon's focus on character is recognized, the danger of misappropriation persists; abstract the
Sermon from its context within the story of Jesus as narrated
in Matthew and it becomes all too easy to interpret it in
terms of abstract themes or principles. But abstracted
principles can quickly become as impersonal and rigid as
abstracted rules. They are, at the same time, both too precise
and too imprecise, or rather, they convey an inappropriate
form of precision: they are too precise inasmuch as, like
rules, they admit to rigid interpretation and application;
they are too imprecise inasmuch as, once abstracted from

---

imperfect – not as that which undermines or contradicts the imperfect (see
for example *ST* I–II 107 2). James M. Gustafson comments upon the
peculiarly Anabaptist notion of Jesus as the bringer of a New Law in
contrast to the view shared by both Thomas and Calvin that Jesus (in
himself and in his teaching) is the ultimate interpreter of the Old Law. For
Gustafson this is simply one instance of an underlying commonality
between Roman Catholic and Reformed approaches to ethics (James M.
Gustafson, *Protestant and Roman Catholic Ethics*, p. 19); cf. *Institutes* II viii 6.
[5] 'We miss all this when we reduce the Beatitudes to maxims of positive
thinking, new rules for getting by well. How many moralistic sermons
have we heard urging people to be peacemakers, or meek, or feeders of
the poor? The indicatives become moralistic imperatives, new rules which
lead to conventional forms of ethical activism, anguish, or security,
depending on the particular species of self-deception at work in the
practitioner': Stanley Hauerwas and William H. Willimon, *Resident Aliens:
Life in the Christian Colony* (Nashville: Abingdon Press, 1989), p. 85.

the narrative of Jesus, they fail to penetrate the specific and personal manner of virtue as defined in him. So, for example, Joseph Fletcher's attempt to reduce Christian ethics to the single theme of 'love' fails, not just because 'love' is itself so vague a concept, but more specifically because the person of Jesus, the focus for any valid Christian ethic, simply cannot be reduced to any single principle. The gospel is the story of a person, not a catalogue of abstracted principles, no matter how noble or compelling:

> It is important at this point to make clear that I am not arguing that the emphasis on love in current Christian ethics is wrong because it involves a misunderstanding of love, though that is certainly part of my case. Rather I am trying to make a more radical point: that even if love is freed from its sentimental perversions, it is still not an adequate principle, policy, or summary metaphor to capture the thrust of the Gospel for the Christian's moral behavior. Love is dependent on our prior perceptions of the truth of reality that can finally be approached only through the richness of the language and stories which form what we know. The Christian is thus better advised to resist the temptation to reduce the Gospel to a single formula or summary image for the moral life. Christian ethics and the Christian moral life are as rich and various as the story we hold and the life we must live to be true to it.[6]

In his otherwise impressive and helpful book, *The Moral Vision of the New Testament*, Richard B. Hays identifies the themes of Community, Cross, and New Creation as three focal images 'that all the different canonical tellings share'.[7] Simply as a comment on New Testament themes this may be valid, and were one to isolate organizing themes within the New Testament these three would be as good as any and better than most – but why bother? Does not this

---

[6] Stanley Hauerwas, *Vision and Virtue*, p. 120, commenting on Joseph Fletcher, *Situation Ethics*.
[7] Richard B. Hays, *The Moral Vision of the New Testament*, p. 194.

rather miss the point? Surely the purpose of the Gospel narratives is to identify 'truth' as a person: the purpose of Scripture is not to provide us with 'focal images' any more than it is to furnish us with rules or propositions; it is to narrate the character of God – in a preliminary and provisional manner in the Old Testament, and in an ultimate manner in the New Testament. The themes of the New Testament find their focus, and therefore their integration, in the person of Jesus himself as narrated: to focus on the themes themselves jeopardizes this focus and, consequently, risks the forfeiture of integration.

Like the Pharisees who, in this story, were so concerned with the minutiae of Sabbath observance, we instinctively feel more comfortable with an ethic that is codified than with one that is narrated; we know where we are only when every 'i' is dotted and every 't' is crossed. But whenever our focus shifts from the person as narrated to a law, a principle, or a theme, we risk denying the gospel by displacing the ultimate with the penultimate, the truly absolute with the provisional. This is fatal. The Church's tolerance, or even support, of slavery – not to mention its acceptance of any form of racism or sexism – was directly a consequence of a preoccupation with the penultimate at the expense of the ultimate. And, sadly, we need not look back beyond the beginnings of the nineteenth century to find examples of slavery being justified on a supposedly biblical basis.[8] This apparent

---

[8] See, for instance, the following passage quoted by Bernard Hoose: 'For Harris, speaking to a Protestant audience, the Bible was the only possible guide. Tradition, habits, "mere human reason and sense" – all were fallible. Anyone "with any pretensions to Religion" must immediately assent to the final authority of Scripture. And any person who professed to acknowledge the Bible as the unerring Word of God must assent to every Scriptural decision, without reserve and without questioning God's hidden justice ... Having boxed his readers within this framework of orthodox Protestant assumptions, Harris proceeded to show that slavery had been positively sanctioned by God during the period of natural law, in the time of Abraham and Joseph; during the period of Mosaic law; and during the earliest Christian dispensation': David B. David, *The Problem of Slavery in the Age of Revolution 1770–1823* (Ithaca: Cornell University Press, 1975), pp. 531–44, quoted in Bernard Hoose, *Received Wisdom? Reviewing the Role of Tradition in Christian Ethics* (London: Geoffrey Chapman, 1994) pp. 28f.

concern for biblical authority in reality undermines the true authority of Scripture by failing to take due account of the Christological focus of Scripture as heard within the Church. If any text of Scripture is heard and interpreted other than as focused and qualified in Scripture's central story it is misheard and misinterpreted. Here, in the humanity of Jesus, every other definition of humanity is rendered provisional and every hierarchical division of humanity is annulled; no man and no woman is any less defined by the humanity of Jesus than is any other man or woman (Gal. 3.28).[9]

The Council of Chalcedon confessed Christ not only as 'truly God' but also as 'truly human'; of 'one substance with the Father', but also as of 'one substance with us'. Herein is expressed the faith of the Church that God is truly defined in the gospel story since it is here, in the gospel story, that he has defined himself. But it is equally the faith of the Church that here in the gospel story God simultaneously has defined true humanity: the humanity that the Father chooses – and consequently the only 'true' and perfect humanity – is precisely the humanity assumed by the Son and indwelt by the Spirit. For Athanasius, in his account of the Incarnation, the divine dilemma is twofold. On the one hand God, in coherence with his love and faithfulness, acts in human history to overcome death and corruption. But this alone would be insufficient to restore God's purposes for humanity and for creation. Consequently, God acts simultaneously in human history to restore his image in fallen humanity.[10] If some more recent accounts of the Atonement, in their concern to focus on the Cross and Resurrection, have tended to focus less on the Incarnation, it may be an outcome of a failure to appreciate this twofold nature of God's dilemma, a further symptom of a marginalizing of sanctification through a focus on justification. The gospel is re-creation as much as rescue, sanctification as much as justification, command

---

[9] 'There is neither Jew nor Greek, slave nor free, male nor female, for you are all one in Christ Jesus.'
[10] Athanasius, *De Incarnatione Verbi Dei*, III 13ff.

as much as mercy. In the humanity of Jesus, God has not only acted to overcome human sin and its consequences, he has also acted to restore his image in fallen humanity. The humanity of Jesus as narrated in the gospel *is* the only 'true' humanity; the humanity of Jesus *is* the command of the gospel:

> Here again we must begin by stating that this is the question that is answered in Jesus Christ. One cannot emphasize enough that in him true man as well as true God is present and manifest. There is no abstract humanity and therefore no correspondingly abstract human self-understanding. Man is no more, no less, no other than what he is through and with and for Jesus Christ.[11]

Barth's pervading concern to maintain the freedom of God's command has led some of his critics to suspect his account of ethics of an imprecision and arbitrariness.[12] In response to this charge it must be recognized again that, in Barth's understanding, the freedom of the divine command is nothing other than the freedom of *this* God who has defined himself and defined humanity in the

---

[11] Karl Barth, *The Christian Life*, p. 19.

[12] So, for instance, '... Barth's claim that the ethical good is determined solely from the command of God is simply fantastic. Ethics is fundamentally reflection on our received human experience as to what is good and bad, right and wrong' (Stanley Hauerwas, *Vision and Virtue*, p. 28). Nigel Biggar defends Barth from this charge by affirming that 'Barth is not an ethical Spiritualist ... if we would hear what God commands us, we must listen in the context of biblical exegesis. We hear the command of God only through and under Scripture' (Nigel Biggar, 'Hearing God's Command and Thinking about What's Right', p. 108). Biggar can therefore conclude that 'God's command is the imperative form of God's Word. God's Word must be heard under Scripture; and because under Scripture, therefore in the Church; and because in the Church, therefore in the World. It is clear, then, that what Barth does not mean by his concept of hearing the command of God is a moment of purely private revelation. It is not a form of solipsistic monologue. Hearing takes place in dialogue – primarily with Scripture and secondarily with one's fellow-hearers, both past and present, both actual and virtual. There *are* public criteria that one can bring – indeed, *must* bring – to bear on another's claim to have heard a command of God' (Nigel Biggar, 'Hearing God's Command and Thinking about What's Right', p. 111).

gospel story.[13] God is free to command *whatever* he wills, but this freedom is specifically to command whatever *he wills*. And, at least for Barth, this God is not arbitrary; he 'cannot disown himself' (2 Tim. 2.13); he cannot be other than himself as defined in the gospel story; he cannot choose or command some other humanity than is defined here. For Barth, autonomous ethics, like human religion, is itself a mark of human sinfulness and pride deriving from our desire to exalt ourselves as moral arbiters and thereby to justify ourselves. Christian ethics, if it is to be truly *Christian*, cannot derive from anything other than the command of God, but, while God as *God* remains utterly free in this command, while his command, like his gracious mercy, cannot be presumed upon or calculated in advance, his command is genuinely *his* command and, consequently, his command, like his gracious mercy, can never be arbitrary or capricious.[14] Christian ethics, if it is to be truly *Christian*, cannot derive from anything other than the command of *this* God who has defined himself and defined humanity in Christ.[15]

However, if there is ground for suspecting Barth's account of ethics of imprecision it is a consequence of his relative lack of attention to the specifics of the Gospels' narration of Jesus and his similar lack of attention to the

[13] As has been intimated previously, when William Stacy Johnson identifies 'the very open-endedness, provisionality, and inclusiveness of Barth's deliberations' as strengths rather than weakness, he seems to be minimizing Barth's understanding of the determinate (rather than indeterminate) nature of the divine command for the sake of establishing Barth's (undoubted) 'nonfoundationalist' credentials (William Stacy Johnson, *The Mystery of God*, p. 154).

[14] 'The intelligibility of Barth's discussion of "The Command of God" as a whole turns upon his refusal to identify his account with some generic "theonomous ethics", and upon his counter-assertion that terms such as "command", "law" or "claim" are Christianly construed by reference to the nameable history of Jesus Christ. Everything hangs upon the fact that God's command is specified in that history, that God "demands our objective obedience in and with the fact that He is gracious to us in Jesus Christ"' (John Webster, *Barth's Ethics of Reconciliation*, pp. 51f.).

[15] '... in all that he does Man acts well only when he acts in response to the deeds of God... The first act of anyone who would know what he must do must *not* be one of reflection, but of hearing' (Nigel Biggar, 'Hearing God's Command and Thinking about What's Right', p. 102).

continuing narrative of the Church as the witness and living echo of this focal narrative; it is an outcome of insufficient attention to the central story (and the subsequent stories) in which this command of God is mediated; it is a further manifestation of the 'immediacy' which Colin Gunton identifies as pervading the entirety of Barth's theological account.[16]

Barth is rightly concerned to interpret the gospel narratives doctrinally in coherence with the manner in which they have been heard and believed within the Church – to fail in this respect is to fail to identify this story as the authentic definition of God and humanity; it is to reduce Christ to a moral teacher and example. But Barth seems so concerned with this doctrinal focus that it threatens to displace the narrative itself, or, rather, it leads to such a concentration upon the narratives of baptism, crucifixion, resurrection and ascension that the narratives of Jesus' life and ministry appear marginalized.[17] Indeed, the very structure that Barth has adopted in his account of the doctrine of reconciliation, by defining humanity in terms of Jesus' exaltation while his self-humbling identifies true deity, militates against a thorough engagement with the particularities of his incarnate life. Here, surely, is an

---

[16] Colin E. Gunton, *A Brief Theology of Revelation*, pp. 16ff., 66ff. It is difficult not to concur that Barth is, at the very least, reticent in his account of the Spirit's mediation of God's mercy and God's command, both in the humanity of Jesus and in the humanity of the Church. The implications of this 'immediacy' will be more fully discussed in chapter eight.

[17] While Nigel Biggar is right to affirm that the Bible 'should not be used moralistically, simply or merely as a source-book of moral rules', his previous comments that 'the Bible's role is primarily that of shaping and monitoring the development of dogmatics, and only then of monitoring the movement from dogmatics to ethics' seems to run close to the displacement of narrative by dogmatic reflection (Nigel Biggar, *The Hastening that Waits*, p. 112). Moreover, in seeking to contrast Hauerwas and Barth, Nigel Biggar appears to overstate the focus on Jesus' life within the *Dogmatics*. Biggar may be correct in observing that 'Hauerwas's own characterization of Jesus' life in the very specific terms of non-violent love is, if anything, more selective than Barth's', but his concern to defend Barth at this point fails to give due weight to Hauerwas's criticism that 'ethics which begin with Christology tend to ignore or use selectively the life of the man Jesus' (Nigel Biggar, *The Hastening that Waits*, p. 143); cf. Stanley Hauerwas, *The Peaceable Kingdom*, pp. 72ff.

instance of systematic *over*-tidiness. Is it not that Christ's priesthood, expressed in his self-humbling, identifies true humanity as well as true deity, just as his kingship, expressed in his exaltation, identifies true deity as well as true humanity? Barth's structure, undoubtedly intended as a necessary corrective, may prove to be as unhelpful an imbalance as the imbalance it seeks to correct.[18]

Simply because the Church *has* heard and believed the gospel story doctrinally, because it *has* acknowledged this Jesus as truly God and truly human, it must give absolute attention to the manner in which this Jesus is narrated.[19] The command of God, which is the proper theme of Christian ethics, is certainly not arbitrary nor imprecise since it is the command of *this* God who has defined himself and defined humanity within *this* narrative. But neither, for this very same reason, can this command be 'immediate': it is mediated to the Church by the Spirit through this story and, similarly, it is mediated by the same Spirit through the life of the Church as an echo of this story.[20]

Any tendency to focus on the doctrinal at the expense of the narrative minimalizes the so-called 'scandal of particularity' and, thereby, issues either in an idealizing of the

---

[18] For a perceptive outline of this difficulty together with its inherent dualistic roots and implications see T. F. Torrance, *Karl Barth: Biblical and Evangelical Theologian* (Edinburgh: T&T Clark, 1990), pp. 133ff.

[19] For Athanasius, it is God's desire to restore his image in humanity as 'an object of our senses' that necessitates a *life* of Jesus as well as an Incarnation, Death and Resurrection: 'For this reason He did not offer the sacrifice on behalf of all immediately He came, for if He had surrendered His body to death and then raised it again at once He would have ceased to be an object of our senses. Instead of that, He stayed in His body and let Himself be seen in it, doing acts and giving signs which showed Him to be not only man, but also God the Word' (Athanasius, *De Incarnatione Verbi Dei*, III 16).

[20] Consequently, one cannot draw the simple distinction that Nigel Biggar draws (still in his attempt to contrast Hauerwas and Barth) between the significance of the gospel narrative 'in its reference to the reality of the living God' and 'its sociological function in forming the identity of the Christian community'. And for Biggar to opine that in Hauerwas's account of a Christian ethic 'acts of prayer and worship feature only incidentally' is grossly unfair (Nigel Biggar, *The Hastening that Waits*, p. 118).

community of the Church or in a disjunction of the Church's story from the gospel story of which it is an echo. The phrase 'scandal of particularity' refers both to the general and theoretical scandal that God should (or *could*) define himself and humanity in *any* particular, and also to the specific and actual scandal that God *has* defined himself and humanity in *this* particular.[21] Thus stated, the two expressions of the 'scandal' represent the distinction between trying to understand in order to believe and believing in order to understand; they represent inimical approaches to the task of theology. Only by doubting that God, in fact, *has* defined himself and humanity in this particular does it make any sense to ask the question whether he *should* or *could* do such. But from where do we derive these assured criteria to pontificate on what God should or should not, can or cannot do? Who do we think we are?

> Who God is and what it is to be divine is something we have to learn where God has revealed Himself and His nature, the essence of the divine. And if He has revealed Himself in Jesus Christ as the God who does this, it is not for us to be wiser than He and to say that it is in contradiction with the divine essence ... We may believe that God can and must only be absolute in contrast to all that is relative, exalted in contrast to all that is lowly, active in contrast to all suffering, inviolable in contrast to all temptation, transcendent in contrast to all immanence, and therefore divine in contrast to everything human, in short that He can and

[21] Daphne Hampson, in her book *After Christianity*, expresses surprise that some theologians, Colin Gunton in particular, confuse these two senses of 'the scandal of particularity'. I suspect that the confusion – if such it is – derives from the differing 'faith' stance of different authors. Colin Gunton clearly stands in the 'faith seeking understanding' tradition and, while he recognizes the 'scandal' as seen by Hampson, he begins with the assumption that this apparently 'scandalous' event has, in fact, occurred. Hampson excludes the possibility of such a 'scandalous' defining event on *a priori* grounds: Daphne Hampson, *After Christianity* (London: SCM Press, 1996), p. 288; cf. Colin Gunton, *The One, The Three and the Many*, p. 180.

must be only the 'Wholly Other.' But such beliefs are
shown to be quite untenable, and corrupt and pagan,
by the fact that God does in fact be and do this in Jesus
Christ.[22]

If, however, we begin with the confession that God has
indeed defined himself and humanity in this particular we
cannot evade the scandal of this particularity – the task of
theology is to grapple with its significance, not evade it.
The scandal of this particularity is, of course, evaded if the
doctrinal interpretation of this narrative is abandoned, if
we deny that God has, in fact, defined himself and
humanity here. But the scandal of this particularity is
similarly evaded if we detach the doctrinal formulation
from the narrative itself, thereby failing to grapple with the
fact that God has defined himself and humanity in *this*
story, in *this* human life, in *this* context. This doctrinal
docetism – for that is what it is – which detaches the
confession of Christ's humanity from its particularities, can
only issue either in a similar idealizing of the doctrine of
the Church, or in a radical disjunction between the
Church's actual humanity and this idealized humanity of
Jesus, as if the Church were not called to be formed in his
likeness, as if the Church were not indwelt and
empowered by his Spirit. It is the Church's faith that it is
precisely in this story as narrated, precisely in the particularities of the story of Jesus, precisely in the particularities
of his context, that God has defined himself and humanity.
   In one respect the particularity of the Incarnation might
appear scandalous inasmuch as all men and women, in
every age, of every race, of every social class, are defined
by God in the humanity of this single, male, first century,
Jewish carpenter and roving rabbi. Though these particularities of Jesus' humanity may be appropriate within his
immediate historical context – and, more especially, within
the context of the covenant history of Israel – they must not
be misconstrued as essential to that humanity in any exclu-
sivist manner: all humanity is defined and included in this

22 *CD* IV/1, p. 186.

humanity; that which is essential and defining in the humanity of Jesus is his relatedness to the Father through the Spirit.[23]

By far the more startling scandal of the Incarnation is that the eternal Son should assume the particularities of *our* humanity, real humanity, weak humanity, sinful humanity. It is this aspect of the humanity of Jesus that persistently has proved most scandalous and offensive in the history of Christian thought, and, though Barth too is insistent that it is *this* humanity that the Son of God assumes,[24] it is this offence that is obscured by the very structure of his treatment of the doctrine of reconciliation: it is not just the true God who is identified in the humiliation, weakness and suffering of Christ; true humanity is defined here also. Certainly this true humanity has its goal in the resurrection and ascension of Jesus, in 'The Homecoming of the Son of Man', but it reaches this goal through a life of obedient service, through suffering, through death.[25] The humanity assumed by the Son of God, the humanity in which true humanity is defined, is not some idealized humanity floating above the

---

[23] It is quite bizarre that the maleness of Jesus and of the first apostles is sometimes cited in defence of an exclusively male priesthood within the Church while the Jewishness of Jesus and of the first apostles is never taken to be similarly determinative. If Christ can represent a woman on the cross it is difficult to see why a woman cannot represent Christ in any form of Christian ministry.

[24] 'It is this humanity that the Son of God assumed ... He was also our flesh. Of course, as His humanity, it became a different thing from ours, for sin ... could not find any place in Him. Yet apart from this single characteristic it is our own familiar humanity out and out, namely, not only with its natural problems, but with the guilt lying upon it of which it has to repent, with the judgment of God hanging over it, with the death to which it is liable. The Son of God could not sin – how could God be untrue to Himself? But all of this, the entire curse of sin, which is what Holy Scripture means when it calls men flesh, this curse the Son of God has taken upon Himself and borne by becoming a man' (*CD* I/2, p. 40; cf. pp. 53ff., 159ff.).

[25] 'Perfection', then is not a state but a dynamic, it is not so much an evaluation of the humanity the Son of God assumed as it is an evaluation of the life he lived within that humanity, the manner in which he reached that humanity's goal: 'Although he was a son, he learned obedience from what he suffered and, once made perfect, he became the source of eternal salvation for all who obey him ...' (Heb. 5.8f.).

weaknesses, struggles, contradictions and pain that are commonplace to us: precisely in this *real* humanity, *true* humanity is defined. The humanity of Jesus, the humanity commanded by God in the gospel, is yet humanity assailed by the world, the flesh and the devil. The exalted Christ can 'sympathise with our weaknesses' because he really 'has been tempted in every way, just as we are – yet was without sin' (Heb. 4.15).[26] The humanity the Father chooses, which is itself the command of the gospel, is narrated in the story of the *real* human life of Jesus: the perfection of this humanity, then, does not consist in some idealized otherness to the conditions of our own human existence but rather in the relatedness of Jesus to the Father, through the Spirit, *under these conditions.*

The scandal of this aspect of the gospel's particularity obviously is undermined by any form of docetism in which the humanity of Christ is deemed to be other than our own. But this scandal is similarly, though more subtly, undermined whenever the particularities of the narrative are obscured or qualified in favour of some idealized notion of Jesus' perfection, as if that perfection were not lived out in these present conditions of fallenness.

The defence of pacifism in Richard Hays' *The Moral*

---

[26] It is Edward Irving, the nineteenth-century theologian and preacher, who is 'notorious' for the view that Christ assumed 'fallen' human nature and was preserved from sin through the indwelling of the Spirit. Hence: 'The point at issue is simply this; whether Christ's flesh had the grace of sinlessness and incorruption from its proper nature, or from the indwelling of the Holy Ghost. I say the latter. I assert, that in its proper nature it was as the flesh of his mother, but, by virtue of the Holy Ghost's quickening and inhabiting of it, it was preserved sinless and incorruptible': quoted in C. Gordon Strachan, *The Pentecostal Theology of Edward Irving* (London: Darton, Longman & Todd, 1973), p. 30. For such views Irving was found guilty of heresy by the London Presbytery of the Scottish Presbyterian Church on 30th November 1830. It is therefore interesting to note the following quotation, from the previous century, in a sermon by Jonathan Edwards: 'It was this nature, with all its weakness and exposedness to sufferings, which Christ, who is the Lord God omnipotent, took upon him. He did not take the human nature on him in its first, most perfect and vigorous state, but in that feeble forlorn state which it is in since the fall . . .': Jonathan Edwards, 'Sermon on Luke xxii 44' in *The Works of Jonathan Edwards*, vol. 2, revised Edward Hickman (Edinburgh: Banner of Truth Trust, 1974), pp. 866–77 (p. 866).

Vision of the New Testament is masterly but this reader at
least is left less than convinced by his attempts to
reinterpret or qualify some of the more awkward passages
within the Gospel narratives. No amount of special
pleading can alter an account in which John the Baptist
doesn't encourage soldiers to leave the army (Luke 3.14), in
which Jesus does clear the Temple forcibly (Luke 19.45ff.),
in which Jesus does encourage his disciples to buy swords
(Luke 22.36). These isolated incidents do not, of course,
detract from Jesus' command that we should 'not resist an
evil person' (Matt. 5.39), they do not give justification to the
Church's unfaithful alliance with violent coercion,[27] but
they do constitute testimony concerning the 'non-ideal' (or
rather, 'fallen') context in which Jesus' life was lived and in
which his true humanity was actualized; they do militate
against the common Anabaptist tendency to treat the
Sermon on the Mount is if it were a series of new, absolute
laws rather than a description of the characteristics of those
who are learning to live coherently with the character of
God.

The story of Jesus sending Peter to retrieve a coin from
the mouth of a fish in order to pay the temple tax may seem
trivial, even to the point of appearing out-of-place in the
Gospel narratives, but it illustrates this underlying point
concerning the context in which Jesus' true humanity was
lived out (Matt. 17.24ff.). 'Ideally' and 'in principle' Jesus
and Peter, as true 'children', should be exempt from the
tax, yet not to pay the tax would offend or scandalize.[28] We,
more likely, may be scandalized by the thought of Jesus

---

[27] 'One reason that the world finds the New Testament's message of
peacemaking and love of enemies incredible is that the church is so
massively faithless. On the question of violence, the church is deeply
compromised and committed to nationalism, violence and idolatry. (By
comparison, our problems with sexual sin are trivial.) This indictment
applies alike to liberation theologies that justify violence against
oppressors and to establishment Christianity that continues to play
chaplain to the military-industrial complex, citing just war theory and
advocating the defence of a particular nation as though that were
somehow a Christian value' (Richard Hays, *The Moral Vision of the New
Testament*, p. 343).
[28]   ἵνα δὲ μή σκανδαλίσωμεν αὐτούς

acting out of expediency, accommodating himself to the 'non-ideal' context of human fallenness, but the reality of his true humanness is identified precisely in this scandalous particularity. There was an occasion then, when this Jesus, who was to go passively to his cross, acting out of 'perfect' obedience to his Father, and prompted by the Spirit, took a whip and cleared the Temple. His 'perfection' was lived out in this present, fallen, 'non-ideal' context and therefore simply cannot be determined in advance by absolute rules or principles. In this respect the story of Jesus coheres with the stories of the Old Testament in which the purposes of God are worked out in the world as it is rather than the world as it will be.[29]

Generally, pacifism tends to be dismissed as impractical and idealistic. This, of course, it most certainly is: it would be difficult to imagine how a society could function without some form of coercive restraint in response to criminality.[30] But my point is that, more seriously than this impracticality, it is implicitly docetic; it idealizes the humanity of Jesus by failing to take sufficient account of the fallenness of the context in which his humanity was actualized; it reduces a living narrative, with all its contradictions and tensions, to an abstracted and absolute rule.[31]

It must be understood that I hesitate to make this point. The appalling history of ecclesiastical coercion is sufficient to drive many to embrace the pacifist vision. Moreover, as Stanley Hauerwas comments, an acceptance of limited violence in the pursuit of justice is fraught with contradictions; simply because we remain less than perfect men and

[29] At the risk of over-generalization, Anabaptist hermeneutics tend to suppose too radical a distinction between the Old and New Testaments. One factor uniting these accounts is the fallenness of their context. The implications of this fallenness will be discussed further in chapter ten of this book.
[30] '... any attempt to develop an ethic of nonviolence ultimately seems to flounder on our sense that something is just not right about such a commitment. That sense of incongruity derives from our feeling that such an ethic is too far out of step with the world in which we have to live' (Stanley Hauerwas, *The Peaceable Kingdom*, p. 135).
[31] Accordingly, Stanley Hauerwas's own concentration on peaceableness may, notwithstanding his own assertions and warnings, run the danger of reducing ethics to a single theme.

women in a less than perfect world we really cannot trust ourselves to act unequivocally for the sake of justice.[32] But reactions nearly always issue in distortions. Coherence with the gospel, and with its scandalous particularity, forbids us to retreat from the tensions and contradictions of the world simply because we are confronted with its tensions and contradictions. Christological docetism issues either in a radical distinction between Christ's humanity and our own, or in a corresponding ecclesiological docetism.[33] Some of the earlier Anabaptist writers were at least consistent in forbidding Christians to act as magistrates,[34] but thereby they exposed their radical view of the Church's relatedness (or rather, non-relatedness) to the world. The implications of this and of other forms of 'two kingdom' thinking will be pursued later in this book – my concern at present is merely to argue that a non-docetic Christology demands a correspondingly non-docetic ecclesiology, that is to say, a non-docetic account of ethics.

In coherence with the scandalous particularity of the narrative of Jesus' true humanity the Church is called to live truthfully and, at least potentially, scandalously. Like Jesus we cannot withdraw from the tensions and contra-dictions of our present context and, as with Jesus, there may be occasions when those tensions and contradictions issue in actions which may appear scandalous. Precisely

---

[32] 'Although I have sympathy with this position and though it certainly cannot be discounted as a possibility for Christians, the problem with these attempts to commit the Christian to limited use of violence is that they too often distort the character of our alternatives. Violence used in the name of justice, or freedom, or equality is seldom simply a matter of justice – it is a matter of the power of some over others' (Stanley Hauerwas, *The Peaceable Kingdom*, p. 114).

[33] The idealizing of a supposed Matthean community by James McClendon, in support of his pacifist agenda, is similarly an example of this tendency to match an idealized Christology with an idealized ecclesi-ology: James Wm. McClendon, Jr., *Systematic Theology: Ethics* (Nashville: Abingdon Press, 1986), pp. 299ff.

[34] So, for instance, the following passage from Pilgram Marpeck: '... how long would his conscience allow him to be a magistrate, assuming that he did not want to forsake the Lord Jesus Christ and Christian patience ... no one can serve two masters ...': Pilgram Marpeck, 'Defence', quoted in *Anabaptism in Outline: Selected Primary Sources*, ed. Walter Klaassen (Scottdale: Herald Press, 1981), p. 263.

because we are called to live in coherence with the gospel story, we cannot absolutely exclude the possibility of limited violence – we are called to live in coherence with the gospel *story*, not with a series of abstracted and absolute rules or principles, whether new or old.[35] The person of Jesus, his *real* humanity which is the scandalous outworking of his *true* humanity, cannot be reduced to rules, principles or themes. Coherence with his person, which is the command of the gospel, cannot therefore be predicted or calculated in advance. But, nonetheless, Christian freedom, like the freedom of God himself, is determinate and not indeterminate, it cannot be reduced to predictable rules but it is a matter of coherence, coherence with the one narrated in this central story. And, because it is a matter of coherence with the one *narrated in this story*, this Christian freedom can never be impotent or merely theoretical. The command of the gospel, which is the call to coherence with the narrated person of Jesus and thereby to obedience to the lived out command of the Father, is also itself the promise of the indwelling and empowering Spirit. The command of the gospel, then, can never be a 'lawless' grace, but neither can it be a graceless 'law'.[36] Christian living, which is a dynamic of coherence, is also a dynamic of indwelling, and to the manner of this dynamic we now turn.

---

[35] In this respect one suspects that Richard Hays, with commendable consistency, too quickly dismisses Barth's view that Peter killed Ananias and Sapphira by his word: cf. Richard B. Hays, *The Moral Vision of the New Testament*, p. 231, cf. p. 235.

[36] 'Set within the context of election to the covenant, the law is no longer primarily accusatory. Rather, it incorporates into the relationship between God and his creatures the imperatival aspect which makes the recipients of grace more than mere beneficiaries' (J. B. Webster, 'The Christian in Revolt: Some Reflections on *The Christian Life*' in *Reckoning with Barth*, ed. Nigel Biggar, pp. 119–144 (p. 124).

Part Three

THE DYNAMICS OF INDWELLING

7
The Indwelling of the Spirit

Much was made in the last chapter of the reality of Jesus' humanity and everything that needs to be said in this present section concerning the possibilities of our human response to the command of the gospel depends upon and derives from the veracity of what has been said concerning the humanity of Jesus. In the study of *Christian* theology, as Karl Barth notes, to be wrong in respect of the person of Christ is to be wrong everywhere else.[1] It ought not to surprise us that docetic accounts of Christology inevitably issue in theologically groundless accounts of *Christian* ethics: an account of *Christian* ethics can only be grounded in an account of Christ and, consequently, any less than adequate account of Christ's humanity will issue in a less than adequate account of our human response to the command of the gospel. It is for this reason that the imaginary librarian introduced in the Preface would not be wholly mistaken to list this book, or any book on *Christian* ethics, within the Christology section of a library. It is not just that the humanity of Jesus is an example for our humanity – though this it certainly is – it is primarily that the humanity of Jesus is definitive and determinative for our humanity. That which he became in his incarnation through obedience to the Father and through dependence upon the Spirit we become through the indwelling of the same Spirit and through participating in his obedience. By the Spirit we have been joined to him, included in his unique relatedness to the Father. Hence, for the Church to affirm the humanity of Jesus as true humanity, and therefore as determinative for our humanity, would be meaningless if his humanity, and the conditions and dynamic of that humanity, were essentially other than our humanity with its conditions and (at least its potential) dynamic.

---

[1] 'I have been very conscious of the very special responsibility laid on the theologian at this centre of all Christian knowledge. To fail here is to fail everywhere. To be on the right track here makes it impossible to be completely mistaken in the whole' (*CD* IV/1, p. ix).

By itself, a 'Spirit Christology' (at least as the idea has generally been expressed) can offer only an inadequate account of Christ's divine identity: who he is as the Son of the Father he is essentially and eternally. Though, even in this respect, if we are to maintain the mutuality of the relatedness of Father, Son and Spirit, it may be appropriate to follow Tom Smail's suggestion in affirming the Son as 'eternally begotten of the Father *through the Spirit*' in parallel to affirming the Spirit as the one 'who proceeds from the Father *through* the Son'.[2] But without a form of 'Spirit Christology' it is impossible to express his humanity adequately: unless his *true* humanity, his perfect obedience to the Father, is an outcome of his continual and absolute dependence upon the Spirit, his humanity is a charade, it is neither *true* nor *real*.[3] If Christ's humanity is *real* humanity, lived under the very same conditions as our common humanity, then the possibility of his *real* humanity being this *true* humanity is a possibility of the Spirit. And by living in continual dependence upon the Spirit, and thereby in perfect obedience to the Father, Christ has defined the only *true* humanity, the humanity the Father chooses and commands. Accordingly Richard Sibbes, the seventeenth-century Puritan, writes thus of Christ's dependence upon the Spirit:

Whatsoever Christ did as man, he did by the Spirit. Christ's human nature, therefore, must be sanctified, and have the Spirit put upon it. God the Father, the first person in Trinity, and God the Son, the second, they work not immediately, but by the Holy Ghost, the third person. Therefore, whatsoever is wrought upon the creature, it comes from the Holy Ghost immediately.[4]

[2] Tom Smail, *The Giving Gift: The Holy Spirit in Person* (London: Darton, Longman & Todd, 1994[2]), p. 141.
[3] This interplay between *true* humanity and *real* humanity is a characteristic of Barth's treatment of the Incarnation and recurs throughout the *Dogmatics*; e.g., *CD*. III/2, pp. 19ff.; IV/1, pp. 211ff.
[4] Richard Sibbes, 'A Description of Christ' (1639) in *Works of Richard Sibbes*, vol. 1, ed. Alexander B. Grosart (Edinburgh: Banner of Truth Trust, 1973), pp. 1–31 (p. 17). Lest it be thought that this quotation from Sibbes

Consequently, if we are to participate in this perfect obedience of the Son, and if this perfect obedience is to be echoed in the particularities of our living, this can only issue from our similar dependence upon the Spirit. This is not a possibility for humanity acting independently. If it were such a possibility then Incarnation and Atonement would be unnecessary, the Spirit would be rendered redundant, and there would be a valid foundation for an independent ethic. But the perfect humanity of Jesus exposes all our attempts to live independently as inauthentic and untrue. The possibility of our *real* humanity reflecting his *true* humanity is exclusively and uniquely a possibility of the indwelling of the Spirit. And this possibility, and all the possibilities deriving from it, is the promise of the gospel:

> ... what the law was powerless to do in that it was weakened by the sinful nature, God did by sending his own Son in the likeness of sinful humanity to be a sin offering. And so he condemned sin in our sinful nature, in order that the righteous requirements of the law might be fully met in us, who do not live according to the sinful nature but according to the Spirit. (Romans 8.3f.)

The promise of the gospel is that, through the sheer grace of God, we are now included in the sonship of the Son before the Father; we are defined unequivocally by mercy, unequivocally by love. But the promise of the gospel is also that, in anticipation of the final resurrection and the fulfilment of our humanity, we can live here and now in the power of the Spirit. The Spirit who indwelt and empowered Jesus is the same Spirit who is promised, here and now, to the Christian.[5] According to the apostle Paul's

---

is unusual or exceptional it should be noted that this view of Christ's holiness as an outcome of his dependence upon the Spirit was espoused by Calvin (*Institutes* II xiii 4) and similarly by John Owen in *A Discourse concerning the Holy Spirit* in *The Works of John Owen*, ed. W. H. Goold, vol. III (London: Banner of Truth Trust, 1965), pp. 161ff.

[5] So Richard Sibbes again comments, 'We have not the Holy Ghost immediately from God, but we have him as sanctifying Christ first, and

argument in Romans, it is this promise of the Spirit, which
itself is a consequence of all that has been achieved in the
humanity of Christ, that distinguishes the Christian from
those who, bounded by their own inherent possibilities,
sought to obey the law within the era and bounds of the
Old Testament. God has now achieved that which 'the law
was powerless to do'; the 'righteous requirements of the
law' can now be 'fully met' in those who live 'according to
the Spirit'; we no longer have 'an obligation' to live
according the 'sinful nature' but rather have the possibility
of living 'by the Spirit' (Rom. 8.3f, 12f.). The command of
the gospel, then, does not come to us without, at the same
time, promising the impartation of the ability to fulfil it: the
command of the gospel is simultaneously the promise of
the Spirit. When Peter, on the day of Pentecost, calls his
hearers to repent and to be baptized, it is with the confident
expectation that they too will receive this gift of the Spirit;
the promise of the Spirit's indwelling and empowering is
the context of the call to repentance (Acts 2.38f.).

The gospel promise of the Spirit, therefore, is not
primarily a matter of a 'gift of tongues' or of 'works of
power' but primarily consists in the possibility of a life
that is coherent with the perfected humanity of Jesus.
Through the Spirit's indwelling, our lives can become an
echo of the perfect obedience of Christ.[6] I use the term
'echo' in order to indicate both the incompleteness and the
reference of this work of the Spirit. True humanity is
defined in Christ alone and, though here and now we may
be brought to participate in that which is originally and
uniquely fulfilled in him, we do so in a partial and incomplete manner; the possibility of our living here and now
through the indwelling of the Spirit is no more than an
anticipation of the final resurrection – but it is,
nonetheless, a genuine anticipation; it is an actuality and

---

then us; and whatsoever the Holy Ghost doth in us, he doth the same in
Christ first, and he doth it in us because in Christ' (Richard Sibbes, 'A
Description of Christ', p. 18).

[6] So, for instance, 'It is the work of the Spirit in us to bring about (albeit
provisionally) what he has already accomplished in the Son' (Jeremy
Begbie, *Voicing Creation's Praise*, p. 227).

no mere charade.[7] The means through which this anticipation occurs will be discussed in the next chapter; the
present concern is to affirm the reality of this anticipation.
The reality of this anticipation consists both in a new
perception and in a new possibility. It consists in a
new perception inasmuch as the Christian has been
brought by the Spirit, through the gospel story, to perceive
all reality in a new manner. To recognize the gospel story
as *the* defining story for reality in its entirety is to recognize
all reality differently. Nor is this new recognition merely
a matter of detached rational awareness – as if such a
detached awareness was, in any case, possible; as if
our knowing could be detached from our willing; as if our
minds were compartmentalized.[8] As Jonathan Edwards
insists, to know a matter is to be affected by that matter;
there can be no knowledge without a change of affection;
to perceive a matter differently *is* to be changed.[9] Since the
Spirit is the mediator of this new perception – just as he is,
in reality, the mediator of *every* perception – this new
perception itself is transformative; it necessarily implies
change.

The Christian life is not simply a matter of assuming
a vague loving attitude, but rather it is a concrete

[7] '... God intends ... that man should be entirely united to Him, and this
will be realized in heaven, when God will be *all in all* ... Hence this
precept will be observed fully and perfectly in heaven; yet it is fulfilled,
though imperfectly, on the way' (*ST* II–II 44 6).
[8] 'The Enlightenment imagines neutral human beings, neither delivered
up to injustice, impiety, and ingratitude, nor religious enthusiasts; it
images human beings who *disengage* their wills from their knowing'
(Eugene F. Rogers, Jnr., *Thomas Aquinas and Karl Barth*, p. 157).
[9] In this respect note James M. Gustafson's discussion of Jonathan
Edwards's idea of conversion as implying a 'new sight'. Gustafson
acknowledges that this notion was common amongst the Puritans
(*Protestant and Roman Catholic Ethics*, p. 61). Note also this further
comment by Eugene Rogers: 'Propositions abstracted from the will would
leave our desires unaffected, our subjective ends apart from the objective
final end that God has granted us, our actions therefore finally unintelligible, our lives surd and unredeemed. The propositions of faith on a page
are so many pieces of paper, not identifiable as God's tender until we see
them in use' (Eugene F. Rogers, Jnr., *Thomas Aquinas and Karl Barth*, p.
119).

determination of our being developed through our history. The Christian is one so formed as he assumes the particular description offered him through the Church. This formation is the determination of our character through God's sanctifying work. Sanctification is thus the formation of the Christian's character that is the result of his intention to see the world as redeemed in Jesus Christ.[10]

But the reality of this anticipation consists, not just in a new perception, but also in a new possibility (or range of possibilities). The Christian is not merely one who can now see things differently; the Christian is one who now has the possibility of living differently in response to this new perception. The Holy Spirit, who is the mediator of a new vision of reality through the gospel story, is also the power through which life can be brought into coherence with this new vision.

This possibility of a living coherence inevitably is undermined by any emphasizing of the distinction between justification and sanctification, as if the former could pertain without implying or including the latter. Any presumed foundation for this radical distinction within the New Testament has recently been challenged by the so-called 'new perspective on Paul' proposed by Krister Stendahl, E. P. Sanders and, perhaps most thoroughly, by James Dunn.[11] Without necessarily embracing these proposals in their entirety – it seems implausible, for instance, that any group in any age, least of all the Pharisees whose attitude is recorded in the Gospels, has been free

---

[10] Stanley Hauerwas, *Vision and Virtue*, p. 67.
[11] Krister Stendahl, *Paul Among Jews and Gentiles* (Philadelphia: Fortress Press, 1976); E. P. Sanders, *Paul and Palestinian Judaism: A Comparison of Patterns of Religion* (Minneapolis: Fortress Press, 1985); *Jesus and Judaism* (London: SCM Press, 1985); *Paul, the Law and the Jewish People* (London: SCM Press, 1985); J. D. G. Dunn, 'The New Perspective on Paul' in *Bulletin of the John Rylands Library* 65 (1983), pp. 95–122; *Jesus, Paul and the Law: Studies in Mark and Galatians* (London: SPCK. 1990); *The Theology of Paul's Letter to the Galatians* (Cambridge: Cambridge University Press, 1993); with Alan M. Suggate, *The Justice of God: A Fresh Look at the Old Doctrine of Justification by Faith* (Carlisle: Paternoster Press, 1993).

from a tendency towards self-justification – it must surely be conceded that the context for Paul's teaching is located in the difficulties for Jews and Gentiles of co-existing within the one Church. Paul's concern, then, is not so much with how Jews and Gentiles obtain mercy (an inherently Pelagian notion in any case) but with how, having received mercy, Jews and Gentiles can receive one another and relate to one another within the single body of Christ.

All this is not necessarily to imply that Martin Luther's emphasis on justification by faith alone was wholly misplaced or inappropriate – within the historical and theological context of the Reformation it may well have been a timely corrective – but it is to recognize that, within the context of the New Testament itself, the term δικαιοσύνη (justification) has a richer, more relational and more dynamic reference; it is used in correspondence rather than contrast to the term ἁγιασμός (sanctification) and, at least in some instances, the two terms appear to be inter-changeable.[12] Christ 'has become for us wisdom from God – that is, our righteousness, holiness and redemption' and Christ is not divided (1 Cor. 1.30; cf. 1.13). For God to declare a person righteous is itself a creative event in the power of the Spirit. God's Word is never merely a word – to be declared righteous by the Father is to be included in the righteousness of the Son, is to be made righteous in the power of the Spirit. Faith, because it is a relational trust rather than a matter of merely intellectual assent, implies a change of perception that issues in changes of behaviour and practice.[13] To reduce the concept of righteousness to a

---

[12] 'We speak of two *aspects* of the Spirit's work, not of two works. It is perilous to draw too sharp a line in particular items of experience between repentance and moral learning, between justification and sanctification, between conversion and instruction. When did we ever not have to repent while we learnt? When did obedience not go hand in hand with the need for forgiveness? When did we not find worldliness at the heart of the church we thought to instruct, and belief surprising us in the world we thought to convert?' (Oliver O'Donovan, *Resurrection and the Moral Order*, pp. 104f.).

[13] As was noted in chapter three of this book, the strong emphasis on practical discipleship occurring in several Anabaptist writers was a reaction to a merely forensic understanding of righteousness and a merely intellectual understanding of faith: '... faith is a real divine power, which

legal pronouncement is a relatively late theological novelty
that seriously undermines the ethical force of the apostle
Paul's letters.[14] For Paul, the Christian truly is a new
creation with new possibilities in the power of the Spirit.
Hence Richard Hays comments:

> The danger ... is that the slogan *simul iustus et peccator*
> may underestimate the transformative power of God's
> grace and obscure major emphases of Paul's moral
> vision ... We can overlook this major theological
> theme in Paul only if we assume a priori that his
> doctrine of justification somehow makes obedience
> religiously irrelevant.[15]

It is hardly surprising, in a context where justification and
sanctification increasingly have been categorically divided,
the former being perceived in exclusively forensic terms,
that 'second blessing' spiritualities should arise, proposing
sanctification as a separate and subsequent work of the
Spirit, a second and distinct formative event of Christian
experience.[16] Whether or not the term 'baptism in the
Spirit' is used of this subsequent blessing of sanctification,
the implication remains that one can be justified without,
in any sense, being sanctified; justification is reduced to an
impotent pretence; one can be pronounced righteous
without in any sense being made righteous.[17] Moreover, a

---

renews man and makes him like God in nature, makes him living in his
righteousness, and ardent in love, and in keeping his commandments':
Peter Riedeman, *Account* (1542) in *Anabaptism in Outline: Selected Primary
Sources*, ed. Walter Klaassen (Scottdale: Herald Press, 1981), p. 64.
[14] 'There is no meaningful distinction between theology and ethics in
Paul's thought, because Paul's theology is fundamentally an account of
God's work of transforming his people into the image of Christ' (Richard
B. Hays, *The Moral Vision of the New Testament*, p. 46).
[15] Richard B. Hays, *The Moral Vision of the New Testament*, pp. 44f.
[16] That Pentecostal and Charismatic notions of a 'second blessing' have
tended to focus more on spiritual gifts than on holiness, power to impress
than power to live by, may be symptomatic of a more general lack of focus
on Christian behaviour alongside a desire for the dramatic and
immediate.
[17] Of course, if Christian faith is reduced to mere 'believism', if Christian
conversion is reduced to a matter of mere assent – that is to say, if

Perhaps, in exploration of Wesley's history, you could
say "in using words (the exhott to explain, to convince)
one can get a little ahead of oneself."

further consequence of this tendency is to divorce sanctification, as a work of the Spirit, from any instrumental
means of the sacraments or of Christian discipline; sanctification comes to be perceived as an unmediated event, an
'experience', or even a 'feeling'; notions of progress and
growth are implicitly excluded. The teaching of John *and life
Wesley is usually cited as one of the roots of this notion of history*
a subsequent experience of sanctification; however, a
careful reading of his *A Plain Account of Christian Perfection*
reveals a more nuanced understanding.

As its subtitle suggests, this tract was perceived by
Wesley himself to represent a summary of his consistent
teaching throughout his ministry; if commentators have
identified changes in his thinking on this issue, Wesley
himself seems to have been blissfully unaware of any.[18] In
the first place, while Wesley certainly writes of perfection
as an 'instantaneous change' he concedes that not all
perceive this 'instant'; that, in any case, it 'is not absolute';
that it is 'both preceded and followed by a gradual work';
that '[i]t is improvable'; and that it is 'capable of being
lost'.[19] Moreover, Wesley appears increasingly reluctant to
speak of 'sinless' perfection, repeating throughout the
work that 'there is no such perfection in this life, as implies
an entire deliverance, either from ignorance or mistake, in
things not essential to salvation, or from manifold tempta-
tions, or from numberless infirmities, wherewith the
corruptible body more or less presses down the soul'; that
'there is no such perfection in this life as excludes ... invol-
untary transgressions ... naturally consequent on the
ignorance and mistakes inseparable from mortality'.[20] That

Christian conversion is, in reality, no conversion at all – then, in this
impoverished and impotent context, perhaps the expectation of a future
change that is genuinely a change is to be welcomed. Nonetheless, this
would be an expediency necessitated by a travesty and the underlying
travesty of a conversion that is no conversion must be challenged.

[18] John Wesley, *A Plain Account of Christian Perfection as believed and taught
by the Reverend Mr. John Wesley, from the year 1725, to the year 1777* in *The
Works of the Rev. John Wesley*, vol. XI (London: Wesleyan Conference
Office, 1872), pp. 366–446.

[19] John Wesley, *A Plain Account of Christian Perfection*, p. 442.

[20] John Wesley, *A Plain Account of Christian Perfection*, pp. 383, 396.

is to say, both the word 'instant' and the word 'perfection' are used by Wesley in a distinctive and qualified sense. However, that which positively is clear in Wesley's teaching is that 'Christian Perfection' consists in 'perfect love' and that, while such perfect love should be sought through prayer and through spiritual discipline, it is, nonetheless, entirely a work of grace that is received through faith. And, lest Wesley be accused of separating rather than distinguishing justification and sanctification, he affirms that inward sanctification begins in 'the moment a man is justified ... [f]rom that time a believer gradually dies to sin, and grows in grace'.[21]

In these respects Wesley's view seems to differ little from that of Thomas Aquinas who, while acknowledging that absolute perfection in the sense of loving God 'as much as He is lovable' is impossible for the creature, and that even loving God as much as God possibly can be loved by the creature is possible only in heaven, nonetheless affirms that perfection in the sense of 'the removal of obstacles to the movement of love towards God' can be had in this life – though '[t]hose who are perfect in this life are said to *offend in many things* with regard to venial sins, which result from the weakness of the present life ...'.[22]

My concern here is not to defend Wesley from his critics or to pretend that his account is entirely coherent (though I suspect that it is far more coherent than many of his critics allow). My concern is rather to reclaim Wesley from those who cite him in support of a merely forensic view of justification (Wesley's teaching demands that a real change has occurred in the life of the believer through the power of the Spirit), or from those who accuse him of propounding an effortless sanctification: Wesley's notion of an instantaneous perfection must be qualified, and is qualified by Wesley himself, inasmuch as he anticipates a progress in holy love that is continually dependent upon, and responsive to, the work of the Spirit, but which nonetheless, even in this life, can be brought to complete

[21] John Wesley, *A Plain Account of Christian Perfection*, p. 387.
[22] *ST* II–II 184 2.

expression. In contrast to any impotent believism that entertains no expectation for change, but similarly in contrast to any focus on the dramatic or impressive as marks of the work of the Spirit, Wesley represents an expectation for change and for progress through grace that is appropriated in faith, in discipline, and above all in prayer. Indeed, this prayerful expectation for progress towards perfection in love is perhaps the most potent feature of John Wesley's hymns and of the many more hymns written by his brother Charles. To deny the validity of such prayers is either to imply an impotent conversion, or a carelessness for progress, or a disbelief in the Spirit's power to bring to completion that which has been begun.

To be a Christian, then, genuinely is to have made a new beginning, it is to be reborn in the power of the Spirit, it is to be made righteous inasmuch as the Father himself has pronounced you righteous, including you in the righteousness of the Son. This is now the Christian's identity – not merely in pretence but in reality. However, this genuinely new beginning is only a beginning; just as Jesus himself 'grew in wisdom and stature, and in favour with God and people', so also the Christian should expect to grow in increasing coherence with the pattern of Christ (Luke 2.52). But this progress which comes through discipline and through participation in the Christian community is entirely, at the same time, an outcome of the indwelling of the Spirit. Moreover, this progress is appropriately described as a perfecting in love once the notion of 'perfecting' has been separated from any notion of absolute sinlessness.

> Not that I have already obtained all this, or have already been made perfect, but I press on to take hold of that for which Christ Jesus took hold of me. (Phil. 3.12)

As has already been noted, this understanding of the Christian life as progress towards a perfecting of love through grace is strongly reminiscent of the teaching of Thomas Aquinas. As was acknowledged earlier in this book, what is surprising for many Protestants coming (actually) to read the *Summa* is the little Thomas has to say about natural law (not to mention the even less he has to say about so-called 'proofs' of God's existence).[23] Thomas's principle concern is with an exposition of the virtues and this, though certainly indebted to Aristotle's *Nicomachean Ethics*, is bounded and informed throughout by the goal of human existence as defined in the gospel.[24] It is love, and love as defined in the gospel, that unites the virtues by orientating them to their true goal. Indeed, Paul Wadell, commenting on Thomas, speaks of the virtues as each being particular 'strategies of love'.[25] Since the *true* goal of human life is to see God, it is only through love – that love revealed and defined in the gospel – that the human virtues are directed towards their *true* goal:

> ... it is charity which directs the acts of all other virtues to the last end, and which, consequently, also gives the form to all other acts of virtue.[26]

[23] '... I did not find Aquinas to be first and foremost a "natural law ethicist," but one who saw how theological virtues could help us understand and shape our lives' (Stanley Hauerwas, *The Peaceable Kingdom*, p. xxii).

[24] In chapter eleven of his book *Theology and Social Theory*, John Milbank criticizes Alasdair MacIntyre for proposing virtue as a generally accessible ethical 'foundation' and for failing to recognize the degree to which this difference of 'goal' in Thomas's understanding distinguishes his account of the virtues from that of Aristotle: 'The dominance of the philosophic perspective in MacIntyre will not really allow him to enter as far into the task of explicating the *differentia* of Christian ethics as he would like. What he concentrates on in Augustine and Aquinas is what can be dealt with philosophically ...': John Milbank, *Theology and Social Theory* (Oxford: Blackwell, 1990), p. 328.

[25] 'For Aquinas, the virtues are principally strategies of love. The virtues are works of love because each virtue expresses in a particular way our primary love at work. Thomas never considers the virtues in themselves, but always in relation to the passions from which they emerge and according to which they take their meaning. Because the virtues are anchored in love, and love is a passion, the more we grow in the virtues the more we realize how totally dependent we are on another's love': Paul J. Wadell, *The Primacy of Love: An Introduction to the Ethics of Thomas Aquinas* (New York: Paulist Press, 1992), p. 90.

[26] *ST* II–II 23 8. This unity of the virtues is fundamental for Thomas, hence 'The virtues must needs be connected together, so that whoever has one has all ...' (*ST* II–II 47 14; cf. I–II 65 1).

Certainly for Thomas grace brings about a genuine change in the life of the believer.[27] Indeed, the general Protestant unease with a Roman Catholic *ordo salutis*, as represented in Thomas, is the suspicion that here the order of justification and sanctification has been reversed: justification is dependent upon sanctification; by grace (and, in fairness to Thomas, by grace *alone*) we are brought into conformity with the character of Christ and, in view of this consequent 'merit', we are declared righteous.[28] This may or may not be a misrepresentation of the notion of merit in Thomas's writings but, whatever the case, this Protestant suspicion ought not to detract from what here is clear – both that grace issues in a genuine *change*, and that this change is an outcome of *grace*.[29] For Thomas, the theological virtues of faith, hope and love are not merely human possibilities; the Holy Spirit is not just the perfecter of the theological virtues (though this he certainly is) he is also their source.

It is possible to view this apparent separating of the theological virtues as yet another instance of the underlying division of nature and grace that seems to pervade Thomas's writings.[30] Continually he represents human

[27] 'For St Thomas grace is a reality, a *res*. This helps us see that theology is about *realities*. Grace does not just mean the way God looks on us or divine acceptance, as justification in Luther means that God does not count our sins against us, but it makes a *real* difference to us since it has positive effects, recreating and transforming us. St Thomas calls justification a change (*transmutatio*), by which we are ordered within to God' (Francis Selman, *Saint Thomas Aquinas*, p. 80; cf. *ST* I–II 113 2). Some of the difficulties consequent upon Thomas's use of the term 'grace' will be discussed in the next chapter.

[28] See for instance *Institutes* III xiv 11ff.; cf. *ST* I–II 113 1; 114 3.

[29] 'Aquinas insists that "man is justified by faith not as though man, by believing, were to merit justification, but that he believes whilst he is being justified." We are ordained by God to an eternal life of friendship with God, not by our own strength but by the help of grace. In this sense, "merit" but names the process by which God's grace becomes ours because of God's unwillingness to leave us alone': Stanley Hauerwas and Charles Pinches, *Christians among the Virtues: Theological Conversations with Ancient and Modern Ethics* (Notre Dame: University of Notre Dame Press, 1997), p. 126.

[30] 'It is therefore evident that all virtues are in us by nature, according to aptitude and incohation, but not according to perfection, except the theological virtues, which are entirely from without.' *ST* I–II 63 1; cf. '... all virtues, intellectual and moral, that are acquired by our actions, arise

happiness as twofold: one 'proportionate to human nature' and the other 'surpassing' human nature, obtained 'by the power of God alone'.[31] Moreover, in his discussion of the source of the virtues, Thomas pulls back from the most straightforward reading of Augustine's definition of God as the cause of *all* virtue.[32] These sections can certainly be interpreted as implying a division between grace and nature, as implying an independency for human agency with respect to the *non*-theological virtues, and, therefore, as fundamentally inconsistent with Thomas's view of God as universal efficient cause.[33] Yet it is perhaps more accurate to interpret these passages in the light of Thomas's refusal to affirm divine agency at the expense of human agency – though, in this regard, we must surely affirm that God does nothing *without us*.[34] *No* virtue or merit, then, is

---

from certain natural principles pre-existing in us ... instead of which natural principles, God bestows on us the theological virtues, whereby we are directed to a supernatural end ... Wherefore we need to receive from God other habits corresponding, in due proportion, to the theological virtues, which habits are to the theological virtues, what the moral and intellectual virtues are to the natural principles of virtue' (*ST* I–II 63 3).

[31] *ST* I–II 62 1.

[32] 'God is the efficient cause of infused virtue, to which this definition applies; and this is expressed in the words *which God works in us without us*. If we omit this phrase, the remainder of the definition will apply to all virtues in general, whether acquired or infused ... Infused virtue is caused in us by God without any action on our part, but not without our consent. This is the sense of the words, *which God works in us without us*. As to those things which are done by us, God causes them in us, yet not without action on our part, for He works in every will and in every nature': *ST* I–II 55 4 – commenting on Augustine, *De Libero Arbitrio* ii 19: 'Virtue is a good quality of the mind, by which we live righteously, of which no one can make bad use, which God works in us, without us.'

[33] Sadly, I do not think we can exclude the possibility that an inadequately Trinitarian account of creation leaves Thomas without the means of carrying through his concept of God as universal efficient cause. It is this lack which raises again the possibility of our acting 'independently' or 'by nature'. That Thomas sees the Spirit as the source of the theological virtues, but not similarly as the source of the *non*-theological virtues, betrays the possibility that the Spirit (and the Son) are limited in their roles to redemption; they have no real place in an account of creation.

[34] 'Man's meritorious work may be considered in two ways: – first, as it proceeds from free-will; secondly, as it proceeds from the grace of the Holy Ghost' (*ST* I–II 114 3). 'Human acts have the nature of merit from two causes: – first and chiefly from the Divine ordination, inasmuch as acts are

an outcome of merely human agency – the Holy Spirit initiates and perfects every human virtue – but neither is human agency abrogated by this initiating and perfecting through the Spirit. The point at issue is rather that the theological virtues, which bring true unity to all the virtues by directing them to humanity's true goal, are simply unavailable to unregenerate humanity; they issue from an actual change in the human condition in response to the gospel; they are entirely dependent upon a *particular* operation of the Spirit. Here too the Spirit's presence and power does not abrogate human agency – as with Christian conversion, he works through human knowing and human willing – but here he works in a special and distinctive manner; and without this special and distinctive operation in relation to the gospel the theological virtues remain unattainable and the *non*-theological virtues remain without their true and ultimate orientation.

The notion of common grace, that develops within the Reformed tradition and comes to its fullest expression in Dutch Neo-Calvinism, is a means of affirming the presence and operation of the Holy Spirit generally in the world and in humanity. Though, especially in Dutch Reformed circles, there has been some debate as to whether such work of the Spirit consists in constraint as well as restraint – a debate chiefly concerned to deny that human action resulting from such constraint is *ultimately* meritorious – the intent of the notion is to affirm that every good action or attitude, together with the restraint of some evil actions and attitudes, issues from the presence of the Spirit generally in the world.[35] While this is a distinctive notion within this tradition it is, nonetheless, entirely consistent with the older understanding of divine causality as expressed by Thomas, by Calvin and by Edwards. The advantage of this Reformed expression of the older

---

said to merit that good to which man is divinely ordained. Secondly, on the part of free-will, inasmuch as man, more than other creatures, has the power of voluntary acts by acting of himself' (*ST* I–II 114 4).

[35] For an outline of this Dutch Reformed debate see the discussion in G. C. Berkouwer, *Studies in Dogmatics: The Providence of God*, trans. Lewis B. Smedes (Grand Rapids: Eerdmans, 1952), pp. 70ff.

doctrine is that it is explicitly Pneumatological – it is the Spirit who explicitly is the mediator of the Father's presence and action in the world and in humanity. The disadvantage of the notion, at least as it has sometimes been expressed, is that, like the older understanding of divine causality, it is insufficiently orientated to the Son and informed by the gospel; it tends to assume a disjunction between creation and redemption.[36]

This notion of common grace informs a response to the not uncommon (though highly pompous) question of why those who are ignorant or careless of the gospel are yet capable of unquestionably virtuous actions and attitudes: humanity may be God-forsak*ing* but, in the light of the gospel and of the humanity assumed by the Son, it can never be utterly God-forsak*en*; the Holy Spirit indwells creation and humanity generally, orientating creation and humanity towards the Son, the goal and fulfilment of creation, even though the majority of humanity remains unaware of this all-pervading presence and activity. From this perspective of faith, then, *every* virtue, *all* beauty, *all* goodness, *all* harmony, issues from the indwelling Spirit. The Spirit, who has come to indwell the Christian in a particular manner, lives and breathes in all creation and all humanity – and he does so, not in a general or indeterminate manner unrelated to the gospel, but rather in a manner that is provisional and of which the human subject remains unconscious. And, because the human subject remains unconscious of this presence and enabling, the resultant virtues lack the conscious coherence and integration that derives from the gospel and, consequently, some other basis of moral coherence and integration is sought.[37]

That which distinguishes the Christian from the non-Christian is not just a consciousness of this dynamic, and

---

[36] For a thorough consideration of the dangers inherent in such notions of divine causality, and the manner in which they can be Christologically corrected, see Karl Barth's discussion of the *Concursus Dei* in *CD* III/3, pp. 94ff.

[37] This issue of moral coherence will be more fully discussed in chapters eleven and twelve of this book.

therefore a consciousness of its goal, but also a confident expectation that this goal will be reached, that what has been provisional will be perfected. Certainly the Christian, like Christ, is called to live as one who is conscious of this dynamic and who remains dependent upon the presence and power of the Spirit. Just as Jesus continually directed attention away from himself to the Father and the Spirit as the source of his words and actions,[38] so also the Christian continually should confess 'not I, but the grace of God that was with me' (1 Cor. 15.10). The Christian, then, acknowledges the Spirit's presence and power as the source of *every* virtue, *all* beauty, *all* goodness, and *all* harmony:

> And every virtue we possess,
> And every victory won,
> And every thought of holiness,
> Are his alone.[39]

But this consciousness of the Christian brings with it a humble yet confident expectation that 'he who began a good work . . . will carry it to completion until the day of Christ Jesus' (Phil. 1.6). To become a Christian is not only to be brought by the Spirit to an awareness of the gospel story, it is also to be brought into increasing coherence with that story through the Spirit's indwelling.[40] In the light of

---

[38] Donald Baillie's understanding of Christ as the ultimate instance of the paradox of grace rests on this recognition of the disclaiming claims of Jesus: D. M. Baillie, *God was in Christ: An Essay on Incarnation and Atonement* (London: Faber & Faber, 1956).

[39] Henriette Auber (1773–1862), 'Our Blest Redeemer, ere He breathed His tender last farewell . . .' in *The Baptist Hymn Book* (London: Psalms and Hymns Trust, 1962), no. 236. Quoting this same verse of the hymn J. I. Packer comments, 'Most of the time there is nothing humanly abnormal about our experience to force on us any awareness that the Spirit is at work in us – not, at least, until we look back on what we said and did, and see that mere nature cannot account for it . . . in all our service of others, from the simplest forms of practical help to the most delicate spiritual guidance and the most forthright dissuasives from sin, we are activated by the Spirit – whether we know it or not. It is the Spirit's power that generates all the goodness of the Christian's good works: J. I. Packer, *A Passion for Holiness* (Cambridge: Crossway Books, 1992), p. 227.

[40] '. . . the Christian concept of morality is essentially bound up not just with *my* possible action but with an action of God, wrought in or available

the gospel story no man or woman is defined primarily in terms of their gender, their race, their sexuality, their background or their abilities: God has defined all humanity in the single humanity of Jesus; his *real* humanity is the only *true* humanity. But the Christian is one who is being brought into conformity with Christ, one whose *real* humanity is being shaped into this *true* humanity through the indwelling Spirit. This prospect of coherence is the new possibility presented to the Christian.

Of course, the Christian is free *not* to live in the light of this possibility, to live other than in conscious dependence upon the Spirit, to live other than by the desire for coherence – the indwelling Spirit does not abrogate human agency even here – but to do so is to live in denial of one's true identity.[41]

But what the Christian cannot do is to claim impotence, to claim that a denial of this identity was inevitable, to claim that circumstances or background, nurture or nature, necessitated unfaithfulness. The *true* humanity of Jesus was realized in *real* humanity, humanity no less *real* than our own, and in a context no less *real* than our own. In this *real* humanity Jesus lived in dependence upon the Spirit and in obedience to the Father and, consequently, *true* humanity was perfected in him. The Christian is presented with this same possibility, is confronted with this same command to obedience, but is also assured of this same indwelling power. The command of the gospel is, at the same time, the promise of the empowering presence of the Spirit. The Christian who is called to live coherently is also promised the possibility of living coherently. And it is to the process and means through which this coherence is realized and enacted that we now turn.

---

to us in living the moral life. ... It is the Christian claim that if we only repent of our condition of sin and turn to Christ with complete trust he will live in and through us, transforming our attitude to the world and enabling God to be loved for himself through us' (Keith Ward, *Ethics and Christianity*, p. 243).

[41] 'Every way of life not lived by the Spirit of God is lived by 'the flesh', by man taking responsibility for himself whether in libertarian or legalistic ways, without the good-news that God has taken responsibility for him' (Oliver O'Donovan, *Resurrection and the Moral Order*, p. 12).

8
The Indwelling of the Story

That Karl Barth includes an account of Christian baptism
within the uncompleted fourth volume of his treatment of
the Doctrine of Reconciliation is intended to indicate, not
only the responsive and prayerful nature of Christian
ethics, but also the ethical nature of baptism: baptism is a
genuinely human, and therefore a genuinely ethical,
action; in baptism, the Christian responds to God in prayer,
in faith, and in obedience.[1] If this represented the totality of
Barth's argument here it would hardly be controversial
and would merely reiterate that which he had said
previously.[2] But this closing 'Fragment' of the *Church
Dogmatics* is distinctive for what it denies rather than for
what it affirms. In this, his final attempt to give an account
of Christian baptism, Barth radically distinguishes baptism
with the Holy Spirit from baptism with water and
maintains that the latter is *merely* a human action.

This had not always been Barth's view. In *The Teaching
of the Church regarding Baptism*, an English translation and
edited version of an address to theological students in
1943, Barth speaks of water baptism as 'in essence the
representation of a man's renewal through his participation by means of the power of the Holy Spirit in the
death and resurrection of Jesus Christ'.[3] Here water
baptism is itself the witness and sign of baptism with the
Holy Spirit; it is the latter that occurs in the former,[4]
indeed, the power of baptism is the power of Jesus
Christ.[5] Even here, however, Barth is careful to maintain
that the power of Christ is never dependent upon

---

[1] *CD* IV/4, pp. 41ff.
[2] In his earlier work, *The Teaching of the Church regarding Baptism*, Barth
spoke of baptism as 'plainly a human act': Karl Barth, *The Teaching of the
Church regarding Baptism*, trans. Ernest A. Payne (London: SCM Press,
1948), p. 16.
[3] Karl Barth, *The Teaching of the Church regarding Baptism*, p. 9.
[4] Karl Barth, *The Teaching of the Church regarding Baptism*, pp. 12f.
[5] Karl Barth, *The Teaching of the Church regarding Baptism*, p. 19.

baptism,[6] that this power of Christ in baptism is not 'causative or generative' but 'cognitive' in its aim.[7] But by 1967 Barth had come to abandon any form of 'sacramental' understanding of water baptism, and, though this change was influenced partly by the exegetical work of his son Markus,[8] it is clear that Barth's principal intention is to maintain the integrity of water baptism as a truly human and truly ethical action; Barth simply could not now conceive of how any action can be truly and fully human if it is, at the same time, an action of God:

> If, like faith, love, and the whole action of the Church, especially its preaching, it is basically a divine action, how can it be understood and taken seriously as a human action?[9]

Stated so blatantly, Barth's assertion is breathtaking: how can any theology that reflects upon the Incarnation question the integrity of a human act on the grounds that it is, at the same time, a divine act? Barth's categorical separation of baptism with the Holy Spirit from water baptism can only be a further instance of that 'immediacy' which Colin Gunton perceives as vitiating the *Dogmatics*,[10] an 'immediacy' which, in this case at least, issues in apparent dualism: accordingly, Spirit baptism not only may occur without reference to water baptism, it does so necessarily; it occurs without any form of mediation; it occurs in a vacuum. While Barth may recognize correctly that the

---

[6] Karl Barth, *The Teaching of the Church regarding Baptism*, p. 21.
[7] Karl Barth, *The Teaching of the Church regarding Baptism*, p. 29.
[8] *CD* IV/4, p. x.
[9] *CD* IV/4, p. 106.
[10] Colin E. Gunton, *A Brief Theology of Revelation*, pp. 16ff., 66ff. A further instance of this 'immediacy' may occur in Barth's discussion of the threefold form of the Word of God (*CD* I/1, pp. 88ff.; cf. *CD* IV/3, pp. 114ff.). Barth is concerned to affirm the dependency of Scripture and Church proclamation (and even, perhaps, the 'words and truths of creation') upon the Word of God itself but, even by speaking of a threefold form of the Word of God, he gives the impression that the Word itself can come immediately, without the human words of Scripture, or of proclamation or of any other form of mediation. If this is implicitly dualistic it raises more fundamental questions concerning the degree to which Barth's entire account *really is* shaped Christologically.

word μυστήριον is never used in the New Testament in
relation to 'Christian obedience, nor love, nor hope, nor the
existence and function of the ἐκκλησία, nor its proclamation of the Gospel, nor its tradition as such, nor baptism,
nor the Lord's Supper', and while he may similarly be
correct in suspecting that pagan notions have been
imported into the significance of the term,[11] his consequent
attempt to eliminate every element of divine action from
the New Testament references to baptism reeks of special
pleading. In this respect Barth's insistence that baptism is a
form of prayer is incoherent: what is the significance of
prayer – particularly in this instance – without a humble
expectation of divine response; what is being requested in
prayer if Spirit baptism has already occurred 'immediately'?[12] Even John Webster, who tries so hard to defend
Barth from the charge of dualism consequent upon this
abandonment of a sacramental theology, concedes that
Barth's rejection of a sacramental understanding of
baptism is 'unnecessary'.[13]

If Jesus Christ is truly God and, simultaneously, truly
human, this categorical division of human action from
divine action is not just unnecessary, it is erroneous. The
ethical significance of Christ's faithfulness through
temptation is not invalidated simply because he was led into
the desert by the Spirit (Matt. 4.1). The ethical significance of
Christ's obedience even to death is not invalidated simply
because he 'offered himself unblemished to God' through
'the eternal Spirit' (Heb. 9.14). Barth would certainly not

[11] 'In the vocabulary of Christian theology "sacrament" came to have
irresistibly the sense of μυστήριον derived, not from the New Testament,
but from the Greek and Hellenistic mystery religions. It came to be used
for μυστήριον = re-presentation of the cultic deity = means of grace' (CD
IV/4, p. 109).
[12] Barth can respond to the latter question only by seeing baptism as a
prayer for the continuance of this grace. For a fuller discussion of Barth's
final view of baptism see John E. Colwell, 'Baptism, conscience and the
resurrection: a reappraisal of 1 Peter 3:21'.
[13] John Webster, Barth's Ethics of Reconciliation, p. 172: 'It would not be
impossible to construct an account of Spirit-baptism and water-baptism as
a differentiated unity without threatening either the uniqueness and
incommunicability of the work of Jesus Christ or the full reality of the
human response.'

deny the ethical validity of Christ's human action on the grounds that his obedience to the Father flowed out of his dependence upon the Spirit, that his genuinely human action was, simultaneously, a divine action within him and through him. Indeed, precisely through this dependence upon the Spirit, precisely because his every human action was simultaneously a divine action, Christ's human action is *truly*, as well as *really*, human. To be obedient to the Father in dependence upon the Spirit is to be *authentically* human. Only when human action is dependent upon the Spirit, then, can human action be *authentically* ethical. *Truly* ethical human action necessarily is, simultaneously, divine action.

On the day of Pentecost, Peter calls his hearers to repent and to be baptized; at the same time he assures them that they 'will receive the gift of the Holy Spirit' – the promise of the Spirit is for them and 'for all whom the Lord our God will call' (Acts 2.38f.). In the light of this text alone Barth would be justified in interpreting baptism in terms of prayer – but here the prayer which is baptism is specifically in relation to the gift of the Spirit and it is undertaken specifically in the light of a divine promise. This, of course, is not to imply that the promise of the Spirit is tied to baptism: the promise cannot be manipulated or restricted. That it cannot be restricted is demonstrated in the story of Cornelius, though, while Cornelius and those with him receive the Spirit prior to water baptism, it is, nonetheless, reasonable to identify this receiving of the Spirit as the significance of their water baptism (Acts 10.1ff.). Moreover, while their baptism with the Spirit could not, perhaps, be said to be 'mediated' by their water baptism, it is certainly not 'immediate'; it is mediated through Peter's preaching; it does not occur in some non-mediated vacuum. That this promise of the Spirit cannot be manipulated is less readily demonstrated from the New Testament, though the incident at Samaria demonstrates that there is nothing automatic or mechanical about the promise (Acts 8.4ff.),[14]

---

[14] We are offered no explanation of why the Samaritans did not receive the Spirit when they were baptized by Philip – certainly there is no hint here of any attempt at manipulation (though this follows in the story of Simon the sorcerer).

and countless incidents within the Old Testament demonstrate the futility of attempts to manipulate God through divinely ordained signs or symbols.[15]

As an act of prayer, and as an act of obedience, baptism is authentically a human action – indeed, in the light of the *true* humanity of Jesus and the manner of his baptism, baptism is *the* authentically human action – but because it is an act of prayer, and because it is an act of prayer in response to a specific divine promise, it cannot be *merely* a human action. Or, to put the matter conversely, baptism with the Holy Spirit, which Barth rightly identifies as the true beginning of Christian identity, is not promised as an 'immediate' event; it is mediated through the proclamation of the Church and through the form of prayer that is water baptism. Baptism, then, is a human promise and prayer in the light of a divine promise.[16] Rightly enacted it is free from any attempted manipulation, but rightly enacted it is also free from any uncertainty.[17] As an authentically human action it is not just a response to a divine action, or even just an anticipation of a divine action; through faith it is a means of an authentically divine action, or, to express the matter in more traditional terms, it is a means of grace.

Barth at least perceives the dangers of his newly adopted approach and seeks to distance himself from 'the understanding of baptism which was championed in

[15] Note in particular the story in 1 Samuel 4 of the Israelites' assumption that carrying the Ark of the Covenant into battle will bring victory.
[16] In this regard note John Calvin's definition of a sacrament: 'It seems to me that a simple and proper definition would be to say that it is an outward sign by which the Lord seals on our consciences the promises of his good will toward us in order to sustain the weakness of our faith; and we in turn attest our piety toward him in the presence of the Lord and of his angels and before men. Here is another briefer definition: one may call it a testimony of divine grace toward us, confirmed by an outward sign, with mutual attestation of our piety toward him' (*Institutes* IV xiv 1).
[17] Notwithstanding the dualistic elements of his account, Barth affirms this twofold freedom of baptism as prayer: 'Because and to the degree that baptism is prayer, the participants act in this order. They are free both from any calculating manipulation of God's grace and also from any uncertainty as to its being given. They let God be God, but they let Him be their God, who has called them and to whom they may call in return, who hears them and is heard as they may hear Him, and, hearing, obey Him' (*CD* IV/4, p. 210).

the early Church by groups which stood under Gnostic influence, which was held by Separatists in the age of the Reformation, and which is still espoused by some denominations to-day'.[18] Whenever there has been a belittling of the sacramental dynamic of the Church's life, other symbols, events and experiences – themselves neither divinely ordained nor pregnant with a divine promise – have assumed a pseudo-sacramental significance. The proclamation of the gospel, instead of being accompanied by baptism, is accompanied by 'altar calls' and 'decision cards'. Christian assurance is sought, not in the divine promise inherent in baptism and the Eucharist, but in pious feelings or ecstatic experiences.[19] Having been given specific signs as means of specific promises, having been given specific means of indwelling the gospel story, such pseudo-sacramental inventions are simply perverse.

The concern of the previous chapter was to affirm the reality of the Holy Spirit as the source of a *real* change in the life of the Christian: he is the source and perfecter of virtue; through his indwelling, the life of the Christian is brought into increasing coherence with the *true* humanity of Jesus. The concern of this present chapter is to affirm – in contradistinction to the incipient dualism that characterizes Barth's later writings – that this authentically divine action occurs in, with, and through authentically human action; that it is precisely through the sacramental life of the Church that this divinely sourced transformation takes place.

Baptism as an act of prayer and of obedience, just as any other act of prayer or of obedience, is an authentically human and therefore an authentically ethical action. But baptism as this specific act of prayer and of obedience is foundational for every other act of prayer and of obedience and is therefore *the* authentically human and authentically ethical action. In baptism the Christian is identified with

---

[18]　*CD* IV/4, p. 106.
[19]　Hence Barth comments: 'If … the sacramental view of water baptism is rejected or avoided – often far too hastily and critically – the price which is blatantly paid is that the external work of water baptism, robbed of its glory as a sacrament, is replaced by an "inner work" in the form of experiences, inspirations, illuminations, exaltations or raptures' (*CD* IV/4, p. 106).

Christ, with his death and with his resurrection; in baptism the Christian acknowledges Christ's crucified and risen humanity as the only *true* humanity; in baptism the Christian seeks identification and coherence with this true humanity. This is a truly human action – this is *the* truly human action – but it cannot be a merely human possibility. The Christian can identify with Christ in baptism only because Christ has first, in his baptism, identified fully with sinful and repenting humanity. The Christian can be brought to coherence with the humanity of Christ through baptism only inasmuch as baptism, as a form of prayer, is enacted in the light of the Father's promise to bring the Christian into this coherence through the Spirit. As the definitive moment of the Christian's identification with Christ, then, baptism represents the Christian's initial indwelling of the gospel story, an indwelling effected by the Spirit. Through baptism, and through the indwelling of the Spirit promised in baptism, the Christian is brought to indwell Christ, to indwell his baptism, to indwell his true humanity, to indwell the story of his death and resurrection.

As on the day of Pentecost, baptism is properly enacted in response to the gospel story – to respond appropriately to the gospel story is not merely to hear it but to come to indwell it and to be brought into coherence with it. The Spirit who causes us to hear the gospel story brings us also to indwell it and, as a consequence, to be formed by it and changed by it. The sacraments of baptism and the Eucharist are means through which this indwelling is effected. Indeed, any action that can properly be termed 'sacramental' is so inasmuch as, through prayer and in response to a divine promise, it is a means of indwelling the gospel story.[20] It is for this reason that Christian proclamation ought never to be without the sacraments and the sacraments ought never to be without Christian

---

[20] I am not pretending that this is an adequate or complete definition of a sacrament – to attempt such a definition and to justify it would demand a separate volume. At the very least, more would need to be said concerning the sacraments as specifically 'ordinances'; that is to say, as human acts of prayer and obedience in the light of specific divine promises and in response to specific divine commands.

proclamation: the story is to be indwelt and not just heard, but, unless the story is heard, sacramental indwelling is incoherent. Moreover, baptism and the Eucharist are effective means of indwelling the story only inasmuch as these human actions are simultaneously divine actions, inasmuch as human acts of prayer and obedience occur in the light of a divine promise, inasmuch as the presence and action of the Spirit is real.[21] The truly human cannot be separated from the truly divine – only because there is truly the divine can there be the *truly* human.

The exposition of the Eucharist, proposed by Barth to conclude his projected account of the 'Command of God the Reconciler', remained unwritten and, consequently, one can only suppose that this dualistic disjunction of divine action and human action would have been maintained, that the Lord's Supper would have been defined in terms of *merely* human acts of prayer, of faith, and of obedience. Of course, it has to be admitted that, in this radical disjunction of the divine and the human, particularly in respect of the sacraments, Barth has come to inhabit a distinct 'tradition'. Since the Reformation (though anticipated in previous centuries), partly perhaps in reaction to the extremes of sacerdotalism, partly also perhaps in response to rationalistic reductionism, the significance of baptism and the Lord's Supper as truly divine events has been undermined. Barth's conclusion that water baptism follows after Spirit baptism almost precisely parallels the views of sixteenth-century Anabaptists such as Pilgram Marpeck,[22] and the notion

---

[21] '. . . the sacraments properly fulfill their office only when the Spirit, that inward teacher, comes to them, by whose power alone our hearts are penetrated and affections moved and our souls opened for the sacraments to enter in. If the Spirit be lacking, the sacraments can accomplish nothing more in our minds than the splendor of the sun shining upon blind eyes, or a voice sounding in deaf ears' (*Institutes*, IV xiv 9).

[22] Pilgram Marpeck, 'Confession of 1532' in *The Writings of Pilgram Marpeck*, trans. and ed. William Klassen and Walter Klaassen (Scottdale: Herald Press, 1978), pp. 107–57 (pp. 138ff.). For a comparison of Marpeck and Barth see John Colwell, 'Alternative Approaches to Believer's Baptism (from the Anabaptists to Barth)' in *The Scottish Bulletin of Evangelical Theology* 7 (1989), pp. 3–20.

that baptism is merely an outward witness to personal faith is all too common in present-day Baptist churches. The Zwinglian denial of any 'real presence', interpreting the Lord's Supper as little more than a means of remembering Christ's death, dissolves the sacrament into a *merely* human event and is similarly all too common, and that not just among Baptist churches.

As an act of prayer, of faith, and of obedience the Eucharist, like baptism, is truly a human act. But, since it is an act of specific prayer, faith and obedience, the Eucharist, like baptism, cannot be *merely* a human act. It is an act of prayer, faith and obedience in response to a specific divine promise. Christ promises to be present to his Church through the Spirit in the Eucharist. Christ promises to nourish his Church through the Spirit in the Eucharist. The Eucharist, as a human act of prayer, faith and obedience, occurs in response to this specific promise and invitation:

> Now Christ is the only food of our soul, and therefore our Heavenly Father invites us to Christ, that, refreshed by partaking of him, we may repeatedly gather strength until we shall have reached heavenly immortality.[23]

The Eucharist, then, is an instrumental means through which Christ's promise to nourish us, to sustain us, to form us, is fulfilled. This cannot be a merely human event though it occurs in the context of a truly human event. It is a truly divine event inasmuch as the presence and activity of the Spirit is real. Like Calvin, Thomas Aquinas understands the Eucharist as an instrumental means of grace: neither the sacrament itself, nor the human minister, is the principal agent of this grace; the principal agent of grace is (and can only be) God himself.[24] This is not, however, to

---

[23] *Institutes* IV xvii.

[24] '... the instrumental cause works not by the power of its form, but only by the motion whereby it is moved by the principal agent: so that the effect is not likened to the instrument but to the principal agent ... it is thus that the sacraments of the New Law cause grace: for they are instituted by God to be employed for the purpose of conferring grace' (*ST* III 62 1; cf. 64 1–2).

limit or to deny the real presence, the real power, the real
effectiveness of grace within the sacrament: 'Just as an
instrumental power accrues to an instrument through its
being moved by the principal agent, so does a sacrament
receive spiritual power from Christ's blessing and from the
action of the minister in applying it to a sacramental use';[25]
the power of the sacrament, then, is rooted in a specific
divine promise appropriated in a specific act of prayer,
faith and obedience.

One is struck as much by the similarities between
Thomas and Calvin at this point as by their very real differences.[26] I suspect that those differences derive, at least in
part, from Thomas's tendency to speak of 'grace' where
Calvin tends to speak of 'the Spirit': all too easily grace
comes to be thought of as a 'something' and, thereby, a
'something' at our disposal, to be presumed upon, to be
manipulated. The Spirit, however, as the personal presence
of God in the Eucharist, remains free: he is never simply at
our disposal; he is not to be presumed upon; he cannot be
manipulated.[27] The effectiveness of the Eucharist is
grounded, therefore, not in an impersonal grace tied to the
physical elements or controlled by the minister, but in
the promise of Christ's presence through the Spirit – a

[25] *ST* III 62 4; cf. '. . . if we hold that a sacrament is an instrumental cause
of grace, we must needs allow that there is in the sacraments a certain
instrumental power of bringing about the sacramental effects. Now such
power is proportionate to the instrument: and consequently it stands in
comparison to the complete and perfect power of anything, as the
instrument to the principal agent.'
[26] Such a discussion again warrants a separate volume but it is worth
pondering whether Calvin's language of spiritual rather than bodily
presence fulfils a similar function to Thomas's distinction (following
Aristotle) between substance and accidents: to affirm that the substance of
the elements (notwithstanding their continuing accidents) is determined
by the Word of God, corresponds to the affirmation that Christ is spiri-
tually (rather than bodily) present under these physical signs; i.e., that
which is 'spiritual' is that which is 'substantial', that which is 'physical' is
'accidental'.
[27] I am not suggesting that Thomas's account is guilty of these faults
(though there would seem to be a case to answer). I am rather concerned
to indicate the dangers of referring to an impersonal grace rather than the
personal Spirit – dangers amply exemplified in accounts of the Eucharist
subsequent to Thomas.

presence confidently to be sought in prayer and faith rather than to be presumed upon or manipulated.[28] However, this promise of Christ's presence by the Spirit is appropriated in a prayer that takes the specific form of a re-enacting of a supper which, itself, was a prefiguring of Christ's death – and, to this extent, the Eucharist is rightly perceived as a 're-presenting' of Christ's death. The Eucharist is explicitly then, like baptism, a re-enactment, a means of indwelling the gospel story; through this act of indwelling, which is a form of prayer, this specific promise of Christ's presence is invoked.

For Israel, the Passover meal, which formed the context for Christ's institution of the Eucharist, was similarly a means of indwelling a story. By celebrating Passover, the people of Israel were not merely remembering the events of the Exodus, they were indwelling those events, sharing in those events, identifying with those events; they were affirming their identity with those who first came out of Egypt; they were affirming that their identity too was defined by these specific events of suffering, sacrifice and separation. For Jesus to reinterpret two elements of the Passover supper in relation to his forthcoming sacrifice surely implies a similar intention that these too should be means of indwelling. The bread and the wine are means of

28 In this respect note the following comment from David McCarthy Matzko: 'In the Mass ... if Christ is not present, then the eucharistic meal is unintelligible. Christ's presence and ritual performance sustain the intelligibility even of theories, like transubstantiation or trans-signification, which intend to explain what is going on. ... The grammar and language of bodily movements and verbal expressions acknowledge a social and linguistic space where this particular bread and wine are Christ. Through action we are *oriented* to God's grace. The presence of Christ is *seen* in bread when a set of practices occasions possibilities for *seeing* by conforming the human agents to the events of God. Christ's presence is an event which transpires in space and time, through the worshipping community and by means of ritual action which establishes a world of social, linguistic, and metaphysical possibilities. In the doing of the "Do this in remembrance of me", Christ *is* our bread. Christ is present, and our ritual performance establishes the linguistic and material possibilities for bread and wine to be *recognized* as the body and blood of Christ': David McCarthy Matzko, 'The Performance of the Good: Ritual Action and the Moral Life' in *Pro Ecclesia* VII (1998), pp. 199–215 (pp. 208f.).

sharing in the body and blood of Christ (1 Cor. 10.16); by
eating the bread and drinking the wine we not only
remember that sacrificial death, we participate in it, we
indwell it.

And by indwelling it we are formed by it. Both John
Calvin and Charles Spurgeon urged a weekly celebration
of the Lord's Supper because they both recognized it as
foundational for Christian identity and Christian
formation.[29] A people whose life and worship is centred on
this means of indwelling the story will be a people who are
continually being shaped by that story, a people shaped by
thanksgiving, a people shaped by their knowledge of their
utter dependence, a people shaped by their need to be
sustained by the living Christ. To continue to indwell the
gospel story through the Eucharist is increasingly to come
to view the world in the light of the gospel story and to
come to live in deeper coherence with that story. The
'habit' of Holy Communion prompts habits of holy
character. The point is well expressed in an excellent essay
by David McCarthy Matzko concerning the ethical
significance of the sacrament:

> The proposal of this essay is that certain activities and
> practices orient our lives to the good. By performing
> certain designated actions, we come to understand the
> good, and through these practices, we enter into and
> are shaped by God's redemptive activity ... The
> proposal is that specific actions orient persons to a
> right vision of the world and, as a consequence,
> occasion right conduct. Action shapes vision which in
> turn cultivates action.[30]

Moreover, this repeated act of indwelling is not impotent
but is effective. The human act of prayer which is the
Eucharist is performed in response to a divine promise

[29] For a discussion of Baptist attitudes to Communion see Michael J.
Walker, *Baptists at the Table: the Theology of the Lord's Supper amongst
English Baptists in the Nineteenth Century* (Didcot: Baptist Historical
Society, 1992).
[30] David McCarthy Matzko, 'The Performance of the Good', p. 199.

and, consequently, this authentically human action –
which as a *truly* human action can never be a manipulative
or presumptuous action – is simultaneously an authentically divine action; it is enacted in humble assurance in the
light of Christ's promise to be present and to nourish and
sustain us; it is a coming of the Spirit. And as a coming of
the Spirit it is an effective shaping of our lives in response
to the sacrifice of Christ; as we continue to indwell
the story through the Eucharist, the Spirit, through the
Eucharist, continues to shape us in coherence with Christ.[31]

Precisely in such a definition of the sacraments lies a
definition of the Church. By its constant proclamation of
the gospel the Church exists as the community in which
this story is continually heard – but this, of itself, is insufficiently definitive. The Church is defined and identified by
the Word *and the sacraments*, by hearing and proclaiming
the gospel story, but also by indwelling that story and
being shaped by it. Whenever the Church's sacramental
life is belittled there is immediately the danger that the
gospel will be heard without being indwelt, that faith will
be reduced to mere believism, that the community of the
Church will be reduced to a series of merely secular social
functions.[32] That which is truly the Church is identified,
not merely by its hearing and proclaiming of the gospel,
but by its indwelling of the gospel through the sacraments
as the ordained means of that indwelling. Only through

[31] Matzko makes the point that it is precisely through these acts of
performance that we are brought to recognize the ethically good; ethical
accounts that assume the good to be self-evident inevitably ignore this
need to be brought to a place where the good can be recognized: 'Apart
from their disagreements, Grisez and Richard McCormick, for example,
both depend upon an assertion that basic human goods are self-evident to
any agent, and because they assume goods are self-evident, they provide
no account of how a moral agent becomes *properly situated* in relation to
these goods': 'The Performance of the Good', p. 203; commenting on Jean
Porter, *The Recovery of Virtue: The Relevance of Aquinas for Christian Ethics*
(London: SPCK, 1990).
[32] In this regard, the notice sheet of many Baptist churches is terrifying.
Where Communion is celebrated twice a month and the church
programme is cluttered with a host of regular weekly activities it is
difficult not to conclude that it is these other activities, rather than the
gospel as expressed in the sacraments, that are definitive for the church's
identity.

this active indwelling of the gospel story is the Church itself a sacramental community, a means of the presence of the living Christ. The promise of Christ's presence to his Church is determinate and not indeterminate: it is consequent upon the community coming together in his name (Matt. 18.20); it is prospective of the community being formed in coherence with his character.

This sacramental reality of the Church's identity is similarly both an authentically human and an authentically divine occurrence. Contrary to every form of 'immediacy', the Holy Spirit forms us through our interaction with one another as that interaction is focused on the gospel story and is itself a further means of indwelling that story. Just as the Father works 'mediately' through the Son and the Spirit, so the Spirit works 'mediately' through creaturely agency. The genuinely human events of the community of the Church, its faithfulness, hopefulness and lovingness, are not *merely* human, nor are they in contradistinction to the presence and action of the Spirit; they are simultaneously genuine divine events; they are a means through which the Spirit works to shape us in coherence with Christ. By interaction with one another and with the tradition which itself has been formed through a history of such interactions, we are shaped by one another and, accordingly, we are shaped by the Spirit. Our acquiring of habits of humble obedience and spiritual discipline through human interaction is a means by which the Holy Spirit forms those habits within us. Precisely through the means of the culture of the Church, then, the Spirit effects his sanctifying purposes.[33]

---

[33] Here again Barth's implicit dualism must be resisted, not just in relation to the Church, but, in the light of the Spirit's presence and action in creation, more generally: 'If one has a conviction about the social processes of life being grounded in the purposes and goodness of life's ultimate power and good, then these processes have at least the prospect of being channels of the divine beneficence toward man. If one is convinced that the purposes of God to fulfill and redeem life work through the mundane human experiences of living in communities, then socialization processes indeed have theological significance and dignity. On the other hand, if a radical disjuncture is drawn between socialization and the significant work of God's goodness toward man, so that the call

This genuinely human dynamic of the Church's existence can, of course, degenerate into the *merely* human. Where the reality of the presence and activity of the Spirit is denied or 'demythologized' (which is no more than a sophisticated way of denying his reality), or where the sacramental focus of the Church's life is belittled, there human activity may be *merely* human and the gospel may be reduced to an impotent programme of general social reform. But where the presence and activity of the Spirit is sought in prayer and in sacrament, where the proclaiming and indwelling of the gospel story remains determinative, there the Church itself is formed into a living narration of the gospel story through the living Spirit. And where the Church itself exists as this living narration of the gospel, there men and women can be shaped by the Spirit in coherence with Christ, and there, consequently, the Word of the Church's proclamation to the world can take flesh.

All this may sound irredeemably idealistic. Is there not an unbridgeable credibility gap between the calling of the Church and its present reality? In one respect at least this charge must be repudiated: what is envisaged here is not a perfected Church but a Church in the process of being perfected. Precisely in its weakness, precisely in its failure, precisely in its consciousness of sin, the Church is identified as dependent on the Spirit. Its constant hearing of the gospel and sacramental indwelling of the gospel holds the Church in an assurance of God's unfailing mercy and, consequently, reminds the Church of its unremitting need for that mercy. This awareness of sin and of a continuing need for mercy and grace is testimony to the Church's coherence with the gospel rather than testimony against

---

to a religious or religiously moral life is a vocation which necessarily must be independent from, or even counter to, the socialization processes, then these processes have no theological dignity. If reliance to some degree upon what one has become through participating in a culture is per definition a reliance upon that which is less than God, and thus a form of unfaith, religion as a social phenomenon is sin. But another view is theologically defensible, namely, that becoming a person with the interactions of a particular society can be a process which mediates God's ordering and fulfilling intentions for human life' (James M. Gustafson, *Can Ethics be Christian?* p. 58).

that coherence. The Church's awareness of its own imperfect humanity compels it to set its confidence in the perfect humanity of Jesus; its life may only be a *shadow* of his reality, but it *is* a shadow of his reality; its imperfect faith, hope and love point to his perfect faith, hope and love.

The more profound fear is not of failure but of apostasy, that the Church, through fear of failure, will abandon that which distinguishes it as truly the Church. As long as the Church, even in its failure, continues to hear the gospel and to seek to indwell the gospel, it continues truly to be the Church, despite its failure. However, once the Church, in awareness of its failure, adapts the gospel story, or ceases to see the indwelling of the story as its priority, it ceases truly to be the Church, it ceases to be identified by Word and sacrament. It is, of course, entirely understandable, in the context of modernism and post-modernism, where the Church's faith is either dismissed or marginalized, that the Church should be fearful concerning its future effectiveness – but too often the proposed 'remedy' is more deadly than the pain. Wherever the Church begins to put its confidence in advertizing strategies, management techniques, or feeling-centred counselling therapies, it ceases to be faithful. Wherever social programmes displace sacramental indwelling, the focus of true holiness is jeopardized. Wherever the gospel is offered as commodity instead of proclaimed as command, truth is abandoned. And in each instance the specific promise of the Spirit's presence and activity is forfeited. Indeed, it may well be that where the Church may appear (at least from a secular perspective) to be most effective and flourishing it is, in reality, least faithful. Before trumpeting apparent growth we should pause to consider what actually it is that is growing. To seek growth at the expense of faithfulness is, in reality, to diminish. If the gospel is proclaimed as the supposed remedy for every 'felt' need, it may gain popularity but there can be little expectation for transformation.

Rather than seeking to mimic secular strategies the Church must continually be called to faithfulness – that is to say, not just to believe the gospel story and proclaim it, but also to indwell it and to seek to live coherently in its light; that is to say, simply and truly to be the Church. The renewal of the contemporary Church that is appropriate will not focus on strategies, ecstatic experiences or signs of apparent power, but will rather issue from a more focused indwelling of the gospel story through the common life, worship and sacraments of the Church, and from the consequent presence of the Spirit, shaping the community of the Church in coherence with the gospel it proclaims. Such a Church, which is *truly* the Church, will be *truly* effective since its *truly* human life of prayer and obedience will, simultaneously, be *truly* divine action through the promised presence of the Spirit. Such a Church, in which the gospel habits of truthfulness, hopefulness and loving-ness are being cultivated, will constitute an alternative way of perceiving and of being within society. And such a Church, because it exists *within* society, because it is in the world though not of the world, will, by its mere existence and interacting presence, continually confront and woo the world concerning its true goal and identity before God.[34]

---

[34] Though the reference is to a more general need of 'alternative' communities of virtue, Alasdair MacIntyre exposes the reality of the context in which such communities must be built: 'What matters at this stage is the construction of local forms of community within which civility and the intellectual and moral life can be sustained through the new dark ages which are already upon us. And if the tradition of the virtues was able to survive the horrors of the last dark ages, we are not entirely without grounds for hope. This time however the barbarians are not waiting beyond the frontiers; they have already been governing us for quite some time. And it is our lack of consciousness of this that constitutes part of our predicament' (Alasdair MacIntyre, *After Virtue*, p. 263).

9
Indwelling and Identity

In the light of the *true* humanity of Christ, to live in a truly human manner, and therefore in a truly ethical manner, is to live by the power of the indwelling Spirit. And to live by the power of the indwelling Spirit is to indwell the gospel story through the proclamation, life, and sacramental worship of the Church. Just as there can be no dualistic division between the work of Christ and the work of the Spirit, between that which has been done for us and that which is realized within us, so also there must be no implied division between the work of the Spirit and the genuinely human interactions in and through which that work is accomplished. The dynamic of Christian identity must not be spiritualized in some abstract manner, as if the Spirit's indwelling occurred without prejudice to the life and worship of the Christian community, but neither ought the dynamic of Christian identity be reduced as if it were the outcome merely of social influences, as if the indwelling of the Spirit were unreal or imaginary. Precisely through the life and worship of the Christian community, Christian identity is shaped through the work of the Spirit in coherence with Christ.

It ought to be clear by now that Christian identity (and therefore Christian ethics) essentially is an issue of coherence. The command of the gospel, which is simultaneously the goal of the Spirit's indwelling, is that we should live coherently with the character of Christ, that his *true* humanity should be echoed in the particularities of our lives. To be a Christian, then, is not merely to believe a series of doctrines (as if any doctrine could be truly believed without it affecting us) nor is it simply a matter of adhering to a series of rules (as if the humanity of Christ could be reduced to a series of rules or as if our lives could be reduced to a series of discrete moral choices). To be a Christian, rather, is to be in the process of developing habits of character that, in their integration, bear testimony to the truthfulness of the gospel. To be a Christian is to be orientated by the Spirit towards this goal of coherence – an orientation and an indwelling that occurs through an indwelling of the gospel story as it is narrated in the life and worship of the Church.

As I have argued elsewhere, it is probably in this sense that the Greek term συνείδησις is used within the New Testament.[1] Whereas we tend to speak of conscience, either with reference to a sense of guilt in relation to specific actions in the past (*conscientia consequens*), or with reference to some general ground for our moral decision making (*conscientia antecedens*), it is probable that the New Testament (in accordance with the general use of the term within the ancient world) employs the word with reference to a more general self-consciousness before God, an awareness of an integrated coherence of life, thought and action. To have a good conscience, then, is to be conscious of an overall coherence with what is known of God through the gospel. It is in this sense that conscience can be 'seared', not through guilt over sin but through an abandonment of conscious coherence (1 Tim. 4.2); Christian identity isn't necessarily undermined through an awareness of past wrong but it is necessarily undermined through a refusal to be shaped by the gospel story.

Only if the Church continues to relate its story truthfully, only if the Church continues to seek to indwell its story faithfully, can coherence be maintained. Distortion of the Church's retelling of the story occurs both by omission and by addition. Certainly through conscious or unconscious editing the story can be sanitized, robbed of its vibrancy by being robbed of its offensiveness. Any attempt to render the story more acceptable within a context of liberal modernism apostasizes, from its inception, by admitting a rival canon of acceptability. But, more commonly perhaps, the story is distorted through its voice

---

[1] For a discussion of the significance of the term συνείδησις see Christian Maurer's article '✝ σύνοιδα, ✝ συνείδησις' in the *Theological Dictionary of the New Testament* VII, ed. G. Friedrich; trans. and ed. G. W. Bromiley (Grand Rapids: Eerdmans, 1971), pp. 898–919. I have discussed this issue in 'Baptism, conscience and the resurrection: a reappraisal of 1 Peter 3:21'.

becoming confused in a cacophony of rival stories. Our generation is beset with a myriad of competing stories and media technology offers ever more effective means of indwelling them. The crisis for Christian identity, at least in Western Europe, Australasia and North America, but increasingly world-wide as media saturation is extended, is that rival stories of *Friends, Neighbours,* or *Eastenders* displace the gospel story as the foundational narratives for the lives of Church members, again reducing faith to mere believism and rendering Christian identity as something less than authentically 'Christian'. Christian identity is determined by our indwelling of this story, as distinct from every other story, through our indwelling of the Christian community and its sacramental life in correspondence with our being indwelt by the Spirit.

The obligation of the Church in this (as in every) context is, as has been continually urged by Stanley Hauerwas, simply to be the Church, but to be so truthfully and faithfully.[2] Unintimidated by the beguiling allure of every rival story, the Church must continue to relate its story, shape its worship as the sacramental means of indwelling that story, and allow that worship simultaneously to shape every aspect of its living within the world. It has no other strategy that is truthful and faithful. It must not distort or accommodate its story in any attempt to render it more acceptable or attractive, but neither may it abandon the commitment to allow that story to be foundational for its living. Only through its truthful retelling of the story and faithful indwelling of the story can the Church come to be shaped by the story, can the Church truly be the Church; only thus can habits of faithfulness, hopefulness and lovingness be cultivated.

It is through our indwelling of the gospel story, through our hearing it proclaimed, through our participation in it sacramentally, through our sharing in the living narrative of the Christian community, that our identity as Christians

---

[2] 'The task of Christian ethics, therefore, is simply the task of theology itself – namely to help the churches share their stories truthfully'(Stanley Hauerwas, *Christian Existence Today*, p. 125).

is shaped by the Spirit. Indeed, through our communal
indwelling of the story our own lives, by becoming
integrated with the story, themselves become a retelling of
the story. A mutual hermeneutical dynamic is established:
just as the life and worship of the Church becomes the
means of hearing, interpreting, and indwelling the gospel,
so also the gospel itself becomes the only means of making
sense of our own life stories; without a recounting of the
gospel it becomes increasingly difficult to understand why
this people should live in the manner that they do;[3] even if
their lovingness might, at least in a general sense, be explicable by alternative means (though such explanations will
always be inherently inadequate), there would seem to
be no alternative explanation for their hopefulness and
trustfulness.

In the first place, then, the gospel story is the
hermeneutic of the Christian life, the means through which
the coherence of this particular living narrative is identified. If it should be clear by now that Christian identity is
an issue of coherence it should also be clear that Christian
identity is a dynamic and not a static; it is an interpretation
of the narrative of my life rather than a mere nominal
abstraction. For me to be identified as a Christian is not just
a response to a claim I make about myself, it is also a
reflection on the story of my life as interpreted by that
claim and as a means of interpreting it. My identity is not
just who I claim to have become but who I continue to be
as the narrative of my life is interpreted in the light of the
gospel story.[4] Only as my life is interpreted in the light of

---

[3] 'Our character is the result of our sustained attention to the world that
gives a coherence to our intentionality. Such attention is formed and given
content by the stories through which we have learned to form the story of
our lives. To be moral persons is to allow stories to be told through us so
that our manifold activities gain a coherence that allows us to claim them
for our own. The significance of stories is the significance of character for
the moral life as our experience itself, if it is to be coherent, is but an
incipient story' (Stanley Hauerwas, *Vision and Virtue*, p. 74).
[4] 'Character is the qualification or determination of our self-agency
formed by our having certain intentions (and beliefs) rather than others.
Once it is clear that character is but the concrete determination of our
agency we can understand why no ultimate distinction can be made

God's mercy and forgiveness, but also in the light of God's grace, shaping me in coherence with Christ, does my claim to be a Christian have content, meaning and credibility:

> We attain character not by our constant effort to reach an ideal but by discovery, as we look back on our lives and, by God's forgiveness, claim them as our own. Character, in other words, names the continuity of our lives, the recognition of which is made possible by the retrospective affirmation that our lives are not just the sum of what we have done but rather are constituted by what God has done for us. In short, character is recognized in the discovery of those narratives that live through us, making us more than we could have hoped.[5]

It is the gospel story that provides the hermeneutical key to the life of the Christian and, consequently, 'names the continuity' of the Christian's life, identifying the Christian as 'Christian'. Certainly this continuity of life will be an outcome of the orientation of that life towards a goal, an orientation imparted by the Spirit and represented in the sacramental worship of the Church. But the continuity is expressed, not just in an awareness of this goal, but in the mundane particularities of daily life. A life that is coherent with the gospel story is a life in which the common particularities of work and of human relationships are integrated. To quote again from Stanley Hauerwas:

---

between acquiring character and having character. Character in its particular manifestation cannot be a static possession men have once and for all. Since it is born in intentional behaviour it exists only as a qualification of that continuing behaviour. Men cannot somehow acquire character and then leave it unattended, acting in completely different ways but still claiming to have their previous character. There is a kind of permanence to character, but it is not necessarily unchanging or inflexible. Therefore, the question of acquiring character cannot be dealt with as something that comes at one point to then be forgotten once it is acquired. Rather the question of acquiring character is at the very center of what it means to have character' (Stanley Hauerwas, *Character and the Christian Life*, p. 115).
[5] Stanley Hauerwas and Charles Pinches, *Christians among the Virtues*, pp. 124f.

The moral significance of our lives is not constituted by moving from one significant social problem to another; rather, it depends on our willingness to work at being human through the manifold particularity of our lives. It is a matter not of finding the ultimate truth but of finding what the truth is in the small questions that confront us every day. It is a matter of what we do with our time, whether we are willing to work to make our marriages worthwhile, how well we perform our everyday tasks. The main problem of the moral life is not to come to monumental decisions but to live through the contingencies of our lives.[6]

If Christian identity is a naming of 'the continuity of our lives' in the light of the gospel story, then it must be clear that any 'episodic' interpretation of Christian ethics is inadequate. My identity as a Christian cannot simply be reduced to my response to a series of discrete ethical dilemmas. This is not, of course, to deny that there are dilemmas to which the Christian must respond – the realities of the Christian's context, together with the realities of the Christian's weakness and limitations, make such dilemmas inevitable and ubiquitous – but too often and too easily ethical issues are mistakenly abstracted as the focus of Christian ethics, as if the dilemmas of life could be extracted from the context and continuities in which they occur, as if our response to those dilemmas could be isolated from the narratives of our lives and the communities of worship that identify their coherence. The focus of Christian ethics is the character of Christ as narrated in the gospel story and as echoed in the life of the Church. Dilemmas do not occur in a vacuum but as integrated events within the narrative of our lives to be resolved, not in isolation according to abstracted principles, but with respect to integrity and coherence of character. The approach appropriate to a dilemma in such a context is not a question of what should be done in such a situation but is rather the question of what can be

---

[6] Stanley Hauerwas, *Vision and Virtue*, p. 47.

done coherently in such a situation by such a person whose life narrative is to be comprehended in such a way.

All too readily Christians are allured into discussions of ethical dilemmas, such as that of euthanasia, as if such could be resolved with reference to rules, principles or consequences. In the case of euthanasia appeals are made to the sanctity of life (as a matter of rule or principle) or to the dangers of where this 'slippery slope' might lead (as a matter of consequence). That which is beguiling in such approaches is their apparent accessibility to society as a whole: those who do not share our Christian commitment might not agree with our conclusions but, at least, they will be able to recognize the manner in which those conclusions were reached; questions concerning the sanctity of life and the possible consequences of medical policy are not dependent upon appeals to the gospel narrative and therefore might be persuasive for those whose lives are not consciously formed in response to that narrative.[7] However, notwithstanding the merits or demerits of such arguments, inasmuch as they abandon a distinctively Christian narrative as the focus for ethical living, they lack integrity; they are untruthful and therefore inherently unfaithful. If the gospel story is the hermeneutical key to our lives we ought not to expect our lives, and the ethical decisions reached within their continuities, to be accessible or comprehensible in detachment. While it may be possible for a detached observer to propose some other account for the Christian's attitude to suffering and death such proposals are not merely deficient, they are inevitably delusory. The only truthful account of the Christian's approach to suffering and death is the narrative of the life, death and resurrection of Jesus as that narrative is echoed

---

[7] The common assumption that ethics is primarily a matter of resolving dilemmas itself is suggestive of a rationally detached approach to such dilemmas: '... the assumption that most of our moral concerns are "problems" suggests that ethics can be construed as a rational science that evaluates alternative "solutions." Moral decisions should be based on rationally derived principles that are not relative to any one set of convictions. Ethics becomes a branch of decision theory' (Stanley Hauerwas with Richard Bondi and David B. Burrell, *Truthfulness and Tragedy*, p. 18).

and represented in the life and worship of the Church. If the Christian continues to care beyond the prospects for cure, if the Christian continues to trust and hope when there is no longer any 'medical' basis for such hope, if the Christian refuses to cling on desperately to life as if there was no other prospect for hope, all this is only *truly* explicable in the light of the gospel story and in continuity with a narrative of life that is faithful to that story.[8]

It is in this respect (as has already been noted) that Alasdair MacIntyre's positive proposals may lack coherence. Having undermined every liberal and modernistic foundation for morality, and having stressed the communal (and, therefore, the particular) locus of virtue, MacIntyre seems to propose that virtue, thus located, represents an alternative and generally accessible ethical foundation. John Milbank would appear to be justified therefore in his criticism that MacIntyre has taken insufficient account of the theological distinctiveness of any Christian exposition of the virtues, of the manner in which the account of the virtues in the work of Thomas Aquinas, for all his indebtedness to Aristotle, is radically reorientated by his perception of the true and theological goal of human life.[9] If Christian virtue has any general persuasiveness it is not, as will be argued in the final chapters of this book, an outcome of any 'natural' and universal accessibility. Christian virtue is distinctive to the Christian story and is only inadequately comprehended without reference to that story. It is not that meekness, mercy and a hope that refuses to be intimidated by the prospect of death are uniquely Christian virtues – it is rather that Christian meekness, Christian mercy and Christian hope are distinct and only *truly* comprehensible in their distinctness as informed by the distinct story to which they are a faithful response.

---

[8] For a discussion of the issues involved in this debate, particularly with respect to the dangers inherent when a commitment to care is displaced by a commitment to cure, see Stanley Hauerwas, *Suffering Presence: Theological Reflections on Medicine, the Mentally Handicapped, and the Church* (Edinburgh: T&T Clark, 1988), pp. 23ff.
[9] See chapter eleven of John Milbank's *Theology and Social Theory*.

The Christian story is the hermeneutical key to the life of the Christian.

But on the other hand, the life of the Christian, as it is lived in continuity with the community of the Church, is the hermeneutical key to the Christian story. It is only through the continuities of Christian living, Christian worship and Christian proclamation that the Christian story is validly accessed and comprehended. Here also it is clear that any episodic interpretation of the Christian life is excluded. No single incident within a Christian's life, when isolated from the continuous narrative of that life, is adequate as a hermeneutic of the gospel. Indeed, no individual Christian life, even in its continuity, is adequate as a hermeneutic of the gospel other than in its connectedness with the continuing narrative of the Church. It is precisely in the continuities of this continuing narrative that the gospel story is interpreted and rendered accessible by the Spirit.

This focus on the continuities of Christian identity, then, is jeopardized by any atomistic account of ethics and of the Christian life. Some comment has already been offered on the possibilities of interpreting Barth's account of the divine command in a punctiliar manner and, notwith-standing the attempts of Nigel Biggar and, more recently, John Webster, to defend Barth at this point, it is difficult entirely to eradicate the impression that his understanding of the command of God militates against continuity, connectedness and coherence.[10] If the command of God is,

---

[10] So, for instance, Nigel Biggar comments: 'In his insistence that our duty in relation to God is always to start again, Barth was not at all denying that our relationship with God is formed by our past – that it has (in one sense) a particular history. Rather, he was asserting that we cannot presume upon the goodness or, at least, the sufficient goodness of what we bring from the past; and that, therefore, we must constantly start again in the sense of regularly laying all that we have accumulated open to divine judgment' (Nigel Biggar, *The Hastening that Waits*, p. 138). However, whether this, or Nigel Biggar's response to Professor Hauerwas's other criticisms is finally sufficient, is open to question. Certainly we can never presume upon past goodness but it is not necessary to undermine historical continuity in order to make this point. The lack of the concrete, which includes the lack of apparent interest in history and development, vitiates Barth's account. See Stanley Hauerwas's comments on Barth in *Character and the Christian Life*, pp. 174ff.

in any sense, unpredictable (and we have already noted that William Stacy Johnson makes much of this unpredictability), and if this command of God is immediate, rather than mediated by the Spirit through the culture and worship of the Church, the consequent life narrative of the Christian may be marked by discontinuity as much as by continuity. It is then, to say the least, difficult for Barth to speak meaningfully of Christian character in the sense of a naming of the continuity of our lives.[11] And where continuity is minimized the possibility and prospect of progress and growth is forfeited: progress towards greater coherence is only meaningful if the narrative of life can be considered as a connected continuity.

However, if the life of the Christian, in its connectedness and in its continuity with the life of the Church, is validly a hermeneutic of the gospel story this, at least in some respects, must qualify any distinction between being and doing, between moral goodness and moral rightness. Christian identity is more than the sum of the Christian's actions and attitudes but, if Christian identity and character is truly a 'naming of continuity' there needs to be some continuity to name. This, though, is to approach the dynamic from the wrong direction: it is not that moral rightness constitutes moral goodness but rather that moral goodness inevitably issues in moral rightness. The Christian's identity is formed by the Holy Spirit through the sacramental worship and life of the Christian community in a manner that issues inevitably in habits – and consequently in attitudes and actions – that cohere with the gospel story.

The element of inevitability here, in the first place, indicates that actions derive from identity – only thus can I claim my actions as my own – what I do is an expression of who I am; were this not to be the case it would be incoherent to claim my actions as my own. This is not to undermine that freedom of human action necessary to

---

[11] 'The moral life does not consist just in making one right decision after another; it is the progressive attempt to widen and clarify our vision of reality' (Stanley Hauerwas, *Vision and Virtue*, p. 44).

responsibility, but it is to distinguish between a free action and an arbitrary action.[12] I can be held responsible for an action if, in performing that action, I am free from external compulsion; if that action is authentically mine. But to claim an action as authentically mine is to deny any arbitrariness; it is to acknowledge that action in its connectedness with the narrative of my life even if the coherence and continuity of any single action may be tentative. In his book *Responsibility and Atonement* Richard Swinburne offers a vigorous rebuttal of 'compatibilism', the notion that moral responsibility implies some form of predictability and therefore is compatible with some form of determinism. He concludes that '... men having moral beliefs, are morally responsible for their actions if and only if they have free will in the traditional sense that their intentional actions are not causally necessitated in all their detail by prior causes'.[13] This seems to imply, however, that I am only truly 'free' if I am free to be other than myself. Persons of 'bad character' would, according to this hypothesis, be absolved of responsibility for their actions simply on the grounds that their actions were not truly 'free' in this absolute sense. But no one possesses such 'freedom'. This rebuttal is an extraordinary prescription for self-alienation. A purely arbitrary action, then, is inconceivable; the very connectedness of my actions implies at least a degree of predictability:[14]

> The very aspects of our experience that seem to support the idea of self-agency, freedom, and responsibility

---

[12] 'If freedom is explicable, it must be explained by giving its causes or reasons; but if there are reasons for an act, then that act can be said to be determined by those reasons. On the other hand, if we reject all suggested reasons or causes of an act, so that there is literally nothing to determine the choice which is made, then that choice becomes totally arbitrary; and an arbitrary choice is of no moral worth whatsoever; it is necessarily random and without criteria' (Keith Ward, *Ethics and Christianity*, p. 223).
[13] Richard Swinburne, *Responsibility and Atonement* (Oxford: Clarendon Press, 1989), p. 63.
[14] The classic discussion of issues of freedom and necessity occurs in Jonathan Edwards's discussion of the *Freedom of the Will* in *Works of Jonathan Edwards*, general ed. Perry Miller, vol. 1, ed. Paul Ramsey (New Haven: Yale University Press, 1957).

are paradoxically impossible if man is an indeterminate cause. The indeterminist must deny that a man's action can be explained wholly in terms of his will, motives, desires, or character, for to do so would imply that man is not entirely a free agent. But if acts are completely spontaneous (having no sufficient condition), then how are we to attribute responsibility to anyone? ... not only does free will not contradict determinism, it is inconceivable without it.[15]

But, in the second place, this element of inevitability implies a coherence of action and identity. Indeed, unless actions and attitudes cohere with claimed identity that claim is vacuous, identity is incoherent. In this respect some aspects of Stanley Hauerwas's own account may be open to question. While, as has been argued consistently throughout these chapters, Christian discipleship cannot be reduced to a matter of obedience to rules, if Christian discipleship is identified through its continuities, both internal and external, community rules cannot be categorically excluded: what are rules, after all, other than indicators of continuities? It is this aspect of Hauerwas's work that Jean Porter finds least acceptable:

> We cannot form concepts of particular virtues without some idea of the kinds of actions that correspond to those virtues, even though it is also true that a virtue cannot adequately be understood only as the tendency or capacity to perform a certain kind of action.[16]

---

[15] Stanley Hauerwas, *Character and the Christian Life*, pp. 19f.

[16] Jean Porter, *The Recovery of Virtue: The Relevance of Aquinas for Christian Ethics* (London: SPCK, 1990), p. 105. Similarly, Alasdair MacIntyre notes that, though there is little mention of rules in Aristotle's *Ethics*, it is 'a crucial part of Aristotle's view that certain types of action are absolutely prohibited or enjoined irrespective of circumstances or consequences ... an account of the virtues while an essential part of an account of the moral life... could never be complete in itself. ... Aristotle ... recognizes that his account of the virtues has to be supplemented by some account, even a brief one, of those types of action which are absolutely prohibited' (Alasdair MacIntyre, *After Virtue*, pp. 150ff.); cf. Alasdair MacIntyre, *Whose Justice? Which Rationality?*, p. ix.

If the command of God, which itself is continuous with the true humanity of Christ, is mediated by the Spirit through the continuities of the life and worship of the Church, this command will inevitably issue in the recognition that certain attitudes and actions are continuous and coherent and that certain attitudes and actions are discontinuous, incoherent and, therefore, prohibited. A rule, in this sense, is merely an acknowledgement of continuity and coherence. Such recognition does not undermine the freedom of God, it rather, in Barth's own terms (and in response to any atomistic interpretation of his account), acknowledges his freedom to be genuinely *his*; the freedom to be himself; the freedom to be true to himself and not untrue; the freedom to be coherent rather than incoherent. My identity as a Christian is more than the sum of my actions and attitudes, it is an interpretation of the continuity and coherence of those actions and attitudes, but my actions and attitudes must, at least in their connectedness, admit to such an interpretation. If my actions and attitudes are discontinuous and incoherent with my claimed identity, and with the continuities of Christian identity as recognized within the Christian community, my claimed identity is insubstantial, or, at least, insubstantiable. Moral goodness is more than the sum of morally right actions but, since moral goodness inevitably expresses itself in morally right actions it is incoherent without them.

This is not, however, to reduce an ethic of character to an ethic of rules. I would hope that, by this stage, such a disclaimer was unnecessary – Christian identity is more than the sum of Christian action. But it is to affirm that an ethic of character is not necessarily exclusive of rules so long as those rules are acknowledged as provisional and secondary (and we must continually be vigilant lest the provisional and secondary come to be perceived as the absolute and primary). To admit the possibility (and provisional appropriateness) of community rules is merely to recognize the necessary continuities of the Church's narrative in coherence with the gospel story. Rules in this sense are merely the naming of those obligations recognized by the members of the community of the Church to

one another and to society as a whole; obligations that are
consequent on the manner in which the members of the
community have come to view one another and the world
in the light of the gospel. To recognize such obligations is
not to retreat into legalism; it is to confess that the gospel
takes form as command in the context of its form as mercy;
it affirms us in accordance with God's grace but by that
same grace it truly changes us. If Christian freedom, as the
freedom to be coherent as distinct from any incoherent
arbitrariness, admits an element of predictability then
Christian action, as the outworking of that determinate
freedom, may similarly be marked by predictability and
consistency. The concern of the Church is for that
coherence which derives from faithful indwelling.[17]

But this raises the question of the manner in which
apparently inconsistent actions are to be viewed: if
character is a 'naming of continuity' does any single
discontinuous act undermine character?

The relatedness within the *Summa* between virtue and
habit would suggest that character is not dissolved by any
single incoherent act: '... just as habit is not engendered by
one act, so neither is it destroyed by one act'. But Thomas
goes on to say that '... it is possible for some virtues to be
destroyed by one sinful act ... every mortal sin is contrary
to charity ...'.[18] Throughout his account, Thomas
maintains this distinction between venial sin and mortal
sin, defining the latter as any action 'against charity'.
Consequently, for instance, every act of injustice
constitutes a mortal sin since

> ... every injury inflicted on another person is of itself
> contrary to charity, which moves us to will the good of
> another. And so since injustice always consists in an

---

[17] 'What I mean by casuistry, then, is not just the attempt to adjudicate
difficult cases of conscience within a system of moral principles, but is the
process by which a tradition tests whether its practices are consistent (that
is, truthful) or inconsistent in the light of its basic habits and convictions
or whether these convictions require new practices and behaviour'
(Stanley Hauerwas, *The Peaceable Kingdom*, p. 120).
[18] *ST* I–II 71 4.

injury inflicted on another person, it is evident that to do an injustice is a mortal sin according to its genus.[19]

This distinction between venial and mortal sin, which has remained generally characteristic of Roman Catholic moral theology, appears deficient in Protestant eyes in two respects: on the one hand it appears to minimize the seriousness of sin by discounting the seriousness of venial sin; on the other hand it appears to minimize grace by assuming that any single mortal sin overwhelms it.[20] In practice the difficulties of the distinction have further been compounded by the expansion of the category of mortal sin to the point that the category of venial sin virtually disappears. This may have the merit of heightening the Christian's continual dependence upon mercy but it has the corresponding demerit of undermining the continuity of the Christian's identity, reducing it in practice to an identity that seems continually to be being lost and then regained through the sacrament of penance.

In these respects the development of the more recent notion of a 'fundamental option', as it has been expressed by writers such as Karl Rahner and Joseph Fuchs, may offer a more helpful analysis since it seems to maintain the continuity of Christian identity without necessarily minimizing the seriousness of sin or the Christian's continual dependence upon mercy.[21] Through the connectedness of a Christian's life, through the continuity of their indwelling the gospel story through the life and worship of the Church, their 'fundamental option', the foundational

---

[19] *ST* II–II 59 4.

[20] The similarities between this account and that implied by John Wesley's account of Christian Perfection, however, have already been noted.

[21] Karl Rahner, *Theological Investigations* 17: *Jesus, Man, and the Church*, trans. Margaret Kohl (London: Darton, Longman & Todd, 1981), pp. 100ff. Joseph Fuchs in *Christian Morality: The Word Becomes Flesh*, trans. Brian McNeil (Washington: Georgetown University Press, 1987) pp. 30ff. describes the emergence of this concept of a 'fundamental option' at the 1983 Bishops' Synod in Rome. However, in *Personal Responsibility and Christian Morality*, trans. William Cleves and others (Washington: Georgetown University Press, 1983) pp. 54ff. he speaks rather of 'Christian Intentionality'.

orientation of their life, can be discerned. They may certainly act, speak or think in ways that are inconsistent with this 'fundamental option'; when they do so they need to confess such and seek renewed mercy. Yet the very fact that such actions, words or thoughts can be deemed 'inconsistent' suggests that a 'fundamental option' remains. Only when inconsistency becomes consistent, when a habit of virtue is displaced by a habit of vice, when the *continuity* of a person's life can no longer be deemed to be coherent with the gospel story, only then is Christian identity destroyed.

This analysis not only appears to offer possibilities of a more continuous account of Christian identity, it also offers possibilities of further rapprochement between Roman Catholic and Protestant theology by acknowledging that a continuous dependence upon mercy, far from undermining Christian identity, actually establishes it. To live in coherence with the gospel story is precisely to live in continuing dependence upon mercy, just as it is also to live in continuing expectation that, through the indwelling of the Spirit, deeper coherence with the character of Christ will ensue. The gospel story interprets the life of the Christian in terms of a dependence upon mercy and a growth in grace in coherence with the *true* humanity of Christ. Similarly, the life of the Christian, as in its connectedness it exhibits a dependence upon mercy and a growth in grace, is a rendering and interpretation of the gospel story. Christian identity, as the 'naming of the continuity' of the Christian's life, is established through indwelling, the indwelling of the Christian by the Spirit which is effected through the Christian's indwelling of the gospel story as it is rendered in the life and worship of the Church. This active indwelling, then, identifies the Christian as one who, while remaining dependent upon mercy, can grow in increasing coherence with the character of Christ through the indwelling of the Spirit. But it cannot be stressed too strongly that this coherence which is the continuity of the Christian's identity is the outcome of indwelling – the indwelling of the Christian by the Spirit and the indwelling of the gospel story by the Christian, through participation in the life and worship of the Church, by means of which this indwelling of the Spirit is actualized.

I must acknowledge my indebtedness, however, to Stephen Holmes, a former student and now a colleague, for drawing my attention to the danger of a degree of unconvincing neatness at this point. In the first place the stories of Church history should alert us to the sheer variety of forms that true saintliness can assume, and therefore to the surprising – and in this sense unpredictable – possibilities of authentic coherence. But more negatively, few of us attain this degree of integration; our lives retain a degree of fragmentation notwithstanding our fundamental commitment to live in coherence with the gospel. We have 'blind spots' and, by definition, we are blind to them. We are nonetheless very good at recognizing the 'blind spots' of others; our hearing of the stories of church history is marked with questions such as how, for instance, Jonathan Edwards could continue to keep a slave. Perhaps future generations will be similarly troubled by the ease with which so many of us tolerate violence and pursue material wealth.

The decisive question here, then, is not whether or not we have blind spots, whether or not some aspects of our lives exhibit a lack of integration. The decisive question is how we respond when our attention is drawn to such blind spots; how we respond when we ourselves become convinced of the incoherence of certain attitudes, habits or actions: are our lives orientated by a fundamental desire for coherence, a fundamental commitment to live as disciples of Christ? And in all this we do not live and act as isolated individuals: coherence is pursued within the community of the Church; we indwell the gospel coherently through our coherent indwelling of the life and worship of the Christian community; no one of us is the sole and independent arbiter of what is and what is not coherent with the gospel story; we are part of the Church catholic, the communion of the saints throughout the ages.

Christian identity, then, is not forfeited through sin when that sin is confessed and when mercy is sought, on the contrary, such confession and such seeking of mercy are fundamental to Christian identity. Christian identity is forfeited when sin is no longer acknowledged as sin, when it is not confessed as such, when mercy is not sought. That is to say, Christian identity is forfeited when some rival defining story comes to be indwelt. Such rival stories are ubiquitous – stories that beguile me to define my life other than in relation to the life, death and resurrection of Jesus; stories that beguile me to define my life other than by my constant dependence upon mercy and grace; stories that beguile me to accept myself as defined within the boundaries of my own, discrete story rather than in relation to the gospel story as narrated in the life of the Church.[22]

Any attempt to define my identity by some other means, whether by reference to genetics, to race, to sex, to developmental factors, to education, to wealth, or even to disability, is to repudiate the gospel story as the definitive narrative of my identity.[23] This is not, of course, to deny the particularities of my existence, my genetic makeup, my ethnicity, my sex, my background, my abilities and disabilities; but it is to deny that these factors are either foundational or determinative. Rather the particularities of my life's narrative form the conditions in which my committed indwelling of the gospel takes place. Given these particularities I seek not to be determined by them but rather, within the context and conditions they provide, to be determined by my indwelling of the gospel story through the indwelling of the Spirit. To permit any of these particularities to be determinative for my identity would be to deny the gospel story as the defining narrative of my life. Indeed, were the Church to allow any such factor to determine its view of any individual it would itself, thereby, effectively deny the gospel as its determining narrative; it would apostasize.[24]

---

[22] Stanley Hauerwas speaks of modern tendencies to see the ethical goal as self-acceptance rather than as the good as 'the triumph of the therapeutic over the moral' (Stanley Hauerwas, *Vision and Virtue*, p. 105).

[23] For an excellent discussion of this issue in relation to feminism see Linda Woodhead, 'Spiritualising the Sacred: A Critique of Feminist Theology' in *Modern Theology* 13 (1997), pp. 191–212.

[24] That the Church has committed and does commit such apostasy in respect of each of these particulars is, regrettably, undeniable. The Church too is only truly the Church when it also lives in confession and in hopeful expectation of change.

That to seek to live in coherence with the gospel under such conditions in some respects may be difficult, painful, or even apparently contradictory, is undeniable, but it is the irreducible demand of discipleship. I seek to live dependently rather than independently, in confession of my sin rather than in denial of it, in hopeful expectation of change of that which undermines my coherence with the gospel rather than in self-satisfied acceptance of what has been.

Perhaps the most sensitive manifestation of particularity for the contemporary Church is not the issue of sex or gender but rather the issue of sexuality or sexual orientation. In another context I have discussed the distinctive manner in which sexual orientation may be deemed to be 'given' and the apparent dissonance of homosexuality in the light of Scripture's account of creation and Paul's account of the outcomes of sinfulness in Romans chapter one.[25] I concur that other passages of Scripture seeming to condemn homosexual practice may have particular (and therefore restricted) reference but the account of the creation of humankind as male and female, together with every positive account of human sexuality in Scripture, suggests that sexual intercourse is positively and exclusively intended for the union of man and woman in marriage; that chastity and marriage are the only valid 'expressions' of human sexuality coherent with the gospel narrative.[26] The question for the homosexual, then, as for every other Christian disciple, is whether the gospel story, rather than this 'given' particularity, is to be determinative for identity. Not for a moment should we belittle the pain and cost consequent to such a commitment but neither may we reduce or qualify that commitment. Like every other Christian disciple, the homosexual is called, in the power of the Spirit, to live coherently with the gospel story

[25] John Colwell, 'Christ, Creation and Human Sexuality' in *The Way Forward? Christian Voices on Homosexuality and the Church*, ed. Timothy Bradshaw (London: Hodder & Stoughton, 1997), pp. 88–98.
[26] For a thorough treatment of the biblical texts see Richard B. Hays, *The Moral Vision of the New Testament*, pp. 379ff.; also Anthony Thisleton, 'Can Hermeneutics Ease the Deadlock?' in *The Way Forward? Christian Voices on Homosexuality and the Church*, pp. 145–96.

by indwelling that story through the life, worship *and discipline* of the Church; to find their identity in the true humanity of Christ rather than in any alternative particular; to live in continuous dependence upon mercy and grace. For the homosexual to act inconsistently is no more, but also no less, an issue of mercy and grace than is any other act of inconsistency by any other Christian disciple. Such inconsistencies, inasmuch as they remain *inconsistencies* in relation to the continuities of a person's life, do not themselves dissolve that person's Christian identity. Only when such acts can no longer be deemed inconsistencies, only when the *continuity* of a person's life has become discontinuous with the gospel narrative, does a claimed Christian identity become incoherent. Moreover, the Church similarly is not permitted to define the homosexual in terms of sexual orientation but, as in respect to every other man or woman, of whatever race or background, exclusively as they are defined by the gospel.

Christian identity, then, is a 'naming of continuity' in coherence with the narrative of the gospel. It is the gospel story, as rendered in the sacramental life and worship of the Church, that 'names this continuity' as Christian and thus establishes identity. Correspondingly, it is the indwelling of the gospel story through participation in the sacramental life and worship of the Church, as the means of the Spirit's presence and influence, that issues in this distinctive continuity. The gospel story, therefore, defines the life of the Christian and the life of the Church, while the life of the Church and the life of the Christian is, correspondingly, a retelling and reinterpreting of that gospel story. The world has no access to the gospel story other than as it is narrated in the life, worship and proclamation of the Church. The church is the living hermeneut of the gospel. By its commitment to live faithfully, hopefully, lovingly and thankfully – even though this commitment and its outworking may remain frail and imperfect – it reminds the world of its true foundation and goal. Through its service and being as witness, the Church is a rendering of the gospel to the world. And it is to the possibilities of this rendering being effective and persuasive that we must now turn.

Part Four

UNIVERSALITY AND PARTICULARITY

10
The Priority of the Future

At one point in his discussion of the doctrine of creation Colin Gunton opines that, perhaps throughout the history of Western theology, no writer has expressed the relationship between creation and redemption as effectively as Irenaeus of Lyons.[1] This may seem a rather sweeping assertion but it is supported throughout Professor Gunton's analysis by the observation that, from Augustine onwards, the notion of eternal forms as perceived by God tended to displace the Son and the Spirit as the means through which creation is mediated, effectively limiting the agency of the Son and the Spirit to the work of redemption and, as a consequence, dissolving the continuity of redemption and creation in a manner that inevitably introduces some form of dualism.[2]

It was principally in response to gnostic forms of dualism that Irenaeus was writing and this may underlie the thoroughness with which he asserts the continuity of creation and redemption. The Son and the Spirit, who are the agents or 'hands' of God in redemption, are similarly

[1] 'The importance of Irenaeus in all this is considerable, for his straightforwardly Trinitarian construction of the act of divine creation, in some contrast as it is to the later more sophisticated but also more Platonizing approaches, provides not the answers so much as the essential clues for the reshaping of the tradition that is necessary alike for Christian theology and for culture, oppressed as they both are by varieties of gnosticism' (Colin E. Gunton, *The One, The Three and the Many*, p. 2); this argument is repeated by the author in an article on 'The doctrine of creation' in *The Cambridge Companion to Christian Doctrine*, ed. Colin E. Gunton (Cambridge: Cambridge University Press, 1997), pp. 141–57, and again in Colin E. Gunton, *The Triune Creator: A Historical and Systematic Study* (Edinburgh: Edinburgh University Press, 1998).

[2] 'At the fountainhead of the Western treatment of creation is Augustine's subtly altered account of the matter … in his theology, the mediation by Christ and the Spirit, as well as the teleological directedness of the creation, play too limited a role, a first effect is that the link, so beautifully maintained in Irenaeus between creation and redemption, becomes weakened to the point of disappearing, so that it is rarely adequately treated in Western theology after this time' (Colin E. Gunton, *The One, The Three and the Many*, pp. 120f.).

the agents or 'hands' of God in creation.[3] The purpose of God in redemption is continuous with the purpose of God in creation; the work of God in creation is restored and completed in the work of redemption.[4] Any supposed tension between grace and nature consequently is repudiated: there is no 'grace-less' nature; nature itself is 'graced'.[5]

If this thoroughly Trinitarian expression of the doctrine of creation militates against any discontinuity between creation and redemption it similarly would seem to exclude the possibility of any 'unmediated' knowledge of creation. If the structures and entities of creation are mediated through impersonal eternal forms perceived by God then the possibility of some unmediated knowledge of the structures and entities of creation is admitted. If, however, the structures and entities of creation are personally mediated through the Son and the Spirit, any impersonal, immediate or independent knowledge of those structures and entities would appear to be excluded. The personally mediated nature of creation and of every created reality implies that knowledge of creation itself or of any reality within creation must similarly be mediated personally. Not just a knowledge of redemption, then, but knowledge of anything whatsoever is a gift; it is mediated by the Spirit through the Son;[6] to know any reality is, in some sense, to participate in the divine knowledge of that reality; there is no possibility

---

[3] 'For with Him were always present the Word and Wisdom, the Son and the Spirit, by whom and in whom, freely and spontaneously, He made all things. . . .': Irenaeus, *Against Heresies* in *The Ante-Nicene Fathers*, vol. 1, ed. Alexander Roberts, James Donaldson and A. Cleveland Coxe (Grand Rapids: Eerdmans, 1987), IV xx 1.

[4] Irenaeus, *Against Heresies* IV xxxvii, xxxviii. For an excellent appraisal of Irenaeus' account see Douglas Farrow, 'St. Irenaeus of Lyons: The Church and the World' in *Pro Ecclesia* IV 3 (1995), pp. 333–55.

[5] Note here Colin Gunton's comment: 'One of the reasons Aquinas gives for denying the speculation that the incarnation would have happened even if there had been no sin is that creation is *naturally* ordered to God' (Colin E. Gunton, *The Triune Creator*, p. 121).

[6] 'If there is any revelation in the midst of time, it will be because the Spirit, the agent of eschatological completeness and the one who perfects the creation, enables an anticipation to take place: so mediates revelation that we may say that the mysteries of God are made known in our time' (Colin E. Gunton, *A Brief Theology of Revelation*, p. 120.)

of any independent or immediate knowledge of any reality simply because there is no possibility of the existence of any independent or immediate reality.

Not only as an outcome of these epistemological implications but, more directly, as an implication of this dynamic and teleological understanding of creation, Irenaeus' account would seem to qualify the possibility of any naturally discernible natural law. The notion of natural law, or of any appeal to that which is self-evident, assumes some form of correlation between what is and what ought to be. This 'naturalistic fallacy', that obligation can be inferred from mere existence, was disputed by David Hume, but it is more radically undermined by this recognition that creation is not now, nor ever has been, fully perfected. Unlike Hume, Irenaeus is certainly affirming that creation has a goal – this is the very essence of his account – but his denial that creation reaches this goal other than through redemption repudiates the possibility of this goal being inferred from creation's mere existence. The goal of creation, together with the obligations consequent to that goal, is disclosed in the work of redemption through the agency of the Son and the Spirit. As the authentic goal of creation it is certainly coherent with creation's present existence but it is not discernible simply from creation's present existence. Irenaeus' account, then, would seem to prohibit the idealizing of the present; it is realistic in respect of creation's present imperfections; it militates against the confusion of what is with what ought to be; rather, what ought to be is informed by the future; what ought to be is an anticipation of what will be. The knowability of this goal of creation, together with the obligations consequent to that goal is dependent upon the agency of the Son and the Spirit.

This dynamic of knowing has been alluded to earlier in this book and will inform the discussion of persuasiveness in chapters eleven and twelve. The concern of this present chapter is rather with these 'realistic' implications of Irenaeus' teleological and explicitly Trinitarian exposition of the relatedness of creation and redemption.

It is in this respect that Irenaeus has most frequently been

misrepresented or misunderstood. His notion of 'recapitulation' (ἀνακεφαλαίωσις) is not intended to imply that
redemption simply restores creation and humankind to an
original and perfect state, as if the initial state of creation and
of humankind was itself fully 'perfect'; as if creation were
intended as some static 'given': '*Recapitulation involves a
reversal that takes us ahead again.*'[7] Creation itself, in its very
inception, is orientated to a goal, precisely that goal which is
fulfilled in redemption;[8] creation is not a static, it is a determinate process;[9] neither creation nor humankind was ever
fully perfect, perfection and fulfilment is rather the goal
of creation, a goal now attained only through the work of
redemption, a goal now to be accomplished in the context
of the world's fallenness:[10]

[7]   Douglas Farrow, 'St. Irenaeus of Lyons: The Church and the World', p.
349.

[8]   Notwithstanding the undoubted deficiencies of their contributions, it
is the teleological account of humanity in Augustine's *De Trinitate* and
Civitas Dei, and more especially in Thomas's *Summa Theologica*, that
encourages alternative readings of these works and, to some degree,
mitigates the criticisms of writers such as Prof. Gunton.

[9]   Throughout his Didsbury Lectures Colin Gunton speaks of creation as
a 'project': Colin Gunton, *Christ and Creation: The Didsbury Lectures 1990*
(Carlisle: Paternoster Press, 1992).

[10]   'Irenaeus does indeed confess ... the imperfection of creation, an
imperfection that makes the fall possible, not inevitable. The "imperfection" is this: The love for God which is the life of man cannot emerge
ex nihilo in full bloom; it requires to grow with experience. But that in turn
is what makes the fall, however unsurprising, such a devastating affair. In
the fall man is "turned backwards." He does not grow up in the love of
God as he is intended to. The course of his time, his so-called progress, is
set in the wrong direction' (Douglas Farrow, 'St. Irenaeus of Lyons: The
Church and the World', p. 348). Graham McFarlane draws attention to a
similar (though not identical) account in the writings of Edward Irving:
'Adam, then, is presented as perfect, but incomplete. Creation cannot
have been created perfect in light of both its subsequent demise and the
appearance of Christ. Irving argues, "if the creation had been perfect and
sufficient while yet the Christ was unconstituted, then why should there
be a Christ at all? There cannot be two perfections, there cannot be two
unchangeables, otherwise there were two gods." ': Graham McFarlane,
*Christ and the Spirit: The Doctrine of the Incarnation According to Edward
Irving* (Carlisle: Paternoster Press, 1996) pp. 98f. quoting from *The Collected
Writings of Edward Irving in Five Volumes*, vol. 5, ed. G. Carlyle (London:
Alexander Strahan, 1864) p. 98. Similarly, 'The creation, all good though it
was, is not the accomplishment but only the beginning of God's purpose'
(*The Morning Watch*, vol. V, 7 (1833) p. 63, quoted in Graham McFarlane,
p. 99).

The creation is, we might say, perfect in that it is destined for perfection. That is, it is relatively perfect: created for an eschatological perfecting.[11]

It is not, then, that Christ is made in the likeness of Adam; it is rather that Adam was created in the likeness of Christ.[12] Instead of progressing towards that goal in dependence upon the Spirit, humankind in Adam has fallen away from that goal with cosmic consequences; creation itself, which though created for perfection was never perfected, is now corrupted. The work of redemption, therefore, is not intended merely to restore creation and humankind to that initial but unperfected state by undoing this corruption and its effects; the work of redemption rather is intended both to undo this corruption *and* to bring creation and humankind to that perfection that was originally intended. There is not now, nor has there ever been, a perfected state of creation, nor indeed has there ever been a perfected humanity other than in the *true* humanity of Jesus – and his history, together with the history of the cosmos, is, as yet, unfinished; his *parousia* has not yet occurred; the end of history, which comprises the final perfecting of humanity and of all creation, has yet to take place. As the theme of Christian hope, this final perfecting of creation, which is synonymous with the future of Jesus Christ, is certain and not uncertain – the *true* humanity of Christ has occurred in the midst of human history – but it remains the theme of Christian hope, it is not yet an immediate reality of Christian experience:

> We know that the whole creation has been groaning as in the pains of childbirth right up to the present time. Not only so, but we ourselves, who have the firstfruits of the Spirit, groan inwardly as we wait eagerly for our

---

[11] Colin E. Gunton, *The Triune Creator*, p. 55.
[12] '... it was said that man was created after the image of God, but it was not [actually] shown; for the Word was as yet invisible, after whose image man was created' (Irenaeus, *Against Heresies* V xvi 2). Hence Rom. 5.14: ὅς ἐστιν τύπος τοῦ μέλλοντος. The *NIV* translation of τύπος as 'pattern' here seems especially lame.

adoption, the redemption of our bodies. For in this hope we were saved. But hope that is seen is no hope at all. Who hopes for what one already has? But if we hope for what we do not yet have, we wait for it patiently. (Romans 8.22ff.)

The ethical significance of this perception of creation and redemption, then, is simply a matter of practical realism; it is the refusal to ground any form of hope for creation other than in the redemption of the world by our Lord Jesus Christ. In distinction to every form of Nietzschean Nihilism, but similarly in distinction to every form of Hegelian Idealism, the Christian lives in hope. Modernistic optimism, that 'evolutionism' which clings to the prospect that the world and humanity is 'naturally' and independently 'getting better', has proved remarkably resilient through the course of a century that has had more than its share of unimaginable cruelty and disaster. Stanley Hauerwas characterizes this groundless optimism as 'hope without truth' and it is hardly surprising that such unrealistic and unsubstantiated confidence so readily collapses into negativity and despair.[13] Christian hope, by contrast is grounded in the story of Jesus, a story that has yet to reach its conclusion and which, as itself the significance of creation, exposes the unperfected and uncompleted character of creation. Thus grounded, a hope that is authentically Christian is not dashed by tragedy or penultimate disappointment; it is a response to the betrayal, suffering and crucifixion of Jesus; it expects disappointment but it knows that disappointment is not the final word; rather it looks beyond tragedy 'for the resurrection of the dead, and the life of the world to come'.

To parody this realistic hope as an other-worldly opiate is entirely to misconstrue it: a misrepresentation all the more ironic in view of the hopelessness that has issued from the modernist alternatives that perpetrate the parody.

---

[13] 'Optimism – hope without truth – is not sufficient for dealing with the pretentious powers that determine a person's existence in the world' (Stanley Hauerwas, *Christian Existence Today*, p. 211).

That true Christian hope can cope with the tragic need not imply that it collaborates with the tragic or merely acquiesces to it: as a response to the narrative of Jesus it can challenge and confront the tragic in the confidence that the tragic can never be final. The story of Jesus, as it is narrated in the Gospels and as it has traditionally been heard within the Church, does not admit to being interpreted simply in terms of an acquiescence to evil. Jesus confronts sickness, disease and death, he challenges the hypocrisy of the Pharisees, he purges the Temple, he warns the complacent of a coming judgement, only when he himself is threatened by evil does he passively submit to a torturous death, trusting in 'the one who could save him from death' (Heb. 5.7). To interpret the story of Jesus in terms of a passive acquiescence to evil is to fail to listen to the story in its context and in its entirety; it is to focus exclusively upon a misconstruction of Christ's passion without reference to the sustained confrontation with evil on behalf of others that preceded it and that constitutes its underlying significance. Christian hope, as a response to the story of Jesus, can never issue in a passive acquiescence to evil but rather should issue in a proactive confrontation with evil that, refusing to be intimidated by that evil, endures hopefully even through death itself.

But this interpretation of Christian hope similarly militates against any *simplistic* notion of the Church as an anticipation of the future. The Christian community may have 'tasted ... the powers of the coming age', but we have only 'tasted' them (Heb. 6.5); we may have been sealed with the Spirit as a 'deposit guaranteeing our inheritance' but that inheritance lies in the future (Eph. 1.13f.); creation is still waiting 'for the children of God to be revealed' (Rom. 8.19); the Church has not yet been brought to its final perfection; creation has not yet reached its goal; 'the kingdom of the world' has not yet become 'the kingdom of our Lord and of his Christ' (Rev. 11.15). The Church, then, can only anticipate the future in a strictly qualified sense. Like its Lord, it is not 'of the world' and must live in a manner that is true to its future identity – what ought to be is an anticipation of what will be – but like its Lord it has been 'sent ... into the world', the world as it presently is, not as it will be (John 17.16ff.). For the Church to seek to withdraw from the world, or to seek to live in the world as if the future were already fully present, would be as 'untruthful' as any repudiation of its true, but future, identity. To live in coherence with the gospel story is not only to live in response to the *true* humanity of Jesus but is also to live in response to the *realities* in which that true humanity occurred. The Church thus lives incoherently if it pretends that the world, and the Church itself within it, has already attained its goal, as if evil had already been overcome, as if death had already been finally destroyed, as if the conditions consequent upon creation's fallenness no longer pertained. The Church, then, is called to anticipate the future in a manner appropriate to the conditions of creation's present fallenness – and herein lies the most profound dilemma for the Church's truthfulness and faithfulness.

In an impassioned plea for vegetarianism as a 'faithful response' to the gospel, Stanley Hauerwas argues that the 'burden of proof' rests with those Christians who continue to eat meat or who, with Barth, consider vegetarianism to constitute a 'wanton anticipation' of the 'kingdom of God':

> This can be understood in much the same way that just war theory reflection works in the Christian community: presupposing that non-violence is the fundamental stance of Christians. Christian just war theory is most appropriately understood as a theory of exceptions, exceptions for allowing Christians to engage in limited forms of violence in order to protect the neighbor. Analogously, those Christians who cannot abstain entirely from eating animals need to develop similar criteria for 'just' meat-eating.[14]

One cannot but question whether, both in relation to meat-eating and in relation to just war theory, Professor Hauerwas has given sufficient consideration to the actual

[14] Stanley Hauerwas, *In Good Company*, p. 197.

THE PRIORITY OF THE FUTURE

nature of Barth's objection: the distinction between them would seem to lie precisely in the manner in which each conceives the future to be anticipated in the present. And, in this respect, the 'burden of proof' would seem to rest rather with Professor Hauerwas and those who, with him, would urge a total disavowal of meat-eating or of coercive restraint. It is not easy to see how a commitment to vegetarianism derives from a faithful reading of Scripture. It is one thing to concede that all meat-eating is a provisional concession within the context of the world's fallenness – this would seem to be the outcome of any straightforward reading of the narrative of Genesis – and that, consequently, it *may* have no place within that new creation which issues from the fulfilment of redemption (though such a conclusion is not without its difficulties: are we to infer that the development of all carnivores, of cats, of dogs, of hawks, was the outcome of a 'wrong' turning in evolution; that there will be no carnivores *of any sort* in the new creation?). But it is another thing altogether to conclude that, in this respect, the Church should anticipate the future by repudiating this provisional concession: there would seem to be nothing in the narrative of the gospel or in the Church's traditional reading of that narrative that would lead to such a conclusion. The Church is called to anticipate the future in this present, in a context where this provisional concession still pertains. Indeed, that same process which might lead us to repudiate meat-eating ought similarly to lead us to repudiate clothing, since this too, according to the Genesis narrative, is a provisional concession to human fallenness.

Now all this, to a degree, is tongue-in-cheek: I write as a cheerful carnivore with an axe to grind (or, at least, a knife to sharpen). I must, therefore, admit my bias and concede that, in our present context, vegetarianism may well be the appropriate ethical response to the appalling atrocities of factory farming. Indeed, to repudiate such systematized cruelty could well derive from a faithful indwelling of the gospel. I certainly do not intend to 'invalidate' this response but I do want to question where the burden of proof might lie. If vegetarianism issues from a valid indwelling of the gospel it does so, not because the Church is called to repudiate this provisional concession of meat-eating in anticipation of the future, but rather because the Church is called to repudiate a present and particular corruption of that concession. If truthful and faithful living issues from the Church's reading and indwelling of the gospel story, then the burden of proof concerning meat-eating lies with Professor Hauerwas.

In similar fashion, the development of just war theory represents the Church's (admittedly provisional and fallible) attempt to live both truthfully and realistically, in anticipation of the future within the context of creation's continued fallenness. Here too, and for similar reasons, the burden of proof would seem to lie with those who, like Stanley Hauerwas and Richard Hays, would urge pacifism as the only valid indwelling of the gospel. Too easily those who would align themselves with the just war tradition are caricatured as approving of violence or as uncommitted to peaceableness. In contrast Professor Hauerwas, in the previous quotation, rightly identifies just war theory as 'a theory of exceptions'. Far from condoning violence or colluding with violence, the just war tradition, rightly understood, seeks to limit violence as a tragic and provisional exception, necessitated by the fallenness of this present context. Indeed, while I must admit to being no historian, I find it difficult to think of any national or international conflict that has wholly satisfied the conditions of just war theory and which, therefore, could be condoned by the Church. This, of course, exposes the underlying difficulty of the theory itself: its proponents too easily become corrupted by the violence of human fallenness to which the theory is a concession; concerns for power and for self-interest infiltrate concerns for justice and the strict conditions of the theory are distorted. Nonetheless, as was noted earlier in this book, it was out of an indwelling of this tradition that Bishop George Bell opposed the Allied policy of blanket bombing during the last 'World War'. No form of attack on a civilian population can be condoned with reference to just war theory and it is difficult to see how, with modern weapons of mass destruction, such attacks could be precluded. Goals such as 'punishing Saddam Hussein' or 'dissuading Serbia' simply are invalid goals according to just war theory; indeed, just war theory can apply only to action that is specifically defensive (pre-emptive action against a perceived threat strains the meaning of 'defensive'). This is without raising questions of appropriate and valid authority for action – questions that now need to be addressed in an international context.

However, the fact that just war theory can be, and has been, interpreted in a self-interested and self-justifying manner, that a response to fallenness can itself be distorted by that fallenness, does not of itself invalidate this attempt by the Church to live truthfully in the context of creation's fallenness. Within the narrative of the Old Testament, forceful restraint in response to human violence is as much a provisional concession to creation's fallenness as is meat-eating. Nor is there anything in the New Testament to suggest that this concession has been withdrawn: notwithstanding the mitigating protests of Professor Hays and others, Jesus forcefully clears the Temple. Certainly he passively submits to his own death but, as far as I am aware, no advocate of the Church's tradition of just war theory has ever sought to justify *self*-defence. As I hope is clear, this implies no comprehensive condoning of violent coercion – Stanley Hauerwas is right to remind us of how easily the demands of justice and the desire for power become confused – and, as I will argue in the final chapter of this book, for the Church to seek to anticipate the future kingdom *through* coercion is for the Church to apostasize,[15] but there appear to be no grounds within the New Testament, or within the Church's traditional reading of the New Testament, for the repudiation of every form of coercive restraint in response to human sinfulness, for the abandonment of societal laws, or – contrary to the opinion of some Anabaptist writers – for the withdrawal of the

---

[15] 'A theological justification of revolution is verbal posturing that can only mire the church deeper in the illusion that it can be the church of the poor while continuing to lust after the power of this world' (Stanley Hauerwas, *Vision and Virtue*, p. 7).

Christian community from the magistracy or from other aspects of this process of legal restraint. Christ's *true* humanity occurred in *real* humanity. The Church is called to anticipate the future but in a manner that does not ignore or negate the realities of the present, the realities of creation's continuing fallenness, the realities of the violence of human sinfulness. The Church's traditional reading of the narrative of Scripture would suggest that the burden of proof lies with those who would argue otherwise.

It is at this point that the arguments of Stanley Hauerwas are most vulnerable. I hope that, in the course of this study, I have adequately acknowledged my own indebtedness to Professor Hauerwas and the degree to which my own thinking has been shaped in response to his insights as much as in response to the insights of any Christian thinker, past or present. Nonetheless, it is in this final section of this book that I am attempting to frame some critical responses to certain key aspects of his contribution. Stanley Hauerwas's appreciation of the indispensability of the Church as the community in which the gospel is not only heard and proclaimed, but also indwelt and lived, has already been noted. Scripture must be rescued from the tyranny and distortion of individual interpretation; its message is only truly heard within the continuities of the Christian tradition and of the living community of faith.[16] Yet such is Professor Hauerwas's commitment to non-violence that, in other contexts, he opines that only through a commitment to non-violence will the reader of Scripture recognize that Scripture teaches non-violence; that the *non*-non-violent reader will be incapable of hearing Scripture.[17] So then, Scripture can

---

[16] The cruciality of hearing Scripture in the context of the Church is fundamental to Irenaeus' response to the Gnostics: 'Where, therefore, the gifts of the Lord have been placed, there it behoves us to learn the truth. ...' Irenaeus, *Against Heresies* IV xxvi 5. For an excellent summary of Irenaeus' arguments see Robert W. Jenson, 'Hermeneutics and the Life of the Church' in *Reclaiming the Bible for the Church*, ed. Carl E. Braaten and Robert W. Jenson (Edinburgh: T&T Clark, 1995), pp. 89–105 (pp. 97f.).

[17] 'The reader must be a pacifist first; then he or she will see that the text teaches nonviolence. But can a nonpacifist reader ever be changed by

only be heard rightly within the community of the Church, and Scripture can only be heard rightly by those committed to non-violence – but the Church traditionally has embraced no such tradition of non-violence so where, then, can Scripture validly be heard? This fatal incoherence is ably exposed by Stanley Hauerwas's colleague at Duke University, Richard Hays:

> The logic of Hauerwas's hermeneutical position should require him to become a Roman Catholic. The Roman Catholic Church, however, historically teaches positions on major ethical issues (such as just war and the role of women in the church) that Hauerwas cannot accept. Thus, he refuses to have his mind and character formed by that tradition and chooses instead to live, anomalously, as a Protestant with no clear theological rationale for his ecclesial practice and no empirical community to exemplify his vision of ecclesial politics. There is no tradition of high-church Mennonites; the idealized tradition to which Hauerwas appeals is an idiosyncratic fiction. When challenged by friends to explain by what authority he, as an unordained person, preaches, he can only say, 'I wish I had a good response to that troubling question.' He cannot appeal to the authority of the New Testament, because his theoretical program insists that the authority of the New Testament is mediated only through a traditioned community to whose traditions he chooses not to submit. Indeed, his very act of preaching is, paradoxically, an act of defiance against the authority that his theology advocates.[18]

With deference to Professor Hays, while there may be no high-church Mennonite tradition, there is a more general

---

reading such a text? Seemingly, Hauerwas's account leaves no possibility for such an event to occur. Nor does he explain how the overwhelmingly nonpacifist Christian tradition can be challenged or corrected by a minority reading such as the one that he offers.' (Richard B. Hays, *The Moral Vision of the New Testament*, p. 259).

[18] Richard B. Hays, *The Moral Vision of the New Testament*, p. 265.

'high chapel' tradition, including a high-church Baptist tradition: a tradition which, rejecting sectarianism, defines itself as distinctive within the Reformed tradition of the church catholic.[19] It must be admitted however, that, unlike the Mennonite tradition, this broader Reformed and catholic tradition has no historical commitment to pacifism. Stanley Hauerwas is a Methodist and, as such, one would expect him to relate to this broad high-church tradition; his appreciative (though not uncritical) respect for the Roman Catholic tradition, rooted in his time on the staff of the University of Notre Dame, is (I would argue) entirely coherent with this broader high-churchmanship. Moreover, it is similarly coherent to seek to indwell such a tradition critically, albeit humbly and submissively. What is incoherent is to indwell a tradition as the only means of hearing Scripture while simultaneously implying that this very tradition is, through its non-commitment to non-violence, incapable of hearing Scripture.

None of this necessarily invalidates Stanley Hauerwas's arguments in favour of non-violence (or in favour of vegetarianism for that matter). If, while seeking to indwell a tradition and to submit to that tradition, I find myself critical of some aspects of that tradition; I live untruthfully if I remain silent. This argument is most persuasive, however, when, acknowledging the overwhelming tradition of the Church, it objects that such a hearing of Scripture and response to Scripture is no longer viable or faithful in this present context.[20] Richard Hays' reading of Scripture is less overtly rooted in an ecclesiology but this does not render his advocacy of non-violence more persuasive. On the contrary, it renders him more vulnerable to the charge of idiosyncrasy; he is not sufficiently acknowledging the context in which he hears that which he claims to hear. But in both cases, given the overwhelming

---

[19] For a discussion of some manifestations of this tradition earlier this century see the chapter entitled 'Word and Sacraments: the Spirituality of Orthodox Dissent' in Ian M. Randall, *Evangelical Experiences*, pp. 174–205.
[20] The advantage of this non-absolutist argument is that it enables a distinction to be drawn between the coercive restraint of the legal process and military intervention.

THE PRIORITY OF THE FUTURE 203

tradition in which the Church has heard the message of
Scripture in these respects, the burden of proof lies with
those who would urge the repudiation of every form of
coercive restraint.

Rightly heard, the Church's tradition of just war theory
is not a compromise with the violence of the world but is
rather a realistic means of restraining that violence in an
anticipatory manner; or, to use Barth's phraseology, it is a
refusal to anticipate the kingdom in a manner that actually
would be untruthful and unfaithful.[21] Certainly the Church
is called to live hopefully – if optimism is hope without
truth then maybe pessimism is truth without hope –
because the Church knows its future it can live hopefully in
the present, not overwhelmed by present tragedies and
violence, sickness and despair, but confidently anticipating
a goal that is certain because it has been identified in the
gospel story. But for the Church to live faithfully it must
live truthfully in respect of its present as well as in respect
of its future; its hope is rooted, not in some untruthful
Idealism but in the reality of the true humanity of Jesus.
And, as has continually been affirmed, the *true* humanity of
Jesus occurred within the realities of human history. In
response to those realities Jesus passively submits to
suffering and death, but in response to those realities he
does not respectfully request traders to vacate the Temple
premises; his *true* humanity does not absolutely exclude
the possibility of coercion in response to human sinfulness.

Within this context of tragedy and disaster, Christians are
not infrequently challenged with the question of why God
doesn't do something. The response to the challenge, of
course, is that God has done something and is doing
something though it may not be the something that the
questioner would either choose, recognize or expect. God
has acted and is continually acting in that manner that is
coherent with his purpose in creation and redemption. To
affirm God's omnipotence is not to suggest that he is capable

---

[21] For an appraisal of Barth's 'chastened non-pacifism' see John H. Yoder,
Karl Barth and the Problem of War (Nashville and New York: Abingdon
Press, 1970).

of any and every indeterminate act, it is rather to attest his absolute freedom to be himself, to act in any and every way that is coherent. God cannot deny himself; he cannot act incoherently; having created this universe and this humanity within it he cannot now act in any manner that would be incoherent with this purposeful act of creation. Or, to put the matter another way, God, who by definition cannot be limited by any factor external to himself, is limited by his own nature, purposes and actions; God has limited himself by his own act of creation. The affirmation that this is the best of all possible worlds, without prejudice to what may or may not have been Leibniz's intention, need not imply some untruthful Idealism that takes no account of the fallenness of creation;[22] it is rather the affirmation that this world, with its sin and suffering, its tragedy and despair, is nonetheless the best *possible* world; it is not an affirmation that this is the best of any indeterminate range of possibilities; it is rather the affirmation that this is the best of all possibilities for this one who is truly God.[23]

---

[22] Bertrand Russell summarizes Leibniz's argument thus: 'There are an infinite number of possible worlds, all of which God contemplated before creating the actual world. Being good, God decided to create the best of the possible worlds, and He considered that one to be the best which had the greatest excess of good over evil. He could have created a world containing no evil, but it would not have been so good as the actual world. That is because some goods are logically bound up with certain evils ... Free will is a great good, but it was logically impossible for God to bestow free will and at the same time decree that there should be no sin': Bertrand Russell, *History of Western Philosophy and its Connection with Political and Social Circumstances from the Earliest Times to the Present Day* (London: George Allen & Unwin, 1946), pp. 612f. The difficulty here (with Russell if not with Leibniz) is that the goodness of God is not explicitly defined by the gospel story: such a definition does not invalidate Leibniz's conclusion but it radically changes the nature of the argument; it renders the conclusion an inference from the particular (the gospel story) rather than a deduction from a general (and detached) logic.

[23] 'It is by this route that we reach the doctrine of this world being the "best of all possible worlds", not by some facile optimism which ignores the reality of suffering. God was, therefore, responsible for evil in the world, for he was its Creator, but he could not, logically, be morally culpable in the sense that he was the cause of evil deeds. If he had created a world in which there was no possibility of evil, it would be a world in which there was no freedom, and it would not, by definition, be the best of all possible worlds': Brian Horne, *Imagining Evil* (London: Darton, Longman & Todd, 1996), p. 83.

That God is not and cannot be arbitrary has already been argued in chapter five of this book in a manner which excluded such a notion as a possible means of explaining away the horrors and ravages of the books of Joshua and Judges in particular. Genocide does not become an inherently 'right' act simply because God says so; rather, because God is 'good' genocide could never be an inherently 'right' act. But because God is 'good', because his goodness excludes the possibility of any arbitrary or incoherent act, God himself is constrained to act, for the present, within the conditions and limitations of the universe as he has created it; he 'cannot' act in any manner that is incoherent with his goal for creation or with his purposed manner of attaining that goal. Such a recognition does not exclude the possibility of a 'miracle': for Jesus to heal the sick and to rise from the dead is entirely consistent with God's goal in creation and with the manner he has chosen through which to attain that goal. But such a recognition does admit the possibility that, in the light of God's ultimate goal and his chosen manner of attaining it, some actions are excluded as possibilities even for God: God himself cannot act as if the universe had already arrived at its ultimate goal; God himself cannot act as if creation were not fallen. To affirm that God always acts in the best *possible* way is to admit that an indeterminate range of possibilities is not available to God.

I am certainly not suggesting that this recognition represents a comprehensive means of coping with the moral difficulties raised by some passages of the Old Testament: I am merely acknowledging that God too is committed to act within the realities of the world as it is; that God's 'best' is not an indeterminate ideal but a realistic possibility; that God's ultimate best is attained through the event of redemption and that, other than in this event, even God can only act in penultimate ways. And if this is true of all God's present action within creation it is certainly true of his action through the Church by his Spirit. Jesus has not yet returned in glory; creation has not yet reached its goal. Here and now the Church, empowered and indwelt by the Spirit, is called to act always in the best *possible* way. This 'best', then, while certainly not excluding the possibilities of pacifism or vegetarianism, does not necessarily establish them either as the *only* valid possibilities.

Through its indwelling of the gospel story, and through its being indwelt by the Spirit, the Church is fashioned in faithfulness. This faithfulness is not expressed in any unrealistic or idealistic optimism, nor in any unhopeful or acquiescent pessimism, but in a realistic hopefulness that seeks to be truthful both to its future identity and its present context. In a society where Modernist Idealism shows every sign of collapsing into nihilistic despair, the winsomeness of the Church's hopeful realism may seem to have persuasive potential, but that potential must be comprehended within the parameters of that dynamic of knowing that has already been outlined.

11
The Commonality of Perception

> Mankind in general seem to suppose some general
> standard or foundation in nature for an universal
> consistence in the use of the terms whereby they
> express moral good and evil; which none can depart
> from but through error and mistake. This is evidently
> supposed in all disputes they may have one with
> another, about right and wrong; and in all endeavors
> used to evince or prove that anything is either good or
> evil, in a moral sense.[1]

This conclusion to Jonathan Edwards's account of *True Virtue*, taken in isolation, would appear merely to express again that common assumption of the Enlightenment that there exists some rational and independently accessible foundation for morality; that without reference to any dynamic of revelation or to any particular and distinctive tradition, that which is morally good and that which is morally evil is evident to all men and women in every place and in every age. This Modernist notion is precisely the assumption that has been questioned throughout this book and is rejected by the key authors with which this book has been seeking to interact. Yet the rejection of this assumption, together with the corresponding focus on the indwelling of the gospel story through an indwelling of the Christian community as the only valid foundation for *Christian* ethics, raises in acute form the question of how the Church, formed by the Spirit through the indwelling of this story, can speak persuasively within a world that does not share this distinctive and dynamic moral foundation.

The temptation, of course, is for the Church to retreat into some self-absorbed moral ghetto. Presuming that the

---

[1] Jonathan Edwards, *Dissertation II: The Nature of True Virtue* in *Works of Jonathan Edwards*, general ed. John E. Smith, vol. 8, *Ethical Writings*, ed. Paul Ramsey (New Haven: Yale University Press, 1989), pp. 537–627 (p. 627).

world does not share (or, at least, does not recognize) this moral foundation, the Church could easily abandon altogether the attempt to speak of its ethical concerns to the world, focusing rather on its commitment to be shaped by its story in an exclusive and inherently sectarian manner. That the Church should focus on its indwelling of its story is not in dispute; what is disputed is this underlying pessimism concerning the persuasiveness of its lived-out narrative: the continuity of creation and redemption expressed by Irenaeus and explored in the previous chapter, a continuity which, though differently expressed in his account of virtue and beauty, is implicit in the writings of Jonathan Edwards, may give ground for some confidence concerning the persuasiveness of the Church's story.[2]

Clearly Paul Ramsey, the editor of the Yale edition of Jonathan Edwards's *Ethical Writings*, interprets Edwards as assuming a '*natural* moral competence' common to all men and women irrespective of any 'common' work or presence of the Holy Spirit.[3] Yet the question must be raised of whether Ramsey has adequately grasped either the significance of the later Reformed notion of 'common grace' or the quite distinctive sense in which Edwards, in

[2] Note that this relatedness of beauty and virtue has already been identified by Thomas: '... spiritual beauty consists in a man's conduct or actions being well proportioned in respect of the spiritual clarity of reason. Now this is what is meant by honesty, which we have stated ... to be the same as virtue that moderates according to reason all that is connected with man. Wherefore *honesty is the same as spiritual beauty*' (*ST* II–II 145 2).
[3] 'So for Edwards ordinary morality was a rather splendid thing. Here we need not and should not appeal to the grace or gifts of the Holy Spirit that are "common" to the godly and ungodly alike: common illuminations, common awakenings, common inspiration, common convictions, common religious experience, common humiliations, etc. These restraints or aids accompany the redemption God is working in every age from the Fall to the end of the world. Edwards was not one to use prevenient grace, restraining grace, or common grace to account for the *natural* moral competence of fallen humanity, and to avoid the belief that we good people are only "miserable sinners" and not totally deprived of true virtue': Paul Ramsey, 'Editor's Introduction' in *Works of Jonathan Edwards*, gen. ed. John E. Smith, vol. 8, *Ethical Writings*, ed. Paul Ramsey (New Haven: Yale University Press, 1989), pp. 1–121 (p. 33).

this context, employs the term 'natural'. Consistently here, Edwards interprets a 'law of nature' in terms of an 'instinct' given to humankind by God;[4] moreover, this given instinct must be comprehended in the context of Edwards's radically dynamic account of the relationship between God and creation and of the means by which anything at all might be known: the universe is continually being re-created by God and, therefore, any 'given instinct' must continually be being given; that anything whatsoever is known or perceived is an outcome of its being 'given' to our perception by God. Fundamental to Edwards's account of virtue is its identification with beauty,[5] but if in any sense, for Edwards, 'beauty is in the eye of the beholder' it is so inasmuch as both the object perceived and the aesthetic response of the affections to that object are continually being 'given' by God.

Oliver O'Donovan's criticism that, by beginning his account of virtue with reflections on a love for 'being in general', Edwards reduces the love of God to a deduction from a prior and more general definition of love and virtue, seems to derive from a similar failure to read Edwards's account of *True Virtue* both in its own continuities and in continuity with Edwards's wider effort.[6] This dissertation

---

[4] 'The *cause* why secondary beauty is grateful to *men* is only a *law of nature*, which God has fixed, or an *instinct* he has given to mankind ...' (Jonathan Edwards, *True Virtue*, p. 565; cf. p. 567); or later (p. 620): '... they who see the beauty there is in true virtue, don't perceive it by argumentation on its connections and consequences, but by the frame of their own minds, or a certain spiritual sense given them of God.'

[5] 'Whatever controversies and variety of opinions there are about the nature of virtue, yet all ... mean by it something *beautiful*, or rather some kind of *beauty* or excellency... virtue is the beauty of the qualities and exercises of the heart, or those actions which proceed from them' (Jonathan Edwards, *True Virtue*, p. 539). For a further discussion of these ideas see Roland Delattre, *Beauty and Sensibility in the Thought of Jonathan Edwards* (New Haven: Yale University Press, 1968); cf. Roland Delattre, 'Beauty and Politics: Toward a Theological Anthropology' in *Union Seminary Quarterly Review* 25 (Summer 1970), pp. 401–19.

[6] 'If one starts by treating "being in general" and announces that one will regard God as a special case of such being, any subsequent assertions that the universe is "as nothing" beside the divine being will inevitably tend to be discounted. One has already *derived* the love of God from a prior love of the universe. The finest Christian theological assertions

On the Nature of True Virtue was prepared by Edwards in 1755 alongside a parallel dissertation *Concerning the End for Which God Created the World*.[7] In 1765, after his death, the two dissertations were published together in a single volume, which is precisely the way in which Edwards intended them to be read: a valid conception of *true* virtue derives, not from any general notion of beauty or order, but from a knowledge of the nature of the true God and of his ultimate goal for the universe;[8] the beauty of creation derives from the beauty of God himself;[9] 'benevolence to Being in general', which constitutes true virtue,[10] is a response to, and a participation in, the overflowing of God's Triune self-love:

> ... the communication of God's virtue or holiness is principally in communicating the love of himself ... And thus we see how, not only the creature's seeing and knowing God's excellence, but also supremely esteeming and loving him, belongs to the communication of God's fullness. And the communication of God's joy and happiness consists chiefly in communicating to the creature that happiness and joy,

---

about the relation of God to his creation will lose their force and significance if they are used merely as the *minor* premiss of an argument which takes as its major premiss the identity of virtue with love of the universe' (Oliver O'Donovan, *Resurrection and the Moral Order*, p. 228).

[7] Jonathan Edwards, *Dissertation I: Concerning the End for which God created the World* in *Works of Jonathan Edwards*, gen. ed. John E. Smith, vol. 8, *Ethical Writings*, ed. Paul Ramsey (New Haven: Yale University Press, 1989), pp. 403–536.

[8] 'The one is the mirror image of the other; the "end" for which God created the world must be the "end" of a truly virtuous and holy life': Paul Ramsey, 'Editor's Introduction' in *Works of Jonathan Edwards*, gen. ed. John E. Smith, vol. 8, *Ethical Writings*, ed. Paul Ramsey (New Haven: Yale University Press, 1989), pp. 1–121 (p. 5).

[9] '... all the beauty to be found throughout the whole creation, is but the reflection of the diffused beams of that Being who hath an infinite fullness of brightness and glory' (Jonathan Edwards, *True Virtue*, pp. 550f.).

[10] 'True virtue most essentially consists in benevolence to Being in general. Or perhaps to speak more accurately, it is that consent, propensity and union of heart to Being in general, that is immediately exercised in a general good will' (Jonathan Edwards, *True Virtue*, p. 540).

which consists in rejoicing in God and in his glorious excellency ...[11]

For Edwards, as for Irenaeus, the universe is purposeful; its God-given goal is both made known and made actual through the work of redemption. The single and ultimate goal of the universe, according to Edwards, is *both* the glory of God *and* the making known of that glory.[12] That this twofold purpose is, in fact, a single and indivisible purpose issues from the very nature of divine goodness, that it is good, in and of itself, that divine goodness should make itself known.[13] Consequently, the work of creation and the demonstration of God's goodness within creation and as the end of creation, is an overflowing of the mutual love of the eternal Trinity; the overflowing of God's goodness within creation, which constitutes true virtue, is an overflowing of the love of Father, Son and Spirit:

> ... it is also evident that the *divine virtue*, or the virtue of the divine mind, must consist primarily in *love to himself,* or in the mutual love and friendship which subsists eternally and necessarily between the several persons in the Godhead, or that infinitely strong

[11] Jonathan Edwards, *The End for which God created the World*, p. 528.

[12] 'For it appears that all that is ever spoken of in the Scripture as an ultimate end of God's works is included in that one phrase, "the glory of God"; which is the name by which the last end of God's works is most commonly called in Scripture: and seems to be the name which most aptly signifies the thing ... There is included in the exercise of God's perfections to produce a proper effect, in opposition to their lying eternally dormant and ineffectual ... The manifestation of his internal glory to created understandings. The communication of the infinite fullness of God to the creature ... These at first view may appear to be entirely distinct things: but if we more closely consider the matter, they will appear to be one thing, in a variety of views and relations' (Jonathan Edwards, *The End for which God created the World*, pp. 526f.).

[13] 'As God's perfections are things in themselves excellent, so the expression of them in their proper acts and fruits is excellent, and the knowledge of these excellent perfections, and of these glorious expressions of them, is an excellent thing, the existence of which is in itself valuable and desirable. 'Tis a thing infinitely good in itself that God's glory should be known by a glorious society of created beings' (Jonathan Edwards, *Concerning the End for which God created the World*, p. 431).

propensity there is in these divine persons one to another.[14]

But if this overflowing of divine virtue, which is true beauty, constitutes God's single and ultimate goal both in creation and redemption, it necessarily issues in, and is reflected by, penultimate expressions of beauty and goodness.[15] Edwards therefore is saying no more, but also no less, than that the universe – which is continually being re-created by God and 'given' to our perception by the Spirit – notwithstanding its fallenness, is coherent with the purpose for which it was created, a purpose particularly disclosed in the work of redemption. If Edwards can write in *True Virtue* of an 'inferior, secondary beauty, which is not peculiar to spiritual beings, but is found even in inanimate things', it is because he has understood the universe as continually ordered towards this goal of virtue and beauty.[16] And if Edwards can assume that men and women, generally and in a penultimate manner, may recognize virtue and beauty, it is because he understands recognition itself, which is always aesthetic, as being given by the Spirit; since the idea of any reality is imparted by the Spirit so too is the sense of beauty of any reality. Within this radically theocentric account of metaphysics and epistemology Edwards is unhesitating in affirming an

---

[14] Jonathan Edwards, *True Virtue*, p. 557. The editor, Paul Ramsey, comments in a footnote to this passage 'It is also the case that for JE the love in the Trinity is the paradigm of all virtuous love.'

[15] 'There is a general and a particular beauty. By a "particular" beauty I mean that by which a thing appears beautiful when considered only with regard to its connection with, and tendency to some particular things within a limited and, as it were, a private sphere. And a "general" beauty is that by which a thing appears beautiful when viewed most perfectly, comprehensively and universally, with regard to all its tendencies, and its connections with everything it stands related to' (Jonathan Edwards, *True Virtue*, p. 540).

[16] 'Yet there is another, inferior, secondary beauty, which is some image of this, and which is not peculiar to spiritual beings, but is found even in inanimate things: which consists in mutual consent and agreement of different things in form, manner, quantity, and visible end or design; called by the various names of regularity, order, uniformity, symmetry, proportion, harmony, etc.' (Jonathan Edwards, *True Virtue*, pp. 561f.).

'analogy' between this secondary and derivative beauty and the beauty of true virtue,[17] that in the secondary beauty of the 'mutual consent and agreement of things' there may be 'some image of the true, spiritual original beauty',[18] but to view this as implying some 'natural' or independent foundation for morality is entirely to misapprehend his account.

All this is not intended as a comprehensive defence of Edwards's account of virtue – the Trinitarian structure of his thought, though an advance on the similar epistemology of George Berkeley, could yet have been more thorough and more consistently explicit; that he can be interpreted by Paul Ramsey and others as implying some rationally accessible foundation for morality is evidence of this defect – but it is to recognize the continuity of his account of the relationship between creation and redemption with that of Irenaeus; and it is to recognize in his radically pneumatological account of ontology and epistemology the possibility of a theocentric foundation for a persuasive and coherent ethic. It is the epistemological potential of a Pneumatological, as well as Christological, mediation of creation that underlies Colin Gunton's recognition that we must 'move towards an analogy of relation that generates a kind of analogy of being':[19]

> If Christ is the mediator of creation, then he is the basis of created rationality and therefore of human knowledge, wherever and whatever; we might say, of all human culture. But that point must be developed pneumatologically also, so that all rationality, truth and beauty are seen to be realised through the perfecting agency of God the Spirit, who enables things to be known by human minds and made by human hands.[20]

---

[17] '... a taste of this kind of beauty is entirely a different thing from a taste of true virtue ... [t]hough it be true, there is some analogy in it to spiritual and virtuous beauty ...' (Jonathan Edwards, *True Virtue*, p. 573).
[18] Jonathan Edwards, *True Virtue*, p. 564.
[19] Colin E. Gunton, *The Triune Creator*, p. 206.
[20] Colin E. Gunton, *A Brief Theology of Revelation*, pp. 124f.

This may seem a surprising possibility to be raised by one so overtly influenced by the theology of Karl Barth, but again it identifies Professor Gunton's key criticism of Barth's account and the manner in which, without abandoning the latter's Christocentric understanding of creation, this account can be developed Pneumatologically. Barth's treatment of creation as 'the external basis of the covenant' and his corresponding treatment of the covenant as 'the internal basis of creation' establishes his under-standing of the Christ-centred relatedness of the doctrines – though, granted his conception of this continuity and inter-relatedness, the paucity of references to Irenaeus is surprising.[21] But what is more surprising, not to say unnec-essary and distorting, is the lack of emphasis here on the mediating role of the Spirit (a lack which might explain the minimal references to Irenaeus). Elsewhere, Barth is eager to emphasize the 'being givenness' of God's Word, a 'being givenness' issuing from the presence and activity of the Spirit;[22] what seems to be missing from his account – and what, accordingly, fundamentally distinguishes his account from that of Jonathan Edwards – is a sense of the 'being givenness' of *all* knowledge. For Barth, the Spirit's role in redemption and reconciliation is explicit (though even here he is vulnerable to criticism); what is not explicit (or even always implicit) is the Spirit's mediatorial role in creation and in our knowledge of all created reality. Oliver O'Donovan censures Barth for confusing ontological and epistemological issues in his repudiation of the 'ordinances' of creation but this, I suspect, is further to confuse the issue.[23] If creation is truly the external basis of

---

[21] *CD* III/1 pp. 94ff.
[22] *CD* I/1, pp. 125ff.
[23] 'In the great theological attack upon Natural Law which was spear-headed earlier this century by Karl Barth, we can only regret that the ontological and epistemological issues were never properly differen-tiated. In his pursuit of an uncompromised theological epistemology Barth allowed himself to repudiate certain aspects of the doctrine of creation (such as 'ordinances') which ought never to have fallen under suspicion . . . All this left him with a formal account of the theological basis of ethics which, depending exclusively on the divine command – inter-preted in the existentialist way as particular and unpredictable – , was far

the covenant, and if the covenant is truly the internal basis
of creation, then there can be no 'ordinances' or 'mandates'
of creation alongside Christ himself; the question is
rather one of the knowability of this Christ-grounded and
Christ-orientated creation.

In many respects, Barth's consideration of Jesus Christ
as the 'Light of Life' brings this question into sharp focus.
During the course of his discussion of the doctrine of
reconciliation and, specifically, of the 'prophetic' office of
Christ as the Word of God, Barth raises 'the more compli-
cated question of true words which are not spoken in the
Bible or the Church, but which have to be regarded as true
in relation to the one Word of God, and therefore heard like
this Word, and together with it':[24]

> The simple point is that the creaturely world, the
> cosmos, the nature given to man in his sphere and the
> nature of this sphere, has also as such its own lights
> and truths and therefore its own speech and words ...
> Its witness and declaration may be missed or more or
> less dreadfully misunderstood. But it is given with the
> same persistence as creation itself endures thanks to
> the faithfulness of its Creator. It is given, therefore,
> quite irrespective of whether the man whom it
> addresses in its self-witness knows or does not know,
> confesses or denies, that it owes this speech no less
> than its persistence to the faithfulness of its Creator.
> Like its persistence, its self-witness and lights are not
> extinguished by the corruption of the relationship
> between God and man through the sin of man, his
> pride and sloth and falsehood ... It is true that by the
> shining of the one true light of life, by the self-revel-
> ation of God in Jesus Christ, they are exposed and
> characterised as lights, words and truths of the created

---

too thin to support the extensive responsibility for moral deliberation
which he would claim in practice and sometimes even defend in theory'
(Oliver O'Donovan, *Resurrection and the Moral Order*, pp. 86f.). Barth
discusses 'ordinances' and 'mandates' in response to Brunner and
Bonhoeffer respectively in *CD* III/4, pp. 19ff.
[24] *CD* IV/3, p. 114.

cosmos, and therefore as created lights in distinction from this one light. Yet as such they are not extinguished by this light, nor are their force and significance destroyed. On the contrary, as the cosmos persists in all its forms and media before, during and after the epiphany of Jesus Christ, so it shines, speaks and attests itself before, during and after this event. The truth given it by God in and with its actuality endures. It does not do so independently of the epiphany of Jesus Christ. But it does so independently of man's relationship and attitude to the latter.[25]

As with the words of Scripture and the Church, there can be no question of any 'completing, rivalling, systematising or transcending the one Word'. If such 'words' exist within creation they do so because, as with the words of Scripture and the words of the Church, the 'one Word itself sets them there'.[26] What is less clear, however, is Barth's conception of the accessibility of these 'words' and 'lights' of creation, or, at least, their accessibility in and of themselves. Later in the course of his discussion he acknowledges the possibility of such 'words' and 'lights' being taken up by *the* Word and *the* Light; that is to say, of such 'words' being truly revelatory:

> In the course of this action of the Word of God the eternal light can shine, the Word of the covenant of grace be spoken and the saving truth of God be uttered in the lights, words and truths of creation. The latter can thus be integrated by the Word of God and achieve what they could not be or do of themselves, but can be and do as the Lord of creation wills it. They are instituted into His direct service and set in a relation in which they do not stand of themselves. They can thus be truths which shine as expressions of the one truth.[27]

---

[25] *CD* IV/3, p. 139.
[26] *CD* IV/3, p. 114.
[27] *CD* IV/3, p. 157.

Here, it would seem, Barth has some difficulty with systematic coherence. Contrary to the astonishing claim of Nigel Biggar that 'Barth readily affirms general revelation while rejecting natural theology',[28] Barth hitherto has repudiated any form of 'general revelation', not because (as these passages from *CD* IV/3 evidence) he ever denies the possibility of God's speaking through created reality, but rather because he denies that such speaking could ever be *general* and remain truly revelatory; that there could ever be other true divine words alongside the one true Word; that there could ever be any λόγος ἄσαρκος, any Word of God in abstraction.[29] But if this remains the case, and if creation and covenant remain in the relatedness that Barth has previously identified, what possibly can be the content and dynamic of these 'words' of creation when they are *not* taken into the service of *the* Word? Barth does affirm that 'there can be no question of words which say anything different from this one Word',[30] that '[w]hat we have in view are attestations of the self-impartation of the God who acts as Father in the Son by the Holy Ghost, which show themselves to be such by their full agreement with the witness present in Scripture and accepted and proclaimed by the Church',[31] but is this sufficient in the light of his earlier strictures? Notwithstanding the implicit distinction between these words of creation and *the* Word, Barth, in a manner reminiscent of Edwards, affirms their underlying *harmony*, the one resonates with the others:

> What they say can so harmonise with what He Himself says that to hear Him is to hear them, and to hear them to hear Him, so that listening to the polyphony of

---

[28] Nigel Biggar, *The Hastening that Waits*, p. 155.

[29] *CD* IV/1, pp. 52f.; compare the following comment from *Karl Barth's Table Talk*, recorded and edited by John D. Godsey: 'Do not ever think of the second Person of the Trinity as only *Logos*. That is the mistake of Emil Brunner. There is no *Logos asarkos*, but only *ensarkos*. Brunner thinks of a *Logos asarkos*, and I think this is the reason for his natural theology. The *Logos* becomes an abstract principle': *Scottish Journal of Theology Occasional Papers* No. 10 (Edinburgh: Oliver & Boyd, 1963), p. 49.

[30] *CD* IV/3, p. 115.

[31] *CD* IV/3, p. 117.

creation as the external basis of the covenant, to its questions and answers, its riddles and solutions, is listening to the symphony for which it was elected and determined from eternity and which the Creator alone has the power to evoke, yet according to His Word the will also.[32]

Any lack of clarity in Barth's argument at this point may derive in part from the possibility of reading this account as implying that the event of revelation invariably produces a *single* effect; the assumption that revelation necessarily issues in reconciliation. Perhaps it is this element of confusion that underlies Nigel Biggar's comparison of Karl Barth with Karl Rahner. Biggar rightly recognizes that Barth follows Augustine in deeming all human loves to be disordered unless they are orientated to '*caritas* or love for God'. But Biggar also deems that 'Barth is willing to entertain the possibility of subordination to the Word of God apart from explicit Christian confession';[33] that he, therefore, 'espouses something akin to Karl Rahner's 'anonymous Christianity', except that where Rahner wishes to establish it as a condition elected by some, Barth appears to propose it as one determined for all'.[34] As with every other attempt to resolve Barth's account in a universalistic direction, this confusion issues from a one-sided reading of Barth that refuses to take seriously his consistent repudiation of universalism. In affirming that revelation is, in reality, the *self-revelation* of God, Barth rightly rejects any *general* form of revelation, but if this self-revelation of God were to issue inevitably in reconciliation, and if the 'words' of creation can become the means of the speaking and hearing of *the* Word, then an avowal of universal salvation would appear to be unavoidable. However, as was noted earlier in this book,

---

[32] *CD* IV/3, p. 159; cf. 'The final and trustworthy thing which they cannot say of themselves concerning their being and existence, they now can say as they reflect the eternal light of God, as they answer His word and as they correspond to His truth' (*CD* IV/3, p. 164).
[33] Nigel Biggar, *The Hastening that Waits*, p. 91.
[34] Nigel Biggar, *The Hastening that Waits*, pp. 150f.

while Barth refuses to limit the mercy of God by denying the possibility that all men and women might ultimately be saved, he similarly refuses to limit the freedom of God's mercy by presuming that this inevitably will be the case; God's mercy remains *his* mercy. He remains the free Lord of the effect of his Word; the hearing and stubborn rejection of this Word remains an impossible *possibility*.

If there is a lack of clarity here it derives more profoundly from Barth's tendency to assume the person and work of the Spirit into the person and work of the Son and, similarly, to assume the dynamic of hearing and perceiving into the dynamic of speaking and shining. The concern, then, must not be to reduce the dynamic of speaking and shining to some 'given' static, but it is to distinguish this particular 'being givenness' from the particular 'being givenness' of hearing and seeing; and it is to recognize in both dynamics the distinctive work of both the Son and the Spirit as conjoined mediators of the Father's action. It is divine perception, and divine perception alone, that determines reality and substantiality: the speaking of the true Word may be heard by the Father alone; the shining of the true Light may be seen by the Father alone; that we are brought to participate in this hearing and seeing is a distinct work of the Spirit in relation to the work of the Son. Certainly for Barth there is no possibility that the 'lights' of creation, once pressed into the service of *the* Light, could be accessible to men and women independent of the action of God's Spirit – this would be incoherent given Barth's dynamic understanding of the divine Word – but what of the hearing and perceiving of these 'words' and 'lights' of creation when they have not yet been taken up by *the* Word and *the* Light? Barth wants to affirm that any 'speaking of true words implies a miracle',[35] but it is here that Irenaeus' understanding of creation as mediated by the Son *and* the Spirit, and Edwards's notion of the 'being givenness' both of created reality *and* of the human perception of that reality, have potential for greater precision.

[35] *CD* IV/3, p. 124.

Both the being of created reality and the human perception of that created reality are being given by God, but they are not synonymous; the being of created reality is dependent upon God's perception of that reality, our perception of created reality is a divinely given participation in that divine perception, but – and herein lies the response to misrepresentations of the views of George Berkeley – the being of created reality is not dependent upon our perception of it but upon God's perception of it, a perception which we are brought to participate in by the Spirit.

It would appear that so-called Thomism (of which Thomas Aquinas was probably innocent) and so-called Barthianism (of which Karl Barth was certainly innocent) issue in a corresponding disjunction of creation and redemption, or, at least, in a corresponding disjunction concerning their knowability. The tendency for the former, in contrast to Thomas himself, for whom nature was 'graced',[36] has been to sever nature from grace in a manner that renders nature independently knowable. The tendency of the latter, in contrast to Barth himself, for whom *the* Word can be spoken and heard through the 'words' of creation, has been to sever nature from grace in a manner that reduces nature to silence. The remedy for both faults is anticipated in Irenaeus' understanding of the mediation of creation *and* redemption by the Word *and* the Spirit; a remedy that finds expression in Jonathan Edwards's conception of the 'being givenness' of creation's resonance with true beauty and true virtue. Here, then, is valid ground for affirming that grace perfects nature rather than abolishes it,[37] not because nature itself has any independent substantiality or knowability, but rather because nature, and the knowledge of nature, itself is 'graced'. Since nature's true voice is being spoken through the Word and being heard through the Spirit it cannot be in

---

[36] 'In Thomas to call reasoning natural is mere tautology; to distinguish it from grace is wrong': Eugene F. Rogers Jnr., 'Schleiermacher as an Anselmian Theologian: Aesthetics, Dogmatics, Apologetics and Proof' in *SJT* 51 (1998), pp. 342–79 (p. 358).

[37] *Gratia non tollit naturam sed perfecit.*

conflict with, or be abolished by, that which is being given to be heard in redemption. Only in the event of perceiving the true Light is the *true* beauty of the 'lights' of creation recognized; only in the event of hearing the true Word is the *true* harmony of the 'words' of creation understood:

> This does not mean that the unique revelation of God in Jesus Christ denies the fact that God has actually made himself known to people in the world from the beginning of the creation, although without revealing his own Self in the familiar personal way as he has done in Christ. Nor does it mean that this revelation of God simply extinguishes the lights of the creation or the contingent intelligibility which God has imposed upon it through his Word, but that it cuts through the twisted apprehension of them due to the alienated and self-inturned nature of the human mind whereby it eclipses the light of the creation and falsifies its truth.[38]

The principal distinction between this dynamic of hearing and seeing and the latter Reformed notion of 'common grace' has already been identified. For Irenaeus, in disputation with the Gnostics, creation is mediated precisely by that same Word and Spirit who are the mediators of redemption; for Thomas Aquinas the analogy of being must imply an analogy of goodness and, since God alone is good and God is 'simple', goodness is ultimately indivisible;[39] for Jonathan Edwards all beauty and virtue

---

[38] Thomas F. Torrance, *The Christian Doctrine of God, One Being Three Persons* (Edinburgh: T&T Clark, 1996), p. 25; cf. '... revelation in Christ does not *deny* our fragmentary knowledge of the way things are, as though that knowledge were not there, or were of no significance; yet it does not *build on* it, as though it provided a perfectly acceptable foundation to which a further level of understanding can be added. It can only expose it for not being what it was originally given to be' (Oliver O'Donovan, *Resurrection and the Moral Order*, p. 89).

[39] 'Everything is therefore called good from the divine goodness, as from the first exemplary effective and final principle of all goodness. Nevertheless, everything is called good by reason of the similitude of the divine goodness belonging to it, which is formally its own goodness, whereby it is denominated good. And so of all things there is one goodness, and yet many goodnesses' (*ST* I 6 4).

within creation is a reflection of the single beauty and virtue of the divine Trinity; for Karl Barth creation has no internal basis other than the covenant and, therefore, any true 'word' of creation must harmonize with *the* true Word. The discordant note sounded by the notion of common grace derives from the implications of the word 'common'. Within the context of Federal Calvinism and its categorical dividing of law and gospel, Adam and Christ, creation and redemption, the term 'common' can only imply some grace other than the grace of the gospel, other than the grace of our Lord Jesus Christ, other than the grace of redemption. The radical nature of this 'other grace', anticipated perhaps in Calvin's conjecture of a 'double decree',[40] is most starkly illustrated by Beza's table of the decrees of election in which humanity, and the totality of human history, is divided and ordered by the distinct decrees of election and reprobation.[41] The notion of common grace, as expressed for instance in the writings of the Dutch Reformed theologian Abraham Kuyper, is merely an outworking of this earlier systematic disjunction according to which God's 'general' providential dealings with creation and humanity are quite distinct from his 'particular' dealings with 'the elect'.[42]

As always, the fundamental issue underlying this notion of common grace is a distinctive doctrine of God: here again we encounter a conception of God as essentially arbitrary; one who categorically divides humanity on no discernible basis and whose subsequent actions are merely an outworking of this primary arbitrary division. But notwithstanding the fatal flaw of this account (which finds not dissimilar expression in other manifestations of

---

[40] For instance, see *Institutes* III xxi 5.

[41] *Summa totius Christianismi, sive descriptio et distributio causarum salutis electorum, et exitii reproborum, ex sacris litteris collecta*, reproduced in Alister E. McGrath, *A Life of John Calvin: A Study in the Shaping of Western Culture* (Oxford: Blackwell, 1990), p. 215.

[42] For a description of these developments see G. C. Berkouwer, *Studies in Dogmatics: The Providence of God*, trans. Lewis B. Smedes (Grand Rapids: Eerdmans, 1952), pp. 70ff.: Barth's subordinating of the doctrine of providence to the doctrine of election is the clearest refutation of this dividing of grace.

nominalism) the notion of common grace at least has the merit (and, indeed, the intention against the background of Enlightenment reductionism) of affirming *God's* activity within creation as the basis of beauty and virtue, human culture and 'common' morality. This underlying merit is most clearly identified by Jeremy Begbie who, while acknowledging this same fundamental flaw, finds here at least a basis for affirming the givenness of aesthetic value:

> ... even a cursory glance at the writings of the Dutch Neo-Calvinists reveals at every turn their belief in what we might call the objectivity of value. Beauty, moral goodness and truth are not human inventions, nor merely the expressions of inner preferences, but are built into the very fabric of the created world, and (especially for Kuyper and Bavinck) are rooted in God himself. Thus, beauty – the most distinctive quality which makes art worthy of praise – is not relative to individual taste or cultural inclination; it is something given, something to which the artist must be faithful. This provides the Dutchmen with what they see as a secure foundation on which aesthetic judgements can be based.[43]

This 'givenness', or rather 'being givenness', of aesthetic

---

[43] Jeremy Begbie, *Voicing Creation's Praise*, p. 155. Dr. Begbie's revision of this notion of common grace, and his refutation of Platonic conceptions of beauty, derives from a re-assertion of the continuity of creation and redemption: 'Beauty ... has all too often been abstracted from time and temporal movement, and turned into a static, timeless quality. Suppose, however, we refuse to divorce it from the transformation of the disorder of creation in the history of Jesus Christ. Suppose we begin there. Does this not open up a more dynamic, and more theological paradigm of beauty? ... I am contending here that the most fruitful model of beauty for the artist will be found not by attempting to distil some formal principle from the contingent processes of the created world, but by directing our attention first of all to the redeeming economy of God which culminates in Jesus Christ. This, I submit, would equip us with a concept of beauty much more distinctively Christian than the somewhat pale Platonic notions which are so often offered in theological discussion of art' (Jeremy Begbie, *Voicing Creation's Praise*, pp. 224f.).

value lies at the root of Jonathan Edwards's account of
human conscience, an account that develops a similar
understanding of conscience in terms of coherence or
consistency to that outlined earlier in this book.[44]
Edwards's notion of justice, and indeed of all virtue, is
aesthetic; an awareness of the justice of a matter is an
awareness of the beauty, harmony and proportion of a
matter.[45] Accordingly, while Edwards distinguishes
between 'natural' conscience as a merely inner coherence
(whereby we seek to be consistent with ourselves) and that
'spiritual sense' which issues in a more profound
coherence (whereby we seek consistency 'with Being in
general'),[46] he affirms the underlying coherence of these
two dynamics,[47] an underlying coherence rooted in their
God-givenness. Here again Edwards speaks of a *natural*
principle of conscience in a quite distinctive sense: any
awareness of inner consistency, or of a consistency with the
natural beauty and harmony of creation, is itself a
perception (or 'instinct') that is being given by the Spirit; its
coherence with 'true virtue' is a consequence of the unity of

---

[44] 'Natural conscience consists ... in a consciousness of our being
consistent or inconsistent with ourselves' (Jonathan Edwards, *True Virtue*,
p. 593).
[45] 'So there is a beauty in the virtue called *justice*, which consists in the
agreement of different things that have relation to one another, in nature,
manner, and measure: and therefore is the very same sort of beauty with
that uniformity and proportion which is observable in those external and
material things that are esteemed beautiful' (Jonathan Edwards, *True
Virtue*, p. 569).
[46] '... approving of actions, because we therein act in agreement with
ourselves ... is quite a different thing from approving or disapproving
actions because in them we agree and are united with Being in general'
(Jonathan Edwards, *True Virtue*, p. 590).
[47] 'Thus has God established and ordered that this principle of natural
conscience, which though it implies no such thing as actual benevolence
to Being in general, nor any delight in such a principle, simply considered,
and so implies no truly spiritual sense or virtuous taste, yet should
approve and condemn the same things that are approved and condemned
by a spiritual sense or virtuous taste' (Jonathan Edwards, *True Virtue*, pp.
595f.). In the light of this underlying and commonly expressed unity it is
probably unhelpful for Paul Ramsey to refer to these as 'two sources of
morality'; in the wider context of Edwards's distinctively theocentric
epistemology the 'natural' is a 'being given' reflection of the 'spiritual'
(see Paul Ramsey's comments at p. 590 n. 3).

its divine source.[48] Indeed, in terms anticipating Barth's discussion of the 'lights' of creation (but without the unnecessary hesitancy of Barth's account), Edwards can expect an awareness of *natural* beauty and *natural* virtue to be means through which an awareness of true virtue is enlivened.[49] Conversely, in terms reminiscent of the apostle Paul's argument in Romans, Edwards recognizes that a failure to acknowledge the divine source of this beauty, and of the awareness of this beauty, inevitably leads to an impairing and corrupting of conscience.[50]

With all this in mind, the quotation with which this chapter began can be re-visited and re-assessed. Far from supposing some independently derived foundation for morality, Edwards is simply observing that '[m]ankind in general seem to suppose' such a foundation.[51] His preceding analysis traces the root for this common supposition, not in any independent rationality or detached observation, but in a universal *being givenness* of aesthetic value; any underlying commonality of value is theistically grounded. Consequently, though this Spirit-given sense of beauty and virtue is inevitably perverted once its divine source is disowned, and though this general sense of beauty and virtue does not of itself and inevitably lead to a

---

[48] '... God in giving to the creature such a temper of mind gives that which is agreeable to what is by absolute necessity his own temper and nature ... therefore, when he gives the same temper to his creatures, this is more agreeable to his necessary nature than the opposite temper: yea, the latter would be infinitely contrary to his nature' (Jonathan Edwards, *True Virtue*, p. 621).

[49] '... God has so constituted nature that the presenting of this inferior beauty, especially in those kinds of it which have the greatest resemblance of the primary beauty, as the harmony of sounds, and the beauties of nature, have a tendency to assist those whose hearts are under the influence of a truly virtuous temper, to dispose them to the exercises of divine love, and enliven in them a sense of spiritual beauty' (Jonathan Edwards, *True Virtue*, p. 565).

[50] '... no wonder that by a long continued worldly and sensual life men more and more lose all sense of the Deity, who is a spiritual and invisible Being. The mind being involved in, and engrossed by sensitive objects, becomes sensual in all its operations, and excludes all views and impressions of spiritual objects, and is unfit for their contemplation' (Jonathan Edwards, *True Virtue*, p. 614).

[51] Jonathan Edwards, *True Virtue*, p. 627.

recognition of *true* beauty and *true* virtue, it inevitably coheres with such; the Spirit-given perception of *true* virtue and *true* beauty resonates with a Spirit-given perception of all created virtue and beauty which is the former's divinely sourced echo and reflection.[52] To repudiate Modernism's presupposition of an independent and rational foundation for morality is not necessarily to deny the possibility of any moral foundation; it is rather to recognize that any valid foundation could never be independent, it could only be mediated by the Son and the Spirit.[53] Moreover, to affirm the continuity of creation and redemption is to expect such a mediation to occur.

If the general intention of the first section of this present book was to repudiate any independently perceived foundation for morality, and the general intention of the second and third sections was to affirm a Christological and Pneumatological foundation for morality, encountered through the narrative of Scripture and the living narrative of the Church and its sacramental life, the general intention of this final section is to affirm the coherence of this distinctively Christian morality with an awareness of creation in general that itself is being given by the Spirit and is orientated to the Son. Herein lies a Trinitarian means of

---

[52] This dynamic resonance of creation and redemption must be contrasted with the static and rational basis of coherence proposed by James Gustafson in the following passage: 'What is ethically justifiable to do (in a purely rational sense) is the Christian thing to do, and vice versa. This is given theological legitimacy by the doctrine of the Trinity in which Christ, the second person, is the one in and through whom all things are created. From this point of view, in principle there is no distinctive Christian morality, but all morality that is rationally justifiable is Christian. The historical particularity of the source of the life of the church has no particular ethical significance, though its theological significance is tremendous, for Jesus is the revelation of God' (James M. Gustafson, *Can Ethics be Christian?* p. 171).

[53] For discussion of the possibilities of a theistic (if not 'fideistic') basis for morality see Paul Helm's *Faith and Understanding*: 'An even more ambitious suggestion to which the faith seeks understanding motif might be applied is the claim that it is only on theistic or supernaturalistic assumptions that certain intellectual problems can be solved. For example, it has been argued that one can best account for the objectivity of moral values on theistic assumptions' (p. 50). See also the discussion in Prof. Helm's final chapter of Plantinga's arguments in *Warrant and Proper Function* (New York: Oxford University Press, 1993).

accounting for a perceived common morality. It certainly cannot be established independently. It simply resonates – but it does so in the power of the Spirit and in coherence with the Son. This resonance can be anticipated simply because creation, and the awareness of creation, are mediated by the same Son and Spirit who are the mediators of redemption. This is not to affirm any *natural* theology or *natural* law, but it is to concur with the possibility of a 'being given' analogy of being that is, in reality, an analogy of grace.[54] The gospel resonates with creation inasmuch as the Spirit gives voice to both.

[54] In this respect, Stanley Hauerwas can speak of co-operation with those outside of the Church in the pursuit of justice as '. . . not based on "natural law" legitimation of a generally shared "natural morality." Rather it is a testimony to the fact that God's kingdom is wide indeed. As the church we have no right to determine the boundaries of God's kingdom, for it is our happy task to acknowledge God's power to make his kingdom present in the most surprising places and ways. (Stanley Hauerwas, *The Peaceable Kingdom*, p. 101); cf. 'What allows us to look expectantly for agreement among those who do not worship God is not that we have a common morality based on autonomous knowledge of autonomous nature, but that God's kingdom is wider than the church' (Stanley Hauerwas, *Christian Existence Today*, p. 17).

12
Persuasiveness and Resonance

It may be a great fault for theological authors to be less than candid concerning their own ecclesiological background and commitment. No writer thinks in a vacuum and the communities that have shaped us and that interpret the narrative of our lives inevitably inform our thinking. I trust that I have already alluded sufficiently to the 'baptist' context of my own thought and to some of the streams of spirituality that have shaped me. As with other denominational groupings, the Baptist tradition within Great Britain is not monochrome: there are baptistic groups that tend towards sectarianism, defining themselves in distinction to the wider church and the world; there are baptistic groups that tend towards a more catholic ecclesiology, defining themselves as bearing a distinctive witness within the wider church and as being in a representative and anticipatory relationship to the world. My own spiritual journey has been marked by a movement from the former to the latter; from a more typically 'Anabaptist' (or Brethren) understanding of the relationship between the Church and the world, to a more classically 'Reformed' ecclesiology. Illustrative of this transition would be the change (or better, reversal) in my attitude to the Church's role in marriage. In my early years of pastoral ministry I would speak specifically of 'Christian Marriage', declining to conduct the wedding of any who were not evidently involved in the life of the Church but, conversely, being willing to preside over the 're-marriage' of a couple where one or both of those involved had previously been married and had been granted a divorce, particularly when the divorcee was either the 'injured party' or had become a Christian since entering the previous marriage. I now find it embarrassing to admit to having once held such an offensive and indefensible (yet all too common) opinion.

But for Adam no suitable helper was found. So the LORD God caused the man to fall into a deep sleep; and

while he was sleeping, he took one of the man's ribs
and closed up the place with flesh. Then the LORD God
made a woman from the rib he had taken out of the
man, and he brought her to the man,
The man said,

> 'This is now bone of my bones
> and flesh of my flesh;
> she shall be called "woman",
> for she was taken out of man.'

For this reason a man will leave his father and mother
and be united to his wife, and they will become one
flesh. (Genesis 2.20ff.)

There is nothing within this creation account, nor in Jesus'
reference to it in confrontation with the Pharisees (Mk.
10.2ff.), to suggest that marriage was ever anything less
than a gracious provision of God for men and women
generally and universally. To speak of 'Christian Marriage'
is to imply that this is not the case: there may, indeed, be a
particular dynamic to a marriage between two Christians –
not least (notwithstanding the overwhelming historical
evidence to the contrary) in an undermining of the patri-
archal outworking of the marriage relationship that
appears to be one of the consequences of the Fall – but the
Church, surely, is called to witness to marriage as this
general and universal provision. Consequently, there
would seem to be no grounds for denying a wedding
service, in the context of the community of the Church, to
any couple seeking God's blessing on their marriage, no
matter how minimal their understanding of God's blessing
might be: marriage is blessed by God generally and universally; his blessing, at least in this respect, is not confined
within the boundaries of the confessing community.[1]

---

[1] Note that, having defined marriage as a sacrament, Thomas
nonetheless affirms that 'marriage between unbelievers is a true marriage'
and even argues that 'a marriage of this kind is a sacrament after the
manner of a habit, although it is not actually since they do not marry
actually in the faith of the Church' (ST III 59 2). Thomas has earlier stated

Moreover, since marriage is this general and universal provision of God, there can be no sense in which a marriage between non-Christians, by whatever rite or process that marriage may have been established, can be of any less validity than a marriage between two Christians: if the Church is at liberty to admit the possibility of re-marriage after divorce this must be without prejudice to any previous Christian commitment or non-commitment by the parties concerned; indeed, if re-marriage after divorce is at all permissible it is so *solely* as an outcome of the mercy of God in the context of human failure – a mercy that embraces the 'guilty' party every bit as much as the 'innocent'.

But if marriage is a gracious provision of God for men and women generally, albeit, as Thomas Aquinas puts it, 'not perfected by its ultimate perfection as there is between believers',[2] we are then confronted by the question of how the Church might witness to this provision, and to the accompanying sexual disciplines implicit in this provision, within a society that does not recognize its defining story – a question all the more pressing when traditional attitudes to marriage and sexual discipline appear to be under such sustained threat.[3] And, of course, this issue of marriage and sexual discipline is merely one instance, albeit a particularly prominent instance, of the general question of

---

that 'the union of Christ with the Church is not the reality contained in this sacrament, but is the reality signified and not contained', but he also recognizes the sacrament of marriage as significant of the resulting 'bond between husband and wife' (*ST* III 42 1) and as significant of the promise of conferred grace (cf. *ST* III 42 3). Calvin (with some justification) questions the sense in which marriage can be termed a sacrament in the sense of being a sign 'of the spiritual joining of Christ with the church' but he perhaps too hastily dismisses the sense in which marriage might be 'an outward ceremony appointed by God to confirm a promise' (*Institutes* IV xix 34).

[2] *ST* III 59 2.

[3] Stanley Hauerwas suggests that this threat derives, not from any loss of significance for the family, but rather through the family having to bear alone the weight once shared by other institutions: '... with the diminishment of other institutions that claim and carry symbols and practices of personal significance, the family has been broken because it has to carry too great a moral load' (Stanley Hauerwas, *A Community of Character*, p. 167).

how the Church can address the world with the gospel in its form as command.

The advantage (not to say, the attraction) of the typically Anabaptist account of the relationship between the Church and the world is that it effectively can evade the question. It is unsurprising, therefore, that with the collapse of a liberal consensus concerning moral foundations this notion of a radical disjunction between Church and world should attract contemporary (and somewhat more nuanced) advocates.

Perhaps the clearest and sharpest expression of an Anabaptist distinction between Church and world occurs in the fourth article of the Schleitheim Confession of 1527 which, while agreed by all those assembled at Schleitheim, is generally considered to derive principally from Michael Sattler, formerly a Prior of St. Peter's Benedictine Abbey in the Black Forest, who was brutally executed barely three months after the gathering that agreed the Confession.[4] The Confession calls for an absolute separation from 'the evil and the wickedness which the devil has planted in the world'; here a categorical disjunction is assumed between 'believing and unbelieving, darkness and light, the world and those who are come out of the world, God's temple and idols, Christ and Belial'; every Christian disciple must separate from 'everything which has not been united with our God in Christ'. It is this principle of separation that underlies the Confession's rejection of all worldly means of violence and coercion together with its refusal of the magistracy and of 'oath taking'.[5] Accordingly we find

---

[4] 'Brotherly Union of a Number of Children of God Concerning Seven Articles' in *The Legacy of Michael Sattler*, trans. and ed. John H. Yoder, (Scottdale: Herald Press, 1973), pp. 34–43: hereafter referred to as *Confession*. Note that both Zwingli and Calvin assumed the *Confession* to be representative of Anabaptist thought: Ulrich Zwingli, 'Refutation of the Tricks of the Baptists' (*In catabaptistarum strophas elenchus*: 1527) in *Selected Works*, ed. Samuel Macauley Jackson (Philadelphia: University of Pennsylvannia Press, 1972), pp. 123–258; John Calvin, 'Brief Instruction for Arming All the Faithful Against the Errors of the Common Sect of the Anabaptists' in *Treatises against the Anabaptists and against the Libertines*, ed. and trans. Benjamin Wirt Farley (Grand Rapids: Baker, 1982), p. 41.

[5] *Confession*, pp. 37f.

Pilgram Marpeck declaring that 'there need be no external power or sword, for the kingdom of Christ is not of this world',[6] and Peter Riedeman (a leading Hutterite) arguing that 'no Christian is a ruler and no ruler is a Christian'.[7] Here, then, is an ideal of the Church in contrast to the world; the boundary between the one and the other is clearly demarked; there can be little or no interaction between the two; the disciplines and processes appropriate to the one are entirely inappropriate to the other; the world is defined more radically by its fallenness than by its createdness. A specific outworking of this disjunction occurs in an anonymous tract on divorce, attributed to Michael Sattler, which recognizes a 'spiritual' form of adultery and implies that marriage can be dissolved if it conflicts with one's first loyalty to Christ.[8] This implicitly 'sectarian' conception of marriage is more rigidly expressed by Dirk Philips who, in response to the text of Ezra 10, not only forbids the marriage of Christian disciples to non-believers but actually encourages Christians to separate from unbelieving partners.[9]

---

[6]   Pilgram Marpeck, 'The Admonition of 1542' in *The Writings of Pilgram Marpeck*, trans. and ed. William Klassen & Walter Klaassen (Scottdale: Herald Press, 1978), pp. 160–302 (p. 209).
[7]   Peter Riedeman, *Account of Our Religion, Doctrine and Faith* (1542), cited in *Anabaptism in Outline: Selected Primary Sources*, ed. Walter Klaassen (Scottdale: Herald Press, 1981), pp. 258–62 (p. 261).
[8]   'Rather the spiritual obligation and marriage with Christ and faith, love, and obedience to God take priority, so that no creature should separate us from God and from the love of Christ' ('On Divorce' in *The Legacy of Michael Sattler*, pp. 101–5, p. 104.)
[9]   'Now, seeing that such impure marriages and intermingling of the children of God with unbelievers in the time of imperfection under the law could not be tolerated, how should it exist before God and his congregation in this time of the perfect Christian being according to the gospel? This each one may reflect upon and consider from the heart': Dirk Philips, 'The Enchiridion' in *The Writings of Dirk Philips*, trans. and ed. Cornelius J. Dyck, William E. Keeney and Alvin J. Beachy (Scottdale: Herald Press, 1992), pp. 59–440 (p. 344); cf. '... it should nevermore come to where anyone called a brother or sister should take an unbelieving person [as a spouse] from the world if they hope to be saved, nor should such be found [among them]' ('About the Marriage of Christians' in *The Writings of Dirk Philips*, pp. 554–76, p. 559). This notion of a 'spiritual adultery' as grounds for divorce seems also to have been held by Peter Riedeman: see George Huntston Williams, *The Radical Reformation* (Philadelphia: Westminster Press, 1962), pp. 516f.

A more circumspect expression of this disjunction between the Church and the world occurs in the Lutheran doctrine of two kingdoms. The understanding of the relationship between Church and State that underlies Martin Luther's writings in response to the Peasants' Revolt,[10] and that comes to more nuanced expression in his 'Warning to His Dear German People' of 1531,[11] is expounded most fully in his treatise on 'Temporal Authority' of 1523.[12] Luther's immediate concern here, as in his other works of a similar nature, is to wrestle with the question of whether, and in what manner, it might ever be appropriate for Christians to resist secular authority. In the course of his denial that the Church can be exempt from the authority of the State – that while defensive action in protection of the gospel may be permissible, insurrection is absolutely forbidden – Luther distinguishes two spheres, and therefore two outworkings, of God's kingly authority: in the temporal sphere or kingdom the world is addressed by the divine law of love, a law expressed in social relationships (including marriage and sexual discipline) that may be upheld through coercive temporal authority; in the spiritual sphere or kingdom of the Church, defined by faith, love remains the ultimate law but here there is no place for coercion since all are equal. The latter kingdom produces righteousness; the former merely maintains peace and restrains evil:

> If all the world were composed of real Christians, that is, true believers, there would be no need for or

---

[10] Martin Luther, 'Admonition to Peace, A Reply to the Twelve Articles of the Peasants in Swabia' (1525), and 'Against the Robbing and Murdering Hordes of Peasants' (1525), trans. Charles M. Jacobs, revised Robert C. Schultz, in *Luther's Works* vol. 46, ed. Robert C. Schultz, gen. ed. Helmut T. Lehmann (Philadelphia: Fortress Press, 1967), pp. 17–43, 49–55.

[11] Martin Luther, 'Dr. Martin Luther's Warning to His Dear German People' (1531), trans. Martin H. Bertram, in *Luther's Works* vol. 47, ed. Franklin Sherman, gen. ed. Helmut T. Lehmann (Philadelphia: Fortress Press, 1971), pp. 11–55.

[12] Martin Luther, 'Temporal Authority: To What Extent it Should be Obeyed' (1523), trans. W. A. Lambert, revised Walther I. Brandt, in *Luther's Works* vol. 45, ed. Walther I. Brandt, gen. ed. Helmut T. Lehmann (Philadelphia: Muhlenberg Press, 1962), pp. 81–129.

benefits from prince, king, lord, sword, or law. They
would serve no purpose, since Christians have in their
heart the Holy Spirit, who both teaches and makes
them to do injustice to no one, to love everyone, and
to suffer injustice and even death willingly and
cheerfully at the hands of anyone.[13]

That which distinguishes Luther's account from that of his
more radical Anabaptist contemporaries is his insistence
that, here and now, Christians inhabit *both* spheres,
submitting to the authority of the one while enjoying the
freedom of the other. Consequently, Christians not only
may participate in the magistracy, in 'oath taking', and in
the coercive responsibilities of the state; Christians actually
have an *obligation* to fulfil whatever secular responsibilities
fall to them. And, since marriage and sexual discipline are
included within the divine law addressed to and through
the temporal sphere, marriage and sexual discipline are
appropriately upheld by temporal authority, an authority
in which Christians appropriately participate.

However, while Luther clearly recognizes both spheres
or kingdoms as addressed supremely by the law of love, he
nonetheless is distinguishing 'two kinds of law':[14] the laws
of temporal kingdoms, while representing God's supreme
law of love, fall short of it and, consequently, those who
merely inhabit the secular sphere or kingdom are
addressed by a lesser and therefore a distinct word. Herein
lies the fundamental difficulty of Luther's account: the
inescapable implication of such a distinction is that law (at
least in this provisional form) can be disjoined from gospel;
that law, as it functions within the temporal sphere, has its
own discrete basis and rationale. And, if the world is
addressed by law *other than as a form of gospel*, this might

---

[13] Martin Luther, 'Temporal Authority', p. 89.
[14] 'For every kingdom must have its own laws and statutes; without law
no kingdom or government can survive, as everyday experience amply
shows. The temporal government has laws which extend no further than
to life and property and external affairs on earth, for God cannot and will
not permit anyone but himself to rule over the soul' (Martin Luther,
'Temporal Authority', p. 105).

further be taken as implying an *ontological* distinction between the world and the Church; an implied disjunction of law and gospel itself implies a corresponding disjunction, not just between world and Church, but more fundamentally between creation and redemption. The story of the relationship between the Church and the State in Germany, particularly through the course of the twentieth century, amply and tragically illustrates the catastrophic consequences of this disjunction. Hence Karl Barth comments:

> That authority and law rest on a particular *ordinatio* of divine providence, necessary on account of unconquered sin, serving to protect humanity from the most concrete expressions and consequences of that sin, and thus to be accepted by humanity with gratitude and honour – these are certainly true and biblical thoughts, but they are not enough to make clear the relationship between this issue and the other, which the Reformation held to be the decisive and final issue of faith and confession ... What has Christ to do with this matter? we ask, and we are left without any real answer, as though a particular ruling of a general, somewhat anonymous Providence were here the last word.[15]

In this respect Eberhard Jüngel's suggestion that the fifth thesis of the *Barmen Declaration* represents a version of this

---

[15] Karl Barth, *Church and State*, trans. G. Ronald Howe (London: SCM Press, 1939), pp. 4f. While Barth's opposition to this 'Two Kingdoms' notion is well known it is surprising how little it is attested within the *Church Dogmatics*: see however the discussion of 'God the Creator as Commander' (*CD* III/4, pp. 32ff.) and the following comments later within the same part-volume: '... there should be no gap in man's activity, but he must actively remember for his part that he is summoned to be present as man in co-operation in the service of the Christian community. Again, as the active recollection of both aspects cannot involve any cleavage or dualism or double kingdom in God's action, since the meaning and purpose of the rule of His fatherly providence are simply the coming of His one kingdom on earth, so the active recollection of man's twofold determination as a Christian and a man cannot divide his activity into two separate spheres under two different laws ...'(*CD* III/4, p. 518).

'Two Kingdom' doctrine would seem to be itself the
outcome of his own Lutheran special pleading.[16] This
article that affirms the State's responsibility for
'maintaining justice and peace' begins with the confession
that this appointment is declared by Scripture. Moreover,
the Declaration begins unequivocally with the claim that
'Jesus Christ, as he is attested to us in Holy Scripture, is the
one Word of God which we have to hear, and which we
have to trust and obey in life and death' and the fifth article
surely must be interpreted in the light of this primary
statement.[17] Indeed, Professor Jüngel himself later admits
that the Church 'will not pervert the Gospel, which
liberates from godless bonds, by reducing it to law and
thereby making it ambiguous'.[18] Given Barth's role in the
framing of the *Barmen Declaration* it is quite unthinkable

[16] 'The *fifth* thesis represents the Barmen version of – do not be shocked!
– the Two-Kingdom-Doctrine of the Reformers. I venture this assertion,
although I know that "just this thesis" stems "word for word" from Karl
Barth, who is to be regarded as a resolute opponent of Luther's Two-
Kingdom-Doctrine. On closer examination, however, it becomes clear
how very much Barth's definition of the relationship between the
Christian community and the civil community is a development of
the Two-Kingdom-Doctrine of the Reformers – albeit a highly original
one': Eberhard Jüngel, *Christ, Justice and Peace: Toward a Theology of the
State in Dialogue with the Barmen Declaration*, trans. D. Bruce Hamill and
Alan J. Torrance (Edinburgh: T&T Clark, 1992), p. 37.
[17] A translation of the Declaration is quoted in full at the beginning of
Jüngel's interpretation (Eberhard Jüngel, *Christ, Justice and Peace*, pp.
xxi–xxix).
[18] 'For this reason Christians, and also the church – in the proclamation
of the Gospel of God's coming kingdom – possess *criteria*, by way of God's
command and God's justice-creating righteousness, for that which is to be
established in the earthly state as justice and peace. As we have already
said, the church will not, thereby, become an active law-giver itself. It will
not pervert the Gospel, which liberates from godless bonds, by reducing
it to law and thereby making it ambiguous. And, in the same way, it will
not pervert the political work of the legislator, the executive, and the
earthly courts by making cumbersome and dubious demands on their use
of power (which is necessarily problematic, ambivalent and ambiguous)
by introducing the unambiguous claims of the kingdom of God. But it will
bring to bear on the legislator *strenuous demands* from the Gospel,
strenuous, evangelical *demands*, which serve as criteria for that which
(within the limits of human insight) is to be regarded as earthly justice
and earthly peace and for that which is to be put in operation, albeit
within the limits of human ability' (Eberhard Jüngel, *Christ, Justice and
Peace*, pp. 71f.).

that any notion of divine law *other than as a form of the gospel* could have been smuggled into the fifth article. Accordingly, John Howard Yoder comments that:

> ... Barth refuses above all other things to deal with the state the way Lutheranism sometimes did, making it a second autonomous realm within the divine economy, for all practical purposes subject to no norms except those which it feels to be desirable for the protection of its own existence. Some people could thus convince themselves that they were being good Lutherans when they failed to resist Hitler. Barth had to avoid giving the state that kind of exemption from Christian examination which Lutheranism, if not Luther himself, permitted.[19]

The continuity and coherence of creation and redemption, as attested by Irenaeus, compels the conclusion that God has but one word for the Church and the world, the word 'Jesus', a word narrated in the gospel story and in the life of the Church. Albeit in very different ways, a radical Anabaptist separation from the world, and a Lutheran account of 'Two Kingdoms', both effectively undermine or even deny this continuity and coherence. That the gospel does indeed take form as command is not denied or negated by this affirmation of the divine word's singularity; what is rather denied and negated is the possibility of this command being anything other than a form of the gospel. The question at issue in this final chapter is not the question of the singularity of this word, the continuity of creation and redemption, the relatedness of law and gospel

[19] John H. Yoder, *Karl Barth and the Problem of War* (Nashville: Abingdon Press, 1970), p. 96. In this respect note also Oliver O'Donovan's comment on the typically Lutheran 'Foundations' of Helmut Thielicke's *Theological Ethics*: 'Given the opposition of law and gospel in the Reformation traditions we can only understand Thielicke's thesis as meaning that the Christian life has to be lived under some other authority than the authority of Christ': Oliver O'Donovan, *Resurrection and the Moral Order*, p. 146, commenting on Helmut Thielicke, *Theological Ethics*, vols. 1–3, ed. (vols. 1–2) William H. Lazareth, trans. (vol. 3) John W. Doberstein (Grand Rapids: Eerdmans, 1966–79).

– it is to be hoped that all this has already been established
– the question is rather one of the appropriate manner in
which the Church might bear testimony to this singular
word, together with the manner in which this singular word
might be heard.

Surprisingly perhaps, John Howard Yoder, a twentieth-
century representative of the Anabaptist tradition, appears
to accept this affirmation of the singularity of the divine
word, maintaining that the distinction between the Church
and the world is a distinction of agents rather than a
distinction of address, a distinction in the manner in which
this one word is heard rather than any distinction in the
word that is spoken.[20] However, this dynamic distinction
of hearing is rendered more complex by Yoder's understanding of the Church's anticipation of the new aeon: with
the introduction of a distinction between the old aeon
and the new – in parallel to the distinction between faith and
unbelief, the Church and the world – Yoder seems to have
smuggled an ontological category under the cover of an
essentially dynamic distinction. It is this 'parallel between
faith and the new aeon' in Yoder's work that Stanley
Hauerwas calls into question.[21] Fundamental to Karl
Barth's account of anthropology is the recognition that

[20] Yoder's arguments are helpfully summarized by Stanley Hauerwas as
follows: 'We must remember the "world" as that opposed to God is not
an ontological designation. Thus "world" is not inherently sinful; rather
its sinful character is by its own free will. The only difference between
church and world is the difference between agents. As Yoder suggests, the
distinction between church and world is not between realms of reality,
between orders of creation and redemption, between nature and super-
nature, but "rather between the basic personal postures of men, some of
whom confess and others of whom do not confess that Jesus is Lord." ':
Stanley Hauerwas, *The Peaceable Kingdom*, pp. 100f.: quoting John Howard
Yoder, *The Original Revolution* (Scottdale: Herald Press, 1971), p. 116. A
similar distinction deriving from the manner in which the one divine
word is heard occurs, from a Lutheran perspective, in Robert W. Jenson's
essay on 'The Church's responsibility for the World' in *The Two Cities of
God: The Church's Responsibility for the Earthly City*, ed. Carl E. Braaten and
Robert W. Jenson (Grand Rapids: Eerdmans, 1997), pp. 1–10.
[21] This, fundamentally, is Professor Hauerwas's criticism of Yoder's
proposal: 'To put the issue in Yoder's own terminology I am suggesting
that his theology of the Church's form of witness to society is not
supported completely by the distinction he draws between the old and
new aeons. To be sure he says both are redeemed in Christ, but if this is

there can be no ontological definition of humanity other
than that identified in Jesus Christ: the Church, here and
now, through the indwelling of the Spirit, may anticipate
the eschatological fulfilment of humanity in Christ but this
anticipation does not constitute any ontological distinction;
the Church and the world are addressed by a single word,
a word that uniquely is ontologically definitive. The
distinction between faith and unbelief – or better, between
apparent faith and apparent unbelief – which constitutes
the distinction between the Church and the world, is at
best elusive and must never be interpreted as implying a
corresponding ontological distinction.

But without recourse to some form of ontological
disjunction between the Church and the world, such as
Yoder's employment of this distinction of the two aeons,
one must question whether merely a dynamic distinction
of hearing, a distinction that Stanley Hauerwas himself
espouses, is sufficient to bear the burden of the ethical
disjunction that characterizes both writers. For some form
of judicial coercive restraint to be appropriate to the world
yet inappropriate to the Church surely requires more than
can be educed merely from a distinction of hearing: either
the world also is being called to abandon every form of
judicial coercive restraint – which, as has previously been
argued, appears to take insufficient account of the world's
fallenness and of the provisionality of God's action in
response to the world's fallenness within the biblical story
– or else this distinction of hearing derives, notwithstanding the protests to the contrary, from an underlying
distinction of address. A distinction of response can derive
from a distinction of hearing; a distinction of *appropriate*

the case can he draw the line between them quite as sharply as he seems
to do in terms of the Christian's stance toward the society and its cares?
Or put in a somewhat different way, how is he sure where the line
between them is to be drawn? The virtue of understanding the dualism of
Christian ethics to be one primarily of possible response of agents is that
it allows for a dynamic understanding of God's redeeming work and the
Christian's response to it. Yoder seems, however, to have severely
qualified this aspect of his theology of social criticism by assuming an
exact parallel between faith and the new aeon, unbelief and the old aeon'
(Stanley Hauerwas, *Vision and Virtue*, p. 220).

response cannot so derive; if the Church responds appropriately to this one word of God by repudiating every form
of judicial constraint, then the world's retention of such can
only be a response of disobedience.

In the light of the coherence of creation and redemption
the Church is called to bear testimony to a singular divine
command that is a form of the gospel. But the singularity
of this divine word has a twofold implication: in contradistinction to any form of sectarianism or 'Two Kingdoms'
notion that implicitly denies this singularity, the world is
addressed by no other and no lesser word than this divine
command which is a form of the gospel; but in contradistinction to any form of sectarianism and in correspondence
with the so-called Magisterial Reformers, the Church is
addressed by this same divine command which, in accordance with the stories of Scripture, takes shape within the
present context of this world's fallenness. Certainly God
calls both Church and world to peaceableness, and
certainly he calls the Church to anticipate the fulfilment of
this call, but not in such a manner as absolves the Church
from the responsibilities of living in this present fallen
context. If some form of judicial coercive restraint is an
appropriate response for the world to the single command
of God, which is a form of the gospel, it is so also, here and
now, in a manner that includes the Church. Every form of
sectarianism which implicitly assumes an ontological and
imperatival disjunction between the world and the Church
more fundamentally implies a corresponding disjunction
between creation and redemption.[22]

Perhaps the most comprehensive rebuttal of any form of
sectarian disengagement occurs in Oliver O'Donovan's
surprisingly robust defence of the notion of Christendom.[23]

[22] In the course of his subsequent discussion of the *Barmen Declaration*,
Eberhard Jüngel also appears to evade Barth's insistence that the Church
is still, at the same time, a part of this fallen world and therefore impli-
cated in both the threat of force and the use of force which is
'characteristic of the not-yet-redeemed world within which the state has
to act' (Eberhard Jüngel, *Christ, Justice and Peace*, p. 50).
[23] Oliver O'Donovan, *The Desire of the Nations: Rediscovering the Roots of
Political Theology* (Cambridge: Cambridge University Press, 1996).

Professor O'Donovan argues that the phenomenon of Christendom should be recognized, not as a *'project'* of the Church's mission, but rather as a *'response'* to that mission and 'as such a sign that God has blessed it'; Christendom 'is constituted not by the church's seizing alien power, but by alien power's becoming attentive to the church':[24]

> The church is not at liberty to withdraw from mission; nor may it undertake its mission without confident hope of success. It was the missionary imperative that compelled the church to take the conversion of the empire seriously and to seize the opportunities it offered. These were not merely opportunities for 'power'. They were opportunities for preaching the Gospel, baptising believers, curbing the violence and cruelty of empire and, perhaps most important of all, forgiving their former persecutors.[25]

This wholly positive conception of Christendom may sound historically one-sided and consequently idealistic, but it represents an important corrective to the common and increasingly ubiquitous 'Anabaptist' dismissal of the phenomenon of Christendom as the Church's greatest apostasy.[26] Whether or not this revisionist reading of Church history – not to mention its assumptions concerning the dispositions of human nature when confronted by the prospect of worldly power – is unrealistically optimistic, that which Professor O'Donovan refuses

---

[24] Oliver O'Donovan, *The Desire of the Nations*, p. 195.
[25] Oliver O'Donovan, *The Desire of the Nations*, p. 212.
[26] For a criticism of this implicit idealism see Tim Gorringe, 'Authority, Plebs and Patricians' in *Studies in Christian Ethics* 11 2 (1998), pp. 24–29 (an edition of the Journal wholly given to responses to this book by Oliver O'Donovan). Note also the following (and most revealing) response from Stanley Hauerwas: 'Being all too cognizant of the sinful proclivities of the human imagination and of the seeming ineradicable human pride which reserves for political life its most virulent manifestations, we find our hope in the prospects of human rule under God to be tempered more by the eschatological "not yet" than encouraged by the eschatological "already"' (Stanley Hauerwas and James Fodor, 'Remaining in Babylon: Oliver O'Donovan's Defence of Christendom' in *Studies in Christian Ethics* 11 2 (1998), pp. 30–55, p. 40).

is any hope-less conception of the Church's mission.[27] Nor is he oblivious to the dangers inherent in the phenomenon, but he identifies the chief danger, not as that of the Church assuming a coercive authority in correspondence to the State, but rather as that of the Church colluding with the State's assumption of its own inherent and autonomous authority, an authority independent of that of Christ:

> The peril of the Christendom idea – precisely the same peril that attends upon the post-Christendom idea of the religiously neutral state – was that of negative collusion: the pretence that there was now no further challenge to be issued to the rulers in the name of the ruling Christ.[28]

There is no question here, then, of any secondary or rival 'word' establishing the State without reference to Christ – the nation-state 'has been in trouble ever since Christ rose from the dead'[29] – but there is also here an assumption

---

[27] It is in this respect that Professor O'Donovan criticizes Stanley Hauerwas: The 'triumph of Christ among the nations Hauerwas is not prepared to see. His Christianity is marked by a return to the catacombs' (Oliver O'Donovan, *The Desire of the Nations*, pp. 215f.). Note however that O'Donovan doesn't see this as sectarianism: 'Was it not the *catholic* church that sheltered in the catacombs and which Augustine thought might be called on at any moment to return to them?' (p. 216).

[28] Oliver O'Donovan, *The Desire of the Nations*, p. 213. Professor O'Donovan later makes this same point with direct reference to the *Barmen Declaration*: 'Of the two perils identified by the fifth chapter of the Barmen Declaration, perhaps the church falls rather less into the temptation of assuming the state's authority, rather more into that of acquiescing with the state's assumption of its own. Political orders, whether or not they are professedly Christian, will tend to want to draw on the social strengths of the church for their support. The church need not always refuse such support; but it must be on guard against the danger that such a posture will distort its mission and message. "Civil religion" poses a more serious objection to the co-operative church-state arrangements of Christendom than religious coercion does. Both, of course, offend against the Gospel, not merely against natural justice: coercion violates the openness of unbelief to come to belief freely while God's patience waits on it; civil religion violates the freedom of belief to believe truly. But civil religion wears the form of the Antichrist, drawing the faith and obedience due to the Lord's Anointed away to the political orders which should have only provisional authority under him' (Oliver O'Donovan, *The Desire of the Nations*, p. 224).

[29] Oliver O'Donovan, *The Desire of the Nations*, p. 241.

concerning the possibilities of the State's knowledge of God and his defining word. In this latter respect Professor O'Donovan exposes the incoherence of Barth's language in the *Barmen Declaration*:

> ... how is this constitutionally pagan state, by definition ignorant of its own righteousness, 'reminded' of what it never knew? And of what, if it knew it, would make it no longer ignorant, and so no longer 'the state as such'? Two ideas appear to have been combined, not entirely happily.[30]

But it is in this respect that Professor O'Donovan's own work appears to be less than fully formulated: throughout the book there is minimal reference to the Spirit and, in particular, to the dynamic by which this kingdom authority of the risen Christ might be known 'generally' among the 'nations'. What the thesis demands is precisely that Pneumatological epistemology proposed by Jonathan Edwards and implicit in Irenaeus' account of creation and redemption: the gospel in its form as command resonates with the nations of the world – and may be 'remembered' by them – since redemption is continuous rather than discontinuous with creation, since the Christ who is the source and goal of redemption is beforehand the source and goal of creation, since the being-givenness by which we come to know the gospel is the work of that same Spirit as the being-givenness by which we come to know anything at all. It is difficult to see how Professor O'Donovan's affirmation of continuity can be maintained without more explicit reference to this underlying continuity of all reality and of all knowledge of reality. The alternative to such a foundation for ethical continuity is epistemological dualism: either a continuance of the dualism of independent rational foundationalism or a retreat into the sectarian dualism that renders the command of the gospel wholly inaccessible to the world.

A similar affirmation of continuity (together with a

---

[30] Oliver O'Donovan, *The Desire of the Nations*, p. 214.

similar lack of any explicit Pneumatological foundation for that continuity) occurs in John Milbank's advocacy of a form of neo-Augustinianism.[31] John Milbank's work is both a detailed (and an exhausting) analysis of social theory and an indictment of the Church's loss of confidence in the foundational nature of its own message:

> The pathos of modern theology is its false humility. For theology, this must be a fatal disease, because once theology surrenders its claim to be a metadiscourse, it cannot any longer articulate the word of the creator God, but is bound to turn into the oracular voice of some finite idol, such as historical scholarship, humanist psychology, or transcendental philosophy.[32]

For Professor Milbank, then, the gospel is the 'metadiscourse' that interprets and qualifies every other discourse; it relates 'the judgement of God' that has 'already happened' in 'the midst of history':[33]

> The *logic* of Christianity involves the claim that the 'interruption' of history by Christ and his bride, the Church, is the most fundamental of events, interpreting all other events. And it is *most especially* a social event, able to interpret other social formations, because it compares them with its own new social practice.[34]

As was noted in an earlier chapter, the rejection of any form of metanarrative, with its connotations of coercion and violence – connotations that John Milbank himself

---

[31] John Milbank, *Theology and Social Theory* (Oxford: Blackwell, 1990). It is remarkable that Augustine can be cited both as a proponent for such continuity and as undermining it: compare Milbank's thesis with, for instance, Colin E Gunton's *The One, The Three and the Many*, p. 55 n. 20. Stanley Hauerwas makes a parallel observation: '... Augustine has the odd position of being claimed by some as the harbinger of the ascendancy of the church in the Middle Ages and by others as the originator of the Protestant rejection of the same church' (Stanley Hauerwas, *After Christendom?* pp. 39f.).

[32] John Milbank, *Theology and Social Theory*, p. 1.

[33] John Milbank, *Theology and Social Theory*, p. 433.

[34] John Milbank, *Theology and Social Theory*, p. 388.

consistently repudiates – is a defining mark of post-modernism. The claim to relate a metanarrative is a thinly veiled claim to control, to coerce, to constrain. Yet, without apostasy, the Church cannot retreat from proclaiming the gospel as *the* foundational story that interprets all other stories since it is the narration of the Christ who is the source and goal of creation itself. As Sara Maitland has affirmed, albeit in a very different book:

> There is, we claim, a universal story. It begins at the beginning (if not before), goes on to the end and then does not stop. There is a Grand Narrative. It is the creative, redemptive and eschatological narrative, centred on the passion, death and resurrection, and developed outwards in all possible directions. It is the workings of God in and with the whole cosmos, and it can be spoken, at least a little, because it has revealed its formal structure in the Word – the creative word and the redemptive word, which (who) is Jesus Christ.[35]

As was suggested earlier in this book, one way of avoiding the unhelpful connotations of metanarrative – a possibility entirely consistent with the argument of this book and with the majority thinkers with which this book has sought to engage – would be to recognize the gospel as underlying story rather than overarching story; as the narrative that undergirds, rather than overrules, every other narrative.[36] The point at issue is not the priority of the gospel in relation to every other story but rather the manner and character of that priority. Jesus is King, but his 'kingdom is not of this world' (John 18.36); he reigns, but the manner of his reigning conflicts with our presupposed concepts of authority:[37]

[35] Sara Maitland, *A Big-Enough God: Artful Theology* (London: Mowbray, 1995), p. 115.
[36] A parallel could perhaps be drawn with Karl Barth's use of the term *Urgeschichte*.
[37] 'Jesus' disavowal of the kingship of this world does not mean that he is not a king. Rather his dialogue with Pilate reveals that he is not the kind of king that Pilates are capable of recognizing. For Pilates are people who have disavowed truth, and in particular, a truth that comes in the form of a suffering servant' (Stanley Hauerwas, *After Christendom?* pp. 91f.).

> Here is my servant, whom I uphold,
>   my chosen one in whom I delight;
> I will put my Spirit on him
>   and he will bring justice to the nations.
> He will not shout or cry out,
>   or raise his voice in the streets.
> A bruised reed he will not break,
>   and a smouldering wick he will not snuff out.
> In faithfulness he will bring forth justice;
>   he will not falter or be discouraged
> till he establishes justice on earth.
> In his law the islands will put their hope.
>
> (Isaiah 42 1–4)

If the phenomenon of Christendom was vitiated by the Church's adoption of the coercive and violent strategies of the nations this was not an inevitable outcome of its proclamation of Jesus' kingship, nor an inevitable outcome of its confession of Christ as the source and goal of the universe and its history; it was rather the consequence of a failure to remember the unique manner of his kingship. It is the crucified Jesus who reigns: he 'will bring forth justice' through 'faithfulness', in a manner that is absolutely coherent with his character; he doesn't need to 'shout' or 'to raise his voice'; he does not further damage that which is damaged already. The gospel, then, is not a dominating narrative, overarching the narratives of human society, it is persuasive narrative: it persuades through its underlying and compelling coherence; it resonates with human stories since it relates the story of the one who is the source and goal of every story; it convinces since it is whispered by the same Spirit who breathes through all creation and who is the giver of every perception.

The Church, then, like its Master, does not need to 'shout'; it has no need of coercive or violent strategies, indeed, it apostasizes the moment it employs them since in doing so it denies the character of its Lord and vacates its defining story; it has no need to dominate nor to seek for power within human society. Its task is simply, through its speech, through its worship, and through its life, to witness to the story that is the gospel; to confess it as the story that underlies every other story and therefore makes sense of every other story. The very attempt to 'shout' or to dominate betrays a loss of confidence in this underlying coherence, a loss of confidence in the ubiquity of the Spirit and the cosmic significance of the Son. And, whether or not this underlying resonance is admitted and owned by the world, the Church will continue to presume the actuality of such resonance: the God-forsaking are not God-forsaken; the reality of the world's fallenness cannot utterly abolish the reality of its createdness and its continuing dependency; the 'spirit' of this age cannot entirely muffle the voice of the Holy Spirit.

It cannot, however, be emphasized too strongly that what is being affirmed here is no 'natural' capacity or 'point of contact' independently inherent in men and women, but rather a being-givenness of perception by the Spirit whose goal is to glorify the Son. The narrative of the gospel resonates in creation, notwithstanding creation's fallenness: the 'light shines in the darkness' and, even though 'the darkness has not understood it', neither has it been able to 'overcome' it (John 1.5).[38] An expectation for resonance would be invalid only if the world's fallenness truly was more decisive than its createdness. This is not a retreat into the independent foundationalism of modernity, but neither is it a capitulation to the foundationlessness of post-modernity; it is an affirmation of the foundation of all reality in the Son and an affirmation of the Spirit's witness to that foundation. Indeed, it is on the basis of this single foundation – the underlying coherence of creation with the narrative of the gospel – that the Church, with respect (for instance) to a repudiation of sexism and racism, may find itself reminded of what the Spirit says in the gospel through the Spirit's speaking through other stories.[39]

---

[38]   Note the ambiguity of the word κατέλαβεν, an ambiguity noted in the margin of the *NIV*.

[39]   'Movements within the world beyond the ecclesial community continually pose a question to the community. They bring before it the question whether particular aspects of its existing self-understanding, beliefs and practices are still to be regarded as authentically Christian, or whether

Merely the collapse of the phenomenon of Christendom does not, of itself, deliver the Church from the temptation to coercive power, but it may at least afford the opportunity for the Church to recall a manner of witness that is faithful. In the context of the world's fallenness, the Church may not be able to evade its societal obligations to participate in the restraining of violence even if, *in extremis*, that *re*straint can only be achieved through some minimal and closely defined use of violence. But the Church may never, without repudiating its defining story, seek to further society's coherence with the goals of that story through violent *con*straint. The Church cannot impose its vision of morality – to do so would itself be immoral – but the Church can, indeed must, play its part in the protection of the weak from the effects of immorality.

To return, then, to the matter of sexual ethics, the specific example with which this chapter began, the Church certainly cannot abdicate a responsibility to protect the weak and the vulnerable from abuse – in this regard it is appropriate for the Church to advocate and support societal legislation (which can never be more than provisional) that aims at restraint for the sake of protection – but the Church must not seek to impose through legislation its positive understanding of marriage and sexual discipline, no matter how attractive (or even utilitarian) such a prospect might be.[40] It may, indeed it should, present its

---

they require critical reappraisal or outright rejection. This process of questioning from outside is one of the ways in which the Spirit leads the community out of distorted and inadequate positions into all the truth (cf. John. 16 13); and it is one of the ways in which oppressive law is distinguished from life-giving gospel as holy scripture is read and interpreted' (Francis Watson, *Text, Church and World*, p. 240); cf. Prof. Watson's earlier reference to John Owen's awareness of this spiritual possibility (p. 237).

[40] 'It can be, and frequently is argued that past generations of Christians have stressed too much the link between sexuality and sin, too little the social and political determinants of human alienation. In so far as such treatment has derived from a generally negative assessment of human sexuality, the current change of emphasis to the social shape of sin would seem to be justified. And yet it can be argued that there is now a danger of over-reaction. If our being made as male and female is at the centre of the way in which we are called to be in the image of God, it may well follow that it is in our sexual relationships – sexual in the broader sense of relations in general between men and women, not only husbands and

case in proclamation, conversation and example. It may, indeed it should, seek to influence and persuade, believing that its witness coheres with the ordering of creation to Christ. But it must not seek to impose its view: to do so would be as much a denial of Christ as are the distortions it seeks to expose and repudiate.

Rather the Church is called, in the first instance, simply to faithfulness, to live in a manner that is coherent with the gospel story. Nor need the Church become discouraged through an awareness of its own frailties and failures (it is no naïve idealism that here is being advocated). As the Church lives hopefully, notwithstanding its evident inconsistencies, as it continues to trust in divine mercy for forgiveness and in divine grace for renewal and recreation, so the Church bears faithful witness to its defining story in recognition that the ultimate fulfilment of that story within its own life is yet to come.

But the Church is also called to prophetic witness, to declare the gospel, which is at the same time the divine command, in its proclamation and conversation as well as in its life. And it is called to declare this gospel, which is divine command, not just as its own defining story, but as the defining story of all creation. It is certainly not called to declare this in any oppressive, manipulative or coercive manner – to do so would be to gainsay the story itself – but it is to do so trusting that its witness will resonate, will attract, will persuade; trusting, that is, not in its own attractiveness and persuasiveness, but trusting rather in the winsomeness of the Spirit who witnesses through the Church's witness and who breathes through all creation. Nor need the Church become discouraged even though

---

wives but parents and children, employer and employee, teacher and taught – that will be found the greater opportunities for both good and ill.

'The negative side, more than apparent in our society, is that at least as much damage and unhappiness, activity that makes for death rather than life, is to be found in human sexual relations as in economic oppression, political tyranny and ecological disaster. This is because the closer our relatedness to another person, the greater potential there is for both good and ill radiating thence to the wider world' (Colin Gunton, *Christ and Creation*, pp. 103f.).

there may be little tangible evidence for such resonance. Its calling is to live and to speak trustfully and hopefully; the outcome of its witness is not its own affair. Perhaps the greater contemporary danger is not that the Church will seek to coerce society to obedience to the command which is the gospel but that the Church, through its indwelling of lesser stories, will itself abandon a coherent and faithful witness in its life and proclamation.

POSTSCRIPT

This book began with the question of the identity of a distinctively Christian ethic and the corresponding question of how such an ethic could be heard beyond the boundaries of the Christian Church. The manner in which the first question has been answered actually compounds the difficulties of the second question. If the gospel in its form as command could be reduced to a series of propositions, and if those propositions were rationally and independently accessible and demonstrable within the world, then the form of the first question would, at least to some extent, disarm the concerns of the second question. But the gospel, even in its form as command, cannot be so reduced: it is irreducibly narrative and narrative that is accessible, not merely by being heard, but more profoundly by being indwelt. Jesus did not merely issue a series of commands, he called men and women to follow him, to be with him. Accordingly, the Church does not confront men and women with a series of commands, it invites men and women to come to indwell its story. The command of the gospel cannot come other than in the context of an invitation to indwell a story by indwelling the community that is being shaped by that story. Or, to put the matter more precisely, the command of the gospel is itself an invitation; an invitation to participate in this transforming story; an invitation, consequently, to view life and creation from the perspective offered by this story.

Since this is the case then, notwithstanding all that has been said in these closing chapters concerning the continuity of creation and redemption and the being-givenness of all perception by the Spirit, the command of the gospel cannot truly be heard in isolation or detachment; it can only truly be heard through this process of indwelling. The disciplines and virtues of Christian living, notwithstanding their resonance within the world as the creation of the Triune God, can only truly be comprehended and embraced through indwelling that community that is being brought to indwell the gospel story by the Spirit:

> Obviously, Christians think what we have learned from our worship about living well is true for anyone. That is why we have the obligation and joy of witnessing to what God has done for us. But the very notion of witness means we cannot presume that those to whom we witness already have learned what we have learned by the necessity of our being gathered.[1]

The gospel is a living narrative: it is only truly heard by being indwelt and it is only truly indwelt through the indwelling presence of the Spirit. The Spirit does not merely cause the story of the gospel to be heard, he draws men and women into that story by drawing them into the sacramental life and worship of the Church. He invites; he gathers; and only thus does he transform. For this reason, any enquiry into the nature of Christ and the gospel story is also an enquiry into the nature of the Church, the nature of the sacraments, the nature of the Spirit: the command of the gospel cannot be accessed other than through these 'means of grace'.

It is for these reasons that this account of the Church's ethical witness is profoundly misrepresented by charges of being confrontational or idealistic:

> ... I would refute the neo-Barthianism of Hauerwas and the post-modern Christendom of Milbank, simply because, as well as being insufficiently dialogical in theological terms, these models are sociological fictions and fantasies which bear no resemblance to the lived experience of Church and culture in Britain today.[2]

[1]   Stanley Hauerwas, *In Good Company*, p. 158.
[2]   Elaine Graham, 'The Ecclesiology of Unemployment and the Future of Work', in *Putting Theology to Work: A Theological Symposium on Unemployment and the Future of Work*, ed. Malcolm Brown and Peter Sedgwick (London: CCBI and The William Temple Foundation, 1998), pp. 40–48 (p. 46).

I hope I have already responded sufficiently throughout this book, and particularly at the close of its final chapter, to this charge of idealism. The Church has not yet arrived at its goal but its non-arrival itself bears witness to the mercy that lies at the heart of its defining story. Precisely in its hopefulness through failure, precisely in its trustfulness through sin, it bears witness to the gospel. Of course the Church, if it is truly the Church, bears visible witness to the transforming power of the gospel, the transforming power of the Spirit. But this transformation, as yet, is incomplete. The Church is on a journey. It has not yet arrived. It bears witness to a goal that remains beyond its present reality. And only in this deferment does the Church truly bear witness to the gospel. Any claim to present completeness would be a denial of its defining story.

But neither is the Church merely confronting the world with a totalitarian command: this is not the manner of the distinctive command that is the gospel story. The Church, rather, addresses the world with an invitation: it calls the world to come and to see; it calls the world to participate in its story and, thus, to participate in this transformation. Of course, the term 'dialogical' may not be appropriate to this invitational process. Ironically, the degree to which this vision of the Church may be fantasy is the degree to which the Church has itself abandoned its distinctive ethic and the consequent necessity of indwelling its story in favour of a 'dialogical' approach to ethical issues rooted in modernism's illusory rationalistic foundation. There is no neutral ground on which to stand. There is no independent rationalistic foundation for detached dialogue. Both Church and world are deluded when they pretend otherwise. But the alternative to detached dialogue is not totalitarian confrontation, it is participatory dialogue; it is gracious invitation. If the Church's gospel takes the form of command, its command takes the form of gospel: by definition it cannot persuade other than by the invitation to indwell.

The Church is constituted by its witness to the gospel story, a witness that has its own coherence and inherent rationality, not through any conformity with some supposed independently derived rational foundation, but through its focus on the Christ who is the true foundation and goal of all reality, and through its being spoken and heard in the power of the Spirit who breathes and speaks through all creation. And this witness of the Church cannot validly take form as command other than as a form of this gospel, as 'good news'. As such, the witness of the Church cannot be coercive or condemnatory; it can only be expressed as gracious invitation. The proclamation of the Church is the story of Jesus, but the Church does not merely call the world to believe the truth of its story – as if any truth could be believed in detachment – it invites the world to indwell the story and thus to be re-orientated to its true and only goal. This and only this is validly the form of the gospel in its form as command.

When Thomas Aquinas orders all the virtues to the theological virtue of love he is not merely adjusting Aristotle's ethical system, he is radically re-orientating it theologically: the love he intends is not indeterminate; it is the love that is narrated in the gospel and that only takes form in human lives by grace. Love thus defined, then, cannot take form here and now without the complementary theological virtues of faith and hope. Consequently, for a community truly to live lovingly requires that it also lives faithfully, trustfully, hopefully, thankfully: only thus can a community claim to be living in truthful response to the gospel. The Church that, refuting all delusory societal claims to neutrality, seeks to live truthfully in this manner – while it certainly may not yet be perfected – nonetheless may claim, in fact, to prefigure the ultimate sociological reality. Only a community thus orientated through worship to God has any claim to sociological ultimacy.

BIBLIOGRAPHY

Athanasius, St. *Athanasius on the Incarnation: The Treatise De Incarnatione Verbi Dei*, trans. and ed. 'A Religious of C.S.M.V.' (London: G. Bles, 1944)

Baillie, D. M., *God was in Christ: An Essay on Incarnation and Atonement* (London: Faber & Faber, 1956)

Barth, Karl, *The Word of God and the Word of Man*, trans. Douglas Horton (London: Hodder & Stoughton, 1928)

——, *The Teaching of the Church regarding Baptism*, trans. Ernest A. Payne (London: SCM Press, 1948)

——, *Ethics*, ed. Dietrich Braun, trans. Geoffrey W. Bromiley (Edinburgh: T&T Clark, 1981)

——, *Church Dogmatics*, vols. I–IV, Eng. trans. eds. G. W. Bromiley and T. F. Torrance (Edinburgh: T&T Clark, 1956–1975)

——, *The Christian Life: Church Dogmatics IV, 4 Lecture Fragments*, trans. Geoffrey W. Bromiley (Edinburgh: T&T Clark, 1981)

Begbie, Jeremy, *Voicing Creation's Praise: Towards a Theology of the Arts* (Edinburgh: T&T Clark, 1991)

Bell, M. Charles, *Calvin and Scottish Theology: The Doctrine of Assurance* (Edinburgh: Handsel Press, 1985)

Berkeley, George, *The Principles of Human Knowledge* in *Works* II, ed. T. E. Jessup and A. A. Luce (London: Thomas Nelson & Sons, 1948ff.), pp. 19–113

Biggar, Nigel, (ed.), *Reckoning with Barth: Essays in Commemoration of the Centenary of Karl Barth's Birth* (London: Mowbray, 1988)

——, *The Hastening that Waits: Karl Barth's Ethics* (Oxford: Clarendon Press, 1993)

Braaten, Carl E., and Jenson, Robert W., (eds.), *Reclaiming the Bible for the Church* (Edinburgh: T&T Clark, 1995)

Burridge, Richard A., *What are the Gospels? A Comparison with Graeco-Roman Biography* (Cambridge: Cambridge University Press, 1992)

——, *Four Gospels, One Jesus? A Symbolic Reading* (London: SPCK, 1994)

Calvin, John, *Institutes of the Christian Religion*, ed. J. T. McNeill, trans. F. L. Battles (Philadelphia: Westminster Press, 1960)

——, *Concerning the Eternal Predestination of God*, trans. J. K. S. Reid (London: James Clarke, 1961)

Clifford, Alan C., *Atonement and Justification: English Evangelical Theology 1640–1790 An Evaluation* (Oxford: Clarendon Press, 1990)

Colwell, John E., *Actuality and Provisionality: Eternity and Election in the Theology of Karl Barth* (Edinburgh: Rutherford House Books, 1989)

——, 'Alternative Approaches to Believer's Baptism (from the Anabaptists to Barth)' in *The Scottish Bulletin of Evangelical Theology* 7 (1989), pp. 3–20

——, 'The Contemporaneity of the Divine Decision: Reflections on Barth's Denial of Universalism' in *Universalism and the Doctrine of Hell*, ed. Nigel M. de S. Cameron (Grand Rapids: Baker Book House, 1993), pp. 139–160

——, 'The Glory of God's Justice and the Glory of God's Grace: Contemporary reflections on the doctrine of Hell in the Teaching of Jonathan Edwards' (Drew Lecture on Immortality, 12 November 1992) published in *Called to One Hope: Perspectives on the Life to Come*, ed. John Colwell (Carlisle: Paternoster Press, 2000), pp. 113–29.

——, 'Christ, Creation and Human Sexuality' in *The Way Forward? Christian Voices on Homosexuality and the Church*, ed. Timothy Bradshaw (London: Hodder & Stoughton, 1997), pp. 88–98

——, 'Baptism, conscience and the resurrection: a reappraisal of 1 Peter 3:21' in *Baptism, the New Testament and the Church: Historical and Contemporary Studies in Honour of R. E. O. White* ed. S. E. Porter and A. R. Cross (Sheffield: Sheffield Academic Press, 1999), pp. 210–27

Edwards, Jonathan, *Freedom of the Will* in *Works of Jonathan Edwards*, gen. ed. Perry Miller, vol. 1, ed. Paul Ramsey (New Haven: Yale University Press, 1957)

——, *Original Sin* in *Works of Jonathan Edwards*, gen. ed. John E. Smith, vol. 3, ed. Clyde A. Holbrook (New Haven: Yale University Press, 1980)

——, *Notes on the Mind* in *Works of Jonathan Edwards*, gen. ed. John E. Smith, vol. 6, *Scientific and Philosophical Writings*, ed. Wallace E. Anderson (New Haven: Yale University Press, 1980)

——, *Dissertation I: Concerning the End for which God created the World* in *Works of Jonathan Edwards*, gen. ed. John E. Smith, vol. 8, *Ethical Writings*, ed. Paul Ramsey (New Haven: Yale University Press, 1989), pp. 403–536

——, *Dissertation II: The Nature of True Virtue* in *Works of Jonathan Edwards*, gen. ed. John E. Smith, vol. 8, *Ethical Writings*, ed. Paul Ramsey (New Haven: Yale University Press, 1989), pp. 537–627

Fish, Stanley, *Is There a Text in This Class? The Authority of Interpretive Communities* (Cambridge, Massachusetts: Harvard University Press, 1980)

Fletcher, Joseph, *Situation Ethics: The New Morality* (London: SCM Press, 1966)

Fuchs, Joseph, *Personal Responsibility and Christian Morality*, trans. William Cleves and others (Washington: Georgetown University Press, 1983)

——, *Christian Morality: The Word Becomes Flesh*, trans. Brian McNeil (Washington: Georgetown University Press, 1987)

Gunton, Colin E., *Enlightenment and Alienation: An Essay towards a Trinitarian Theology* (Basingstoke: Marshall Morgan & Scott, 1985)

——, *The Actuality of Atonement: A Study of Metaphor, Rationality and the Christian Tradition* (Edinburgh: T&T Clark, 1988)

——, *Christ and Creation: The Didsbury Lectures 1990* (Carlisle: Paternoster Press, 1992)

——, *The One, The Three and the Many: God, Creation and the Culture of Modernity: The Bampton Lectures 1992* (Cambridge: Cambridge University Press, 1993)

——, *A Brief Theology of Revelation* (Edinburgh: T&T Clark, 1995)

——, *The Triune Creator: A Historical and Systematic Study* (Edinburgh: Edinburgh University Press, 1998)

Gustafson, James M., *Christ and the Moral Life* (Chicago: University of Chicago Press, 1968)

——, *Can Ethics be Christian?* (Chicago: University of Chicago Press, 1975)

——, *Protestant and Roman Catholic Ethics: Prospects for Rapprochement* (Chicago: University of Chicago Press, 1978)

Hart, Trevor, 'Anselm of Canterbury and John McLeod Campbell: Where opposites Meet?', *Evangelical Quarterly* 62 (1990)

——, *Faith Thinking: The Dynamics of Christian Theology* (London: SPCK, 1995)

Hauerwas, Stanley, *Character and the Christian Life: A Study in Theological Ethics* (Notre Dame: University of Notre Dame Press, 1994; originally published San Antonio: Trinity University Press, 1975)

——, with Richard Bondi and David B. Burrell, *Truthfulness and Tragedy: Further Investigations in Christian Ethics* (Notre Dame: University of Notre Dame Press, 1977)

——, *Vision and Virtue: Essays in Christian Ethical Reflection* (Notre Dame: University of Notre Dame Press, 1981)

——, *A Community of Character: Toward a Constructive Christian Social Ethic* (Notre Dame: University of Notre Dame Press, 1981)

——, *The Peaceable Kingdom: A Primer in Christian Ethics* (London: SCM Press, 1984)

——, *Christian Existence Today: Essays on Church, World, and Living In Between* (Durham, North Carolina: Labyrinth, 1988)

——, *Suffering Presence: Theological Reflections on Medicine, the Mentally Handicapped, and the Church* (Edinburgh: T&T Clark, 1988)

——, with Willimon, William H., *Resident Aliens: Life in the Christian Colony* (Nashville: Abingdon Press, 1989)

——, (ed.) with L. Gregory Jones, *Why Narrative? Readings in Narrative Theology* (Grand Rapids: Eerdmans, 1989)

——, *After Christendom? How the Church is to Behave if Freedom, Justice, and a Christian Nation are Bad Ideas* (Nashville: Abingdon Press, 1991)

——, *Unleashing the Scripture: Freeing the Bible from Captivity to America* (Nashville: Abingdon Press, 1993)

——, *In Good Company: The Church as Polis* (Notre Dame: University of Notre Dame Press, 1995)

——, with Charles Pinches, *Christians among the Virtues: Theological Conversations with Ancient and Modern Ethics* (Notre Dame: University of Notre Dame Press, 1997)

——, *Sanctify Them in the Truth: Holiness Exemplified* (Edinburgh: T&T Clark, 1998)

Hays, Richard B., *The Moral Vision of the New Testament: A Contemporary Introduction to New Testament Ethics* (Edinburgh: T&T Clark, 1996)

Helm, Paul, *Faith and Understanding* (Edinburgh: Edinburgh University Press, 1997)

Hoose, Bernard, *Proportionalism: The American Debate and its European Roots* (Georgetown: Georgetown University Press, 1987)

——, *Received Wisdom? Reviewing the Role of Tradition in Christian Ethics* (London: Geoffrey Chapman, 1994)

Holmes, Stephen R., *God of Grace and God of Glory: An Account of the Theology of Jonathan Edwards* (Edinburgh: T&T Clark, 2000)

Irenaeus, *Against Heresies* in *The Ante-Nicene Fathers*, vol. 1, ed. Alexander Roberts, James Donaldson and A. Cleveland Coxe (Grand Rapids: Eerdmans, 1987)

Johnson, William Stacy, *The Mystery of God: Karl Barth and the Postmodern Foundations of Theology* (Louisville: Westminster John Knox Press, 1997)

Jüngel, Eberhard, *Christ, Justice and Peace: Toward a Theology of the State in Dialogue with the Barmen Declaration*, trans. D. Bruce Hamill and Alan J. Torrance (T&T Clark, Edinburgh, 1992)

Kendall, R. T., *Calvin and English Calvinism to 1649* (Oxford: Oxford University Press, 1979)

Kevan, Ernest F., *The Grace of Law: A Study in Puritan Theology* (London: Carey Kingsgate Press, 1964)

Lodge, David, *Working with Structuralism: Essays and Reviews on Nineteenth- and Twentieth-Century Literature* (London: Routledge, 1981)

Luther, Martin, *Luther's Works* vols. 1–55, gen. ed. (vols. 1–30) Jaroslav Pelikan; gen. ed. (vols. 31–55) Helmut T. Lehmann (Philadelphia: Muhlenberg Press, 1955–75)

Lyotard, Jean-François, *The Postmodern Condition: A Report on Knowledge*, trans. G. Bennington and B. Massumi (Minneapolis: University of Minnesota Press, 1984)

MacIntyre, Alasdair, *A Short History of Ethics* (London: Routledge & Kegan Paul, 1967)

——, *After Virtue: A Study in Moral Theory* (London: Duckworth, 1985[2])

——, *Whose Justice? Which Rationality?* (London: Duckworth, 1988)

Maitland, Sara, *A Big-Enough God: Artful Theology* (London: Mowbray, 1995)

Markham, Ian S., *Plurality and Christian Ethics* (Cambridge: Cambridge University Press, 1994)

Matzko, David McCarthy, 'The Performance of the Good: Ritual Action and the Moral Life' in *Pro Ecclesia* VII (1998), pp. 199–215

McClendon, James Wm., Jr., *Systematic Theology: Ethics* (Nashville: Abingdon Press, 1986)

Milbank, John, *Theology and Social Theory* (Oxford: Blackwell, 1990)

Newbigin, Lesslie, *Foolishness to the Greeks: The Gospel and Western Culture* (London: SPCK, 1986)

——, *The Gospel in a Pluralist Society* (London: SPCK, 1989).

O'Donovan, Oliver, *Resurrection and the Moral Order: An Outline for Evangelical Ethics* (Leicester: IVP, 1986)

——, *The Desire of the Nations: Rediscovering the Roots of Political Theology* (Cambridge: Cambridge University Press, 1996)

Owen, John, *A Discourse concerning the Holy Spirit* in *The Works of John Owen*, ed. W. H. Goold, vol. III (London: Banner of Truth Trust, 1965)

——, *The Death of Death in the Death of Christ* in *The Works of John Owen*, ed. W. H. Goold, vol. X (London: Banner of Truth Trust, 1967), pp. 140–421

2 52

Parker, T. H. L., *Calvin: An Introduction to His Thought* (London: Geoffrey Chapman, 1995)

Placher, William C., *Narratives of a Vulnerable God: Christ, Theology, and Scripture* (Louisville: Westminster John Knox Press, 1994)

——, *The Domestication of Transcendence: How Modern Thinking about God Went Wrong* (Louisville: Westminster John Knox Press, 1996)

Porter, Jean, *The Recovery of Virtue: The Relevance of Aquinas for Christian Ethics* (London: SPCK, 1990)

Rae, Murray, *Kierkegaard's Vision of the Incarnation, by Faith Transformed* (Oxford: Oxford University Press, 1997)

Randall, Ian M., *Evangelical Experiences: A Study in the Spirituality of English Evangelicalism 1918–1939* (Carlisle: Paternoster Press, 1999)

Ricoeur, Paul, *Oneself As Another* (Chicago: University of Chicago Press, 1992)

Rogers, Eugene F., Jnr., *Thomas Aquinas and Karl Barth: Sacred Doctrine and the Natural Knowledge of God* (Notre Dame: University of Notre Dame Press, 1995)

Selman, Francis, *Saint Thomas Aquinas: Teacher of Truth* (Edinburgh: T&T Clark, 1994)

Sibbes, Richard, 'A Description of Christ' (1639) in *Works of Richard Sibbes*, vol. 1, ed. Alexander B. Grosart (Edinburgh: Banner of Truth Trust, 1973), pp. 1–31

Smail, Tom, *The Giving Gift: The Holy Spirit in Person* (London: Darton, Longman & Todd, 1994²)

Thielicke, Helmut, *Theological Ethics*, vols. 1–3, ed. (vols 1–2) William H. Lazareth, trans. (vol. 3) John W. Doberstein (Grand Rapids: Eerdmans, 1966–79)

——, *Between Heaven and Earth: Conversations with American Christians*, trans. and ed. John W. Doberstein (London: James Clarke, 1967)

Thomas Aquinas, *Summa Theologica*, trans. by Fathers of the English Dominican Province (Westminster, Maryland: Christian Classics, 1981)

Torrance, Thomas F., *The Christian Doctrine of God, One Being Three Persons* (Edinburgh: T&T Clark, 1996)

Vanhoozer, Kevin J., *Biblical Narrative in the Philosophy of Paul Ricoeur: A Study in Hermeneutics and Theology* (Cambridge: Cambridge University Press, 1990)

Wadell, Paul J., *The Primacy of Love: An Introduction to the Ethics of Thomas Aquinas* (New York: Paulist Press, 1992)

Ward, Keith, *Ethics and Christianity* (New York: George Allen & Unwin, 1970)

Watson, Francis, *Text, Church and World: Biblical Interpretation in Theological Perspective* (Edinburgh: T&T Clark, 1994)

——, *Text and Truth: Redefining Biblical Theology* (Edinburgh: T&T Clark, 1997)

Webster, John, *Barth's Ethics of Reconciliation* (Cambridge: Cambridge University Press, 1995)

——, *Barth's Moral Theology: Human Action in Barth's Thought* (Edinburgh: T&T Clark, 1998)

Wendel, François, *Calvin: The Origins and Development of His Religious Thought*, trans. Philip Mairet (London: Collins, 1963)

Wesley, John, *A Plain Account of Christian Perfection as believed and taught by the Reverend Mr. John Wesley, from the year 1725, to the year 1777* in *The Works of the Rev. John Wesley*, vol. XI (London: Wesleyan Conference Office, 1872), pp. 366–446

Williams, George H., *The Radical Reformation* (Philadelphia: Westminster Press, 1962)

Yoder, John H., *Karl Barth and the Problem of War* (Nashville: Abingdon Press, 1970)

——, *The Original Revolution* (Scottdale: Herald Press, 1971)

——, *For the Nations: Essays Public and Evangelical* (Grand Rapids: Eerdmans, 1997)

Index of Scriptural References

Name Index

Anselm 16n. 25, 89n. 1, 94, 94n. 13, 96
Aquinas, Thomas *see* Thomas Aquinas
Aristotle 17, 38n. 24, 142, 142n. 24, 158n. 26, 173, 177n. 16, 254
Athanasius 94–5, 95, 96, 116n. 10, 120n. 19
Atkinson, James 44n. 3
Auber, Henriette 147n. 39
Augustine of Hippo 20, 38n. 24, 63n. 65, 142n. 24, 144, 144n. 32, 189, 189n. 2, 192n. 8, 218, 242n. 27, 244n. 31
Aulén, Gustav 94n. 13

Baillie, Donald M. 147n. 38
Barth, Karl viii, 16–17, 16n. 25, 19n. 29, 39–40, 41, 46–7, 49–51, 50n. 19, 50n. 20, 56, 57n. 47, 62n. 33, 64–6, 75, 75n. 12, 78n. 18, 89–90, 93, 93n. 10, 93n. 11, 97, 97n. 23, 97n. 24, 97n. 25, 98–104, 117–22, 120n. 20, 123, 128n. 35, 131, 132n. 3, 146n. 36, 149–54, 156, 156n. 22, 162n. 33, 174–5, 174n. 10, 178, 196, 197, 203, 203n. 21, 214–19, 222, 222n. 42, 225, 235, 235n. 15, 236, 236n. 16, 237, 238, 240n. 22, 243, 245n. 36
Barth, Markus 150
Bavinck, Herman 223
Baxter, Richard 58n. 50
Begbie, Jeremy 64n. 66, 134n. 6, 223, 223n. 43
Bell, George, Bishop 25, 198
Bell, M. Charles 57n. 48, 58n. 49, 96n. 19
Bentham, Jeremy 7, 7n. 8
Berkeley, George 34–7, 38n. 23, 85, 213, 220
Berkouwer, G. C. 145n. 35, 222n. 42
Bettis, J. D. 93n. 11
Beza, Theodore 222
Biggar, Nigel 47n. 13, 47n. 15, 65n.

69, 78n. 18, 102n. 37, 117n. 12, 118n. 15, 119n. 17, 120n. 20, 128n. 36, 174, 174n. 10, 217, 217n. 28, 218, 218n. 33, 218n. 34
Bondi, Richard 16n. 22, 81n. 22, 172n. 7
Bonhoeffer, Dietrich 215n. 23
Braaten, Carl E. 78n. 17, 200n. 16, 238n. 20
Bradshaw, Timothy 184n. 25
Bromiley, Geoffrey W. 99n. 29, 102, 102n. 38, 167n. 1
Brunner, Emil 215n. 23, 217n. 29
Bultmann, Rudolf 46, 46n. 10
Burrell, David B. 16n. 22, 81n. 22, 172n. 7
Burridge, Richard A. 76n. 13, 80n. 21

Calvin, John viii, 51–8, 62, 62n. 61, 63, 63–4, 85, 85n. 31, 96, 96n. 17, 96n. 18, 96n. 19, 113n. 4, 133n. 4, 143n. 28, 145, 153n. 16, 156n. 21, 157, 157n. 23, 158, 158n. 26, 160, 222, 222n. 40, 230n. 1, 231n. 4
Cameron, Nigel M. de S. 94n. 11
Campbell, John McLeod 95n. 13
Clifford, Alan C. 58n. 50
Colwell, John E. 50n. 19, 50n. 20, 51n. 23, 94n. 11, 97n. 22, 98n. 26, 151n. 12, 156n. 22, 184n. 25
Cronin, Kieran 104n. 43

David, David B. 115n. 8
Delattre, Roland 209n. 5
Descartes, René 6, 35n. 17
Doberstein, John W. 60n. 54, 237n. 19
Dunn, James D. G. 136, 136n. 11

Edwards, Jonathan 36–7, 36n. 21, 37n. 22, 85, 97n. 22, 124n. 26, 135, 135n. 9, 145, 176n. 14, 182, 207, 207n. 1, 208–13, 213n. 18,

Subject Index

Abraham 62, 66, 111
accidents, and substance, in the
    Eucharist 158n. 26
Adam, creation in the likeness of
    Christ 193
Amish, attitudes to reconciliation
    91n. 6
Anabaptism
    distinction between the Church
        and the world 127, 231–2
    distinction between Old and
        New Testaments 126n. 29
    dualism 156
    ἀνακεφαλαίωσις (recapitulation)
        192
Ananias (cursed by Peter in Acts)
    128n. 35
anti-foundationalism, and
    foundationalism 34
apostasy
    Church's apostasy in relations
        with the world 246–7
    within the Church 183, 199
atonement
    Anselm's views 94n. 13, 95
    Athanasius' views 94–5
    limited atonement 94n. 12, 96
    Reformation views 95–6
    and the Trinity 96–8
authorial intention 73n. 8

baptism
    baptism in the Holy Spirit,
        effects 50, 51
    Barth's distinction between
        baptism with the Holy
        Spirit and baptism with
        water 149–54
    basis in Jesus' baptism 101–2,
        104
    sacramental nature 154–6
    use of story, in baptism 82
    water baptism 149–50, 153
    see also sacraments
Baptist churches
    denial of real presence 156–7
    tradition 202, 228

Barmen Declaration, relationship
    between the Church and the
    world 235–6, 240n. 22, 242n.
    28, 243
Beatitudes 113n. 5
beauty 223, 223n. 43
    as the nature of virtue 209–13,
        220, 221–2, 224–6
    particular and general beauty
        212n. 15
believism 138n. 17
Bible, as story 69–83, 84–7
biography 80n. 21
    in the Gospels 76–7

casuistry 179n. 17
categorical imperative 9–10
catholicity 31–2
Chalcedon, Council, Christology
    77–8, 116
character, importance of the
    gospel story 169–70
Christendom 241–3, 248
Christian ethics
    Barth's views 98–103, 117–20
    bases
        in Christian belief 3–4
        in stories 88–9
    and Christian identity, as
        coherence of living 166,
        169
    concern with Christology, rather
        than Jesus Christ 76n. 14
    as the demand for life in
        accordance with the person
        of Jesus Christ 128, 131
    development vii–viii
        from within the Christian
            community 31–2
    distinctiveness from society's
        ethics generally 109–10
    effects of the Church's
        proclamation of the gospel
        to the world 251–4
    focused on Jesus Christ in the
        gospel story and as echoed
        in the Church 171–3

dogmatics, relationship to ethics,
    Barth's views 99–100
double decree 96
double effect, principle 105–6
dualism
    in Barth's understanding of
        baptism 150–5
    in sacramental traditions 156–7

election to salvation 56–7
Enlightenment, ethical values 6–7
eternal forms 189, 190
ethics 172n. 7
    as affected by communities 31
    as affected by liberal modernism
        24–6
    development
    as affected by modernism 3, 33,
        34
    and Protestantism 42–3, 58–66
        Calvin's views 51–7
        Luther's views 43–51
    and nominalism 63–6
    objective basis impossible in
        post-modernism 26–34
    within society 4–6
        the Enlightenment 6–7
        natural law 15–22
        situation ethics 8–15
    see also Christian ethics
Eucharist 155, 156, 157–61
    confession as acknowledgement
        of Christian's dependence
        upon Christ's sacrifice 104
    use of story 82
    see also sacraments
euthanasia 172

facts
    and factuality in the Bible 74–5
    recording in stories 71–2
faith
    Anabaptist views 137n. 13
    importance for reason in relation
        to natural law 21n. 35
    and justification 43–51
    proofs 89n.1
    relationship with works,
        Calvin's views 52
    theological virtue 103
Fall
    doctrine 20

Irenaeus' views 192n. 10, 193
foundationalism 22n. 36
    and anti-foundationalism 34
freedom
    God's freedom in the atonement
        98
    and the moral worth of actions
        176–7
fundamental option 180, 181
Fundamentalism 61

gnosticism, Irenaeus' arguments
    against 189–94
God
    concepts about
        in Barth 64–6
        in Neo-Calvinism 64n. 66
        in nominalism 64
    and creation 19
    freedom 178
    glory, as the goal of the universe
        211
    grace, as acceptance of the
        Christian 91–3
    חֶסֶד 110–13
    image restored in humanity
        through Jesus Christ
        116–18, 120n. 19
    justice 62–3
    kingdom, not limited to the
        Church 227n. 54
    knowledge about, through
        piety, Calvin's views 52
    mercy, essential to salvation
        104–8
    nature, as revealed in the gospel
        story 98
    omnipotence 203–5
    perception, as the foundation of
        knowledge 35–41
    purpose as the unity of humanity
        with himself 135n. 7
    relationship to the Christian
        through prayer 102
    relationship to creation 209–13,
        221–3
    revelation
        in Jesus Christ 121–4
        relationship to natural
            theology 20n. 32
        through propositional
            statements in the Bible 75–6
        through stories in the Bible 80

God – *continued*
  as source of the virtues 144
  Trinitarian nature, revealed in
    the gospel story 88
  work in creation and
    redemption 189–90
  see also Holy Spirit; Jesus Christ;
    Trinity
God the Son *see* Jesus Christ
good
  theory of, and liberalism 25n. 3
  within the being of God 65, 66
goodness, in God and creation
    221–2
gospel
  and law 90, 92
  as the means of addressing
    relations between Church
    and world 239–50
  as narrative, effects on Christian
    ethics 251–2
gospel story
  Church's indwelling of the
    gospel story as adherence to
    truth 167–9, 171–2
  importance for the life of the
    Christian 169–71
  as revelation of God as Trinity 88
Gospels
  purpose to reveal the person of
    Jesus Christ through
    narrative 114–20
  representations of Jesus Christ
    76–8, 83
grace 18, 47n. 16, 143
  as acceptance of the Christian by
    God 91–3
  common grace 145–6, 222–3
  effects in baptism 51
  as the perfecting of nature 220
  reception, Calvin's views 52–3

happiness, Thomas Aquinas'
    views 143–4
Hasidim 111
חֶסֶד, indicative of God's character
    110–13
Holy Spirit 49n. 18, 50n. 19
  agency in creation and
    redemption 189–94
  indwelling in Jesus Christ and
    in humanity 131–6, 141–8,
    152

  as mediator of creation,
    Gunton's view 213–14
  as perfecter and source of the
    virtues 143, 145
  role
    in the Church 162–3, 166–8
    and its relations to the
      world 23–4, 243–4, 249, 252,
      253, 254
    in redemption and
      reconciliation, Barth's views
      214, 219–20
    in the world and in humanity
      147–8
      through common grace
      145–6
  and the sacraments 154, 156n.
    21
    baptism 50, 50nn. 20, 21, 149,
      152–3
    the Eucharist 161
  shaping of Christian identity
    within the Church 168–9,
    174–5, 181–5
  as source of recognition of
    reality 212
  testimony, as revelation of God
    in Jesus Christ 85–6
  witness to authority of Christ in
    relationship of the Church
    and the world 247
  work in justification and
    sanctification 136–40
  see also God; Jesus Christ; Trinity
homosexuality 184–5
honesty, as spiritual beauty,
    Aquinas' understanding
    208n. 2
hope
  Christian hope in Jesus Christ
    194–6
  theological virtue 103
human rights 12–15
humanity
  dependence on the Holy Spirit
    131–6, 141–8
  God's working through
    humanity 144
  revelation in Jesus Christ
    116–18, 120n. 19, 122–4,
    124–8, 131

immanence, and transcendence
  98n. 26
individualism 26–7n. 4
injustice 179–80
intention 106n. 46
intentionality, importance for
  character 169n. 4

Jesus Christ 251, 254
  agency in creation and
    redemption 189–94
  as the assurance of salvation
    56–7
  as basis in Christian belief 3–4,
    22
  as basis of Christian ethics 3,
    171–3
  and the Church
    authority in relations between
      Church and world 242–3,
      245–7
    Church's dependence upon
      164
    indwelling of the life of the
      Church through the Holy
      Spirit 16–18, 166–8
    as reconcilation between
      Church and world 237,
      239
  dependence on the Holy Spirit
    132
  and the ethical nature of love 8
  as the form of Adam 193
  futility of attempts to
    reconstruct the historical
    Jesus 73–4
  grace given through justification
    and sanctification, Calvin's
    views 2
  humanity 124–8, 131, 203
    as real humanity through the
      Holy Spirit 148
  indwelling of the Holy Spirit
    131–6, 141–8
  and the just war theory 199
  kingship 245–6
  knowledge about, through
    piety, Calvin's views 52
  as the mediator of creation,
    Gunton's view 213
  as the perfecting of creation
    193–6

person revealed in the Gospel
  narratives 114–20
representation in the Gospels
  76–8, 83
as the revelation of God
  expressed in humanity 121–5
  and God's relation to creation
    221
revelation in stories, Barth's
  understanding 89–91
role in atonement 96
and the sacraments
baptism 149–50, 155
  as basis for Christian baptism
    101–2, 104
the Eucharist 157, 158–9
  Christian's dependence upon
    acknowledged in the
    Eucharist 104
  eucharistic words as evidence
    of universal atonement 97
Sermon on the Mount, as a
  reflection of God's character
  112–14, 125
witness to Father and Holy
  Spirit as the source of his
  words and actions 147
witnessed in the lives of
  Christians 85–6
Word of God, dualism in Barth's
  understanding 150n. 10
as Word of God, and
  relationship to creation,
  Barth's views 215–20
see also God; Holy Spirit; Trinity
Jewishness, Jesus Christ and the
  apostles 123n. 23
John the Baptist 125
Judas Iscariot 97
judgement, as an expression of
  grace 92–3
just war theory 196–9, 202–3
justice, as reflection of social
  situation 10
justification
  Luther's understanding 143n.
    27
  and sanctification 136–40, 143
  in the reception of grace,
    Calvin's views 52–3, 54
justification by faith 43–51